THE ALPHA ENTERPRISE

The key phenomenon in the background to the alpha courses is the decline in conventional religious behaviour and this is at the centre of contemporary religious studies and sociology of religion. For those who are more directly concerned about church decline this book also has a practical significance – do we have something here that works? Hunt tackles the difficult question of whether Alpha courses are working and under what circumstances. This is the only major empirical study I know of the Alpha course.

Professor Christie Davies, University of Reading, UK

The Alpha Enterprise explores the development, growth and impact of the most widely used evangelising programme of recent decades. The Alpha course is run in over seven thousand churches in the UK and over five thousand in the USA. Across the world some four million people have graduated through the course in over 80 countries. Alpha is truly the fastest growing evangelising initiative, creating widespread support as well as stirring strong criticism.

Stephen Hunt critically examines the content and working philosophy of the Alpha course through the experiences of the churches that have run it, as well as the individuals who have experienced it first hand. Hunt charts the history of the programme, its use of group dynamics and media, how it links with the charismatic movement, how it deals with issues such as homosexuality, how it is run not only in churches but in prisons and universities too, and concludes by measuring Alpha's impact and success.

Engaging with debates regarding postmodernity, globalisation, McDonaldisation, consumerism, and secularisation, and based on real-life surveys, *The Alpha Enterprise* sheds new light not only on evangelism but on contemporary Christianity in general and how it engages with a post-Christian culture.

Everyone has heard people quarrelling. Sometimes it sounds funny and sometimes it sounds merely unpleasant; but however it sounds, I believe we can learn something very important from listening to the kinds of things they say.

C.S. Lewis, *Mere Christianity*

The Alpha Enterprise
Evangelism in a
Post-Christian Era

STEPHEN HUNT

ASHGATE

Published by
Ashgate Publishing Limited
Gower House
Croft Road
Aldershot
Hants GU11 3HR
England

Ashgate Publishing Company
Suite 420
101 Cherry Street
Burlington, VT 05401-4405
USA

Ashgate website: http://www.ashgate.com

British Library Cataloguing in Publication Data
Hunt, Stephen, 1954–
   The alpha enterprise: evangelism in a post-Christian era
   1. Christian education 2. Evangelistic work – Church of England
   I. Title
   269.2

Library of Congress Cataloging-in-Publication Data
Hunt, Stephen, 1954–
   The Alpha Enterprise: evangelism in a post-Christian era/Stephen J. Hunt.
      p. cm.
   Includes index.
      ISBN 0-7546-5035-9 (hardcover : alk. paper) – ISBN 0-7546-5036-7 (pbk. :
   alk. paper) 1. Alpha International (Organization) 2. Evangelistic work. I. Title.

BV3752. A46H86 2004
269′.2–dc22

2004002022

ISBN 0 7546 5035 9 (Hbk)

ISBN 0 7546 5036 7 (Pbk)

Printed on acid-free paper

Typeset by Tradespools, Frome, Somerset
Printed and bound in Great Britain by Antony Rowe Ltd, Chippenham, Wilts

Contents

List of figures and tables

Figures

Tables

Foreword

Time-keeping is not my strong point. So as I drove purposefully down the road on a wet April evening I was already slightly late (as usual) for picking up my son from Cubs. But there was no need to panic, I mused, since the ever-enthusiastic Cub leader normally overran the meetings by at least 10–15 minutes. Sure enough, I arrived at the entrance to the church hall to discover a group of parents waiting somewhat tardily for their offspring to come out. But as I joined the small throng to show solidarity in patience, I realized I had walked into a reasonably terse discussion. Each parent was clutching a letter from *Akela*, which reminded parents and Cubs that Sunday was St George's Day, and that Cubs were expected (indeed, the letter stated that it was 'compulsory') to attend church parade. Smart kit and clean shoes were also recommended. The parents stood around discussing the word 'compulsory'. One looked bewildered, and cast around for empathy as he explained that his son played soccer on Sundays, so attendance was doubtful. Another mused that the family were all due to be away for the weekend, and that changing plans for a church parade was neither possible nor desirable. Another looked less than pleased that a 'voluntary' organization such as the Cubs, which she added her son went to by choice, should now be using words like 'compulsory'. There was no question of obligation; attendance and belonging was a matter of preference. (Presumably the oaths her son had taken were simply part of a traditional and quaint ceremony that had little actual meaning.)

At the beginning of the twenty-first century, a small vignette such as this would not be untypical in Western Europe. In the post-war era, a nascent culture of obligation has rapidly given way to one of consumerism. Duty, and the desire to participate in aspects of civic society where steadfast obligatory support was once cherished, has been rapidly eroded by choice, individualism and reflexivity.[1]

Granted, this Foreword is not the place to debate such a cultural turn. But its undoubted appearance on the landscape of late modernity has posed some interesting questions for voluntary organizations, chief of which might be religious establishments. Churches increasingly find themselves with worshippers who come less out of duty and more out of choice. There is, arguably, nothing wrong with that, but under these new cultural conditions churches have discovered that they need to have much more savvy about how they shape and market themselves in the public sphere. There is no escaping the reality: the churches are in competition. For people's time, energy, attention, money and commitment.

It is that last word, 'commitment', that has become such a slippery term in recent times. Few regular or frequent church-goers attend church twice on a Sunday, which was once normal practice. For most, once is enough. Many who do attend on a regular basis are now going less frequently. Allowing for holidays and other absences such as illness, even the most dedicated church-goer may only be present in church for 70 per cent of Sundays in any given year. Many clergy remark on the decline in attendance at Days of Obligation (major saints days, or feast days such as the Ascension). The committed, it seems, are also the busy. The response to this from amongst the more liturgical churches has been to subtly and quietly adapt their practice, whilst preserving the core tradition. For example, the celebration of Epiphany may take place on the Sunday nearest to 6 January, and not on the day itself. A number of Roman Catholic churches offer Sunday Mass on Saturday evenings, in order for Sunday to be left as a family day, or for whatever other commitments or consumerist choices might now fall on the once hallowed day of rest.

It is not my purpose here to venture into a debate about the precise nature of secularization. Whatever that process is supposed to describe, it seems to me that it can never do justice to the intrinsically inchoate nature of religious belief that characterized the Western European landscape and its peoples long before the Enlightenment, let alone the industrial revolution of the nineteenth century and the cultural revolutions of the twentieth century. The trouble with standard secularization theories is that they depend on exaggerating the extent and depth of Christendom. They assume a previous world of monochrome religious allegiance which is now, of course, in tatters. But in truth, the religious world was much more plural and contested before the twentieth century ever dawned. So what, exactly, has changed? Despite my reticence to accede too much ground to proponents of secularization theses, I readily acknowledge that the twentieth century has been the most seminal and challenging period for the churches in all of time. Leaving aside its own struggles with pluralism, post-colonialism, modernity, post-modernity and wave after wave of cultural change and challenge, the biggest issue the churches have had to face up to is, ironically, a simple one: choice. Increased mobility, globalization and consumerism have infected and affected the churches, just as they have touched every other aspect of social life. Duty is dead: the customer is king. It is no surprise, therefore, to discover churches adopting a consumerist mentality, and competing with one another for souls, 'bums on pews', or entering the marketplace itself, and trying to convert tired consumers into revitalized Christians.

In this important and timely study of Alpha courses, Stephen Hunt uses the well-established sociological framework of the spiritual marketplace, in order to illustrate something of the impact of commodification upon contemporary religion. Significantly, he demonstrates that the increasingly consumerist cultural turn adopted by the churches that advocate Alpha does not necessarily lead to an increase in the level of religiosity. Or perhaps put more acerbically, the number of customers for the courses does not necessarily translate into a new army of dedicated converts. Correspondingly, Alpha is more like a creature of its culture, and far less counter-cultural than many of its champions imagine. Its features chime almost too perfectly with post-modern consumer culture: a stress on relationships; a definite nod to the therapeutic; dogma presented with a distinctly 'light' touch; a course to try, but not necessarily a long-term commitment. This is not a criticism, I should add: merely an observation. Alpha is arguably the first example of 'mass branding' for Christianity, replete with its own logo, publications, clothing, cook-books and other non-essential but desirable merchandise such as baseball caps, fleeces, t-shirts, pens and the like. Just as Sidney Carter once lamented those churches that had made their version of Jesus or salvation 'copyright', we now have a version of Christianity that is 'patent pending': the Alpha brand enjoys legal protection, in order to distinguish it from any pale imitator.

Besides the 'marketplace' framework that Hunt deploys in his analysis, this book is also to be welcomed for its firm grounding in ethnography. Hunt's thesis is borne out of many hours of interviews, patient listening and reflection conducted with Alpha consumers, propagators and detractors. This primary research is what gives the book its edge, and locates it within the arena of the sociology of religion. I suspect that a number of readers will have been looking for sharper theological reflections, no doubt to bolster their own critical take on Alpha. Stephen Hunt's book is to be commended for rising above the ecclesial spats that often cloud perceptions and analyses of Alpha. Indeed, this is what good, plain, honest sociology can often best contribute to theological studies: hard data, and thoroughly grounded research that takes account of the social context in any religious movement. In this respect, Hunt has performed a valuable service for those who might want to understand why and how Alpha appears to be so successful. As scholars grapple with the persistence of religion in the modern, secular world, new analytical accounts are constantly needed that explain the tenacity of faith and thereby expose the continued (undeserved) hegemony of secularization theories.

The value of Hunt's approach lies in its grounded ethnography. As a discipline, it comes in all shapes and sizes: some are mainly quantitative, whilst others can be mostly qualitative; some depend on formal questionnaires and clearly proscribed methods; other kinds are more like 'participant observation', and accept the partiality of the observer/interpreter as a given. But fundamentally, as Courtney Bender notes in her prescient study, ethnography is always

> about human relationships: it is built (or broken) through trust and through barter and exchange of various kinds. Although [we] focus on fieldwork relationships, ethnographers carry on simultaneous dialogue and exchange (and human relations) with the scholarly community and

other texts as well. These concurrent dialogues make ethnographic
research unique amongst investigative journeys ... .[2]

Bender describes the delicate balance between stepping into 'streams' of
events and conversations, and the need to stay just outside them. There is an
ambiguity in making 'their' talk 'our' talk, in order to bridge the gap between
the gaze of the ethnographer and the lives that are being lived. Inevitably the
ethnographer is not simply a passive listener, but is an active agent in
conversations, and becomes a reflective partner in dialogue. This requires a
degree of self-awareness in the ethnographer; they must not only be attentive
to the words and moods they study, but also conscious of their own
vocabulary and emotions in a given situation. Ultimately, as Bender quips,
there are really only two kinds of [intellectual] books: (1) a stranger comes to
town, and (2) someone goes on a journey. In ethnography, she notes, one
always finds oneself in the second category, but with some overlap with the
first:

> the ethnographer is always in some sense a pilgrim ... a seeker ... we go
> on trips to undiscovered countries or, armed with notepads and a 'critical
> eye', we make our own countries strange ... [but] fieldwork [also]
> compels us to circle back on ourselves, our ideas, and our worlds, just as it
> also compels us to keep moving toward answers to our questions about
> the worlds of those around us ... .[3]

Hunt's journeying through planet Alpha (he is both a pilgrim seeking answers
and a stranger entering a world he does not belong to), enables the reader to
glimpse, perhaps for the first time, that a form of religion, far from
challenging consumerism, has itself been consumed by it. Again this is not a
criticism so much as a commonsensical observation. Recent work by Giggie
and Winston (2002)[4] shows that modern cities (replete with their pervasive
commercial cultures) and religious traditions interact in dynamic, complicated and unexpected ways, producing expressions of faith that aspire to rise
above the conventional cacophony of everyday city life. Alpha is just such a
product: a faith of the market and a faith for the market. As David Lyon
perceptively notes:

> consumerism has become central to the social and cultural life of the
> technologically advanced societies in the later twentieth century. Meaning
> is sought as a 'redemptive gospel' in consumption. And cultural identities
> are formed through processes of selective consumption.[5]

So, is Alpha doing no more than successfully marketing a specious brand of
Christianity within the wider consumerist cultural milieu, wherein the
'commodification of religion' is taking place? Laurence Moore's seminal
study *Selling God* provides a partial answer. Moore argues that secularization
theories should give way to an understanding of religion in the modern world,
whereby it has become one of a number of 'cultured' and 'leisured' activities
that individuals now purchase or subscribe to. Religion might once have been

somewhat standoffish from consumerism, and only entered the marketplace to censor and condemn it. But now, argues Moore:

> the work of religious leaders and moralists in the market-place of culture [is] immediately entangled in a related but distinguishable enterprise. Rather than remaining aloof, they entered their own inventive contributions into the market. Initially these were restricted to the market of reading material, but their cultural production diversified. Religious leaders ... [started to compete] with the appeal of popular entertainments. By degrees religion took on the shape of a commodity ...[6]

Hunt's important study is devoted to showing just how far that process of commodification has been reified in Alpha. Critics and fans of Alpha alike will gain important new insights by studying Hunt's methodology and findings closely. Social scientists will discover afresh just how complex secularization is in the modern world, and how religion can both consume and be consumed by the processes of free-market capitalism, to its detriment and advantage.

Last, but not least, I am grateful for being given the opportunity to write this Foreword since it allows me to follow up some comments I made on Alpha in an article in *Reviews in Religion and Theology* in 1997. My article (titled on the spur of the moment as 'Join-the-Dots Christianity') was a mischievous, tongue-in-cheek and waspish swipe at the course, critiquing its then profligate self-puffery. Although the article might be said to have landed some important punches (especially about Alpha's rather dogmatic approach to the concept of 'exploring'), my sentiments were taken to be more critical than they were intended. So by way of conclusion, here are three brief reflections on the Alpha phenomenon.

First, I think Alpha represents a seminal moment in the history of evangelicalism within late Western modernity. The course is decidedly 'doctrine-lite', but also dogmatic. It is, however, more simplistic than fundamentalistic. Its appeal to Christian 'basics' reflects its evangelical roots, but it could also be said to be curiously liberal in some regards. By placing a stress on relationships, encounters, experiences and the therapeutic, the Alpha course makes many more concessions to culture than certain conservative evangelical critics would like. Of course, it is precisely this recipe that gives Alpha its appeal. It is culturally-related (not relative) rather than counter-cultural. It is a sign of the times, and not an indictment of the age.

Second, the Alpha course, as well as being a product of its age, is also a product of its context. To be sure, there is no version of Christianity that is without a local accent. At least one lesson from the first Pentecost, as recorded in The Book of Acts, is that Christianity speaks in many tongues, not one. The irony of Alpha is that it is, on the one hand, a global brand. It appears to operate across all cultural boundaries without regard to the particularities of its situational context. On the other hand, the 'Knightsbridge accent' in Alpha is unmistakable. Alpha means Sophie can cruise down Kensington High Street and squeeze in a course on Christianity between a stop at the latest hip restaurant and a trip to Harvey Nichols. Thomas can top-up on Alpha in between a job in the City and a trip to the gym. Alpha is a free-trial pack of Christianity for the busy consumer; not necessarily a course that leads either to converts or commitments.

Third, the claim of Alpha-philes to offer a course that 'explores the meaning of life' is a classic trope. 'Exploration' still remains a constrained and tightly controlled concept. Pedagogically, the course is most weak where it imagines itself to be strong. It refuses to develop a process of deep literacy and serious questioning. It is guilty of what the late lamented Paulo Freire would have called 'the castration of curiosity'. The pre-selected 'basics' not only have ready-to-hand answers, they also shape the questions themselves. Correspondingly, the notion of true exploration is deeply impoverished. But let us not end on such a negative note. Alpha, for all its faults, is a remarkable *tour de force*. It is arguably one of the most recognizable and successful Christian brands of the twenty-first century. Whether you are a consumer or a critic, Alpha's friendly and bathetic form of hegemony deserves some respect. Stephen Hunt's book gives the course its due (as do I), but is thankfully not content to let the matter rest there.

Martyn Percy
Director, Lincoln Theological Institute
University of Manchester

Notes

1 For a useful introduction see Putman (2000).
2 Bender (2003), p. 148.
3 Ibid., p. 151.
4 Giggie and Winston (2002).
5 Lyon (2000), p. 74.
6 Moore (1994), p. 6.

Introduction

A simple depiction of the Alpha course is that of a unique evangelizing programme designed specifically for the contemporary age and one which advertises itself as 'a ten week practical introduction to the Christian faith'. For several years the founders of Alpha have set out the programme as a project which they purport to have been thoughtfully constructed to present the simple principles of Christianity in a relaxed and informal environment to those who would endeavour to know more about the faith. Over the last few years it has constituted a mammoth enterprise. In fact, the endeavour has been supported by thousands of churches in the UK from where it originated and, more recently, by tens of thousands of others across the world – representing practically all denominations and traditions. In the USA its growth has been particularly prolific, if constrained to particular Christian quarters.

The primary long-term aim of Alpha is to win souls in the time-honoured tradition of Christian evangelism. Its short-term goal is to inform and educate people and encourage them to consider the possibility of following a spiritual path in a post-modern age. There is the opportunity to discover, as the Alpha advertising poster suggests, whether or not Christianity really is 'Boring, Untrue and Irrelevant'. Alpha is, to put it succinctly, a crash course in Christianity for beginners, the unchurched, the faithless, and even those already convinced but who wish to refresh their faith or desire to go further in their Christian commitment and journeying. The Alpha course, then, claims to have something for everybody.

Alpha has become almost a household word. Certainly, those who put the much acclaimed programme together would like to think this is the case and that the course has become almost a compulsory church activity. Undoubtedly, Alpha would seem to be gaining recognition with the public at large. The so-called Millennium Alpha initiative, launched in early 2001, was accompanied by a survey conducted by Holy Trinity, Brompton – the church which originally constructed the programme. The research indicated that 12 per cent of those asked (some 900,000 people) recognized the Alpha symbol which appears on posters and leaflets of a man struggling to carry a large question mark – presumably signifying the quest for the answers to the 'ultimate questions' of life. Why am I here? What happens when I die? And what is the meaning of it all?

Some 16 per cent (or 1 in 6) of the UK adult population surveyed by a MORI opinion poll on behalf of Alpha International identified Alpha as a Christian course, while 41 per cent knew someone who had graduated through the programme.[1] If all this is true, and there is no reason to suppose

The Alpha symbol as universally seen on posters, leaflets and literature
Source: *The Alpha Manual*

that it is not, then Alpha has continued to make an impact since its first nation-wide appearance in the UK in the mid-1990s and has retained a considerable hold on many churches, particularly those of an evangelical disposition.

It may be that this apparent relatively high profile enjoyed by Alpha alone justifies the claim that a book should be written about the subject from the point of view of an 'outsider', someone with no vested interest (other than his academic career as a sociologist) and outside of church circles. In fact, this is my second book on the subject. The first and admittedly very slim volume, *Anyone for Alpha* (2001), was offered as a largely 'popular' book for the 'internal consumption' of church-goers in the UK. It was based on the experiences of a small number of churches in south-east England – of those who ran the course in their local church and individuals who had taken or were thinking of subscribing to Alpha as 'guests'.

Table I.1   Alpha Mori opinion poll findings (%)

	September 2000	September 2001	September 2003
Have you heard of a course called Alpha?			
Yes, a Christian course	9	16	20
Never heard of/don't know	86	82	83
Have you ever seen this symbol (Alpha logo)?			
Yes	12	15	not available
No	87	83	not available

The focus of what amounted to a pilot study was largely on whether Alpha was achieving its aim of winning converts. The work provided a rather simplified account of the programme from the point of view of the guest participating in a course. This early research was based primarily on the experiences of Alpha in four churches with different denominational backgrounds and situated in one geographical locality. The volume drew at least some interest. The media regarded it as a valuable source for exploring and sometimes countering a number of the over-enthusiastic claims of the more fanatical Alpha supporters in respect of its impact and level of success. I found myself quoted and misquoted in the newspapers, while also appearing on national and local radio. The latter included a rather contrived and one-sided debate on a local radio 'God slot' with Alpha's principal initiator Nicky Gumbel – described by an Anglican clergyman that I once interviewed as 'probably the second most important man in Christendom after the Pope'.

Elsewhere, my early findings and broad claims regarding Alpha met with a perhaps predictably mixed response. The view of Christian readers was divided. Some interpreted the pilot study as a balanced appraisal that was truly founded on the experiences of those who run the course, as well as individuals who were familiar with it as guests. A number of church people immediately recognized a few of their own encounters of Alpha in the stories of others which I related – dimensions of the course that are rarely brought to light, the negative as well as the positive points. A fair few church men and women, although supporting the aims of Alpha, welcomed constructive criticism believing that it could only benefit the programme and possibly lead to improvements. For example, some acknowledged (as the research indicated) Alpha's underlying middle-class culture. Hence, a number of Christian leaders have subsequently been inspired to find ways of enhancing its wider social appeal. On the other hand, one or two of the problem areas highlighted in the early research persuaded several church leaders that Alpha was not for them. At least one Baptist pastor maintained that it finally convinced him not to run any more courses at his church.[2] It goes without saying that such repercussions were not my intention in conducting research. At the same time, there were those Christians who found my approach unnecessarily negative, lacking in balance, even provocative and cynical. This perceived stance is perhaps inevitable when an agnostic sociologist studies something as sensitive as other people's religion.

This volume brings a more rigorous and focused academic approach, and perhaps more considered reflection in coming to grips with the subject of Alpha through a much larger survey conducted on a national scale (England and Wales to be precise). Its perspective is largely sociological and is not without its difficulties. There are all sorts of methodological and epistemological problems related to how to approach religion in general and contemporary Christianity in particular – at least in the shape of the Alpha programme. Some of the difficulties encountered, such as accounting for and describing people's conversion experiences, are not new to the specialism of the sociology of religion, even if Alpha generates a number of its own unique research dilemmas. These difficulties will be addressed throughout the chapters to come. Moreover, it needs to be said that while I purport to be a sociologist, I make no further claims to be a theologian. It will be necessary to confront a number of theological issues – a study of Alpha demands such an engagement. I trust that I have a sense of place. These theological issues that Alpha raises are complex and I will attempt to negotiate them as respectfully as I can.

The main thrust of this book is to apply state-of-the-art sociological theorizing and several anthropological analytical frameworks to Alpha, and to consider their relevance by way of the empirical data uncovered. The principal concern is in understanding the Alpha 'product' in terms of the dynamics of a 'spiritual marketplace'. To some extent at least, such a theoretical paradigm helps us to understand Alpha as a religious (distinctly Christian) 'supplier' and its parallel contingent of those signed up for the course as 'customers'. In short, there should be room to comprehend the motivations of individuals who have put on Alpha, as well as the levels of satisfaction experienced by those who have passed through it. As crude as these concepts might appear to be they at least provide a starting point by which to come to grips with a unique religious phenomenon and, more broadly, advance theorizing within the context of the discipline that today constitutes the sociology of religion.

Since this book is founded upon a national survey of Alpha courses, its scale hopefully means that the conclusions are more reliable than those produced by the earlier pilot research findings. At the same time it marks an attempt to keep up to date. Things have moved on since I began my initial research in the late 1990s. Alpha has continued to grow on a national and international level. In many parts of the world there is no doubt that it has had considerable impact on the Christian church irrespective of denomination, church tradition, and cultural context. New campaigning initiatives have arisen in recent years which means that additional churches have adopted Alpha and tens of thousands more people across the globe have graduated through the course. There can be little doubting, then, the significance of Alpha for contemporary Christianity, for good or for bad.

I can at this point briefly hint at some of my findings and tentatively raise the issue of my personal attitude to Alpha. This book is not an attempt to 'knock' Alpha and be unduly critical of an evangelism programme which can realistically claim more than a measure of success. I like to think that I have no axe to grind. Nevertheless, I will argue that Alpha's much heralded accomplishments are frequently overestimated. Certainly, there is no doubting its global impact particularly since there is, as yet, no viable or large-scale rival alternative to Alpha. But here we have to be cautious. It is evident that the programme is supported by its own forceful propaganda which is typified by the self-appreciating and self-congratulating headlines of its newspapers and other accompanying material that tend to lack a balanced or critical dimension. For instance, there are headlines in its official newspaper, *Alpha News*, such as 'Alpha Cuts Crime', suggesting that a sizeable number of conversions have led to the decline of criminal behaviour on a national scale and that Alpha has spurred a Christian revival in UK jails and is therefore undertaking something of a public duty in reforming prisoners.[3] This is what is claimed by Alpha supporters, but it ain't necessarily so.

Alpha has also gained the attention of the national media. Two examples of reports in the more 'serious' newspapers may suffice:

> The Rev. Gumbel has a hit on his hands. ... The Alpha achievement is colossal. The churches that were emptying are now filling up again.[4]

> At a time when our churches are losing worshippers, Alpha is packing them in the aisles.[5]

I have frequently been struck by the surprisingly largely warm reception given by Alpha in the secular press in recent years. This has been particularly so since the general coverage of the charismatic movement – from which Alpha is ultimately derived and culturally inspired – over the years by the media has been scarcely cordial. (Media coverage of the so-called Toronto Blessing, an esoteric phenomenon which swept globally through thousands of churches in the mid-1990s, was certainly derisory.) Much of the media representation of Alpha appears to swallow the propaganda that the programme is winning numerous new converts and, that by doing so, wider society is being infused with a new moral spirit. I am, however, yet to be convinced that the near ecstatic triumphalism either by supporters of Alpha in the churches or the media hype strikes the right chord. This is where a more balanced and considered appraisal is called for, one that is perhaps forced to conclude that Alpha, in the context of an increasingly secular society, may be merely a cry in the wilderness with very few hearing the call.

There is little questioning Alpha's impact on UK churches and increasingly in the USA and elsewhere in terms of motivating members to organize courses. Congregations in large cities, down to the village church, have partaken of the initiative. Furthermore, it is by no means confined to a number of churches from particular denominations or evident that it has impacted only a distinct segment of Christendom, although I will argue later that the churches involved may display certain characteristics.

To be sure, there is no doubting either the bustle or the hype of Alpha. Yet things are not always what they seem to be in terms of end results. Moreover, there is evidence of a number of intended and unintended consequences of the Alpha programme that have to be considered in their own right. One is that Alpha has proved to have an ecumenical dimension and in doing so has enhanced the trend over recent decades for churches to come together to discuss their differences and consider the ways forward to Christian unity and to the benefit of all. Alpha has at least advanced this aim since it plays down doctrinal divisions and plays up what is supposed to be the core teachings of the faith, albeit furnished with charismatic teaching and practices.

Over recent years the Roman Catholic church and the range of Protestant denominations have increasingly come to work together in campaigning and propagating initiatives at local, national and, latterly, international levels – strengthening relationships between them and, to some extent at least, overcoming theological and cultural differences. Alpha builds on these foundations but in doing so gives this ecumenical movement a unique 'charismatic' twist. Where once the different strands of Christendom were 'united in the Spirit' they are now joined by the aims and dynamics of Alpha. This by no means suggests that Alpha does not have its critics within the churches. It has, and the nature and significance of the opponents' view will be given scope in this book.

Further research on the Alpha programme can also be justified on the grounds that some issues which were rather tentatively touched upon in the pilot study deserve to be discussed in greater depth in order to cast light on several important aspects of Alpha. One issue is its theological stance and the implications of offering a particular type of Christianity. A number of critics of Alpha have noted its 'fundamentalist' inclinations in what is meant to be an introduction to the faith. 'Fundamentalism' is undoubtedly a slippery term. Nonetheless, claims that Alpha is fundamentalist in nature raise a number of other key questions. What kind of Christianity is being flaunted by Alpha and who selects what constitutes the 'basics' of Christianity?

These questions lead to the further issue as to what is the significance of the topics singled out for exploration and, perhaps more importantly, what is excluded. It seems to me that there is little discussion of the theology being advanced by Alpha. As the programme becomes more popular a greater discussion may follow. Certainly, in the weighty context of university theological schools and seminaries some debate is slowly beginning to emerge. In the early summer of 2002 I attended a theology conference at a Danish university. Many teachers in the theology faculty had told me of the increasing impact of Alpha in Denmark and some of these learned men and women expressed concern. One was amazed at the lack of discussion in Danish churches regarding the theological content of Alpha. He thought that there was a serious danger of this 'introduction to Christianity' becoming, and these are his words not mine, 'the gospel according to Nicky Gumbel' (the director of the course).

In some respects the Christianity advanced by Alpha might appear to be an intolerant form. Some church men and women have argued that it is plainly fundamentalist. 'Fundamentalism', as we have briefly observed, is a difficult concept and is something which has to be detailed in the context of Alpha. Illiberal attitudes to certain topics are arguably evident. For example, its interpretation of the Bible has led a number of critics to suggest that Alpha is homophobic. While the secular world has slowly come to accept the legitimacy and rights of gay people, the programme's literature explicitly states that gay behaviour is a sin and that those who practise it should ideally desist from doing so. There is nothing new in this stance since, in my opinion at least, the Christian church has long opposed homosexuality as part of its unbalanced preoccupation with all things sexual at the expense of condemning other inequities. Nevertheless, the issue of gays, particularly their acceptance within the Christian church, is possibly the hottest current controversy in Christendom other than the ordination of women priests. Using the subject of gay sexuality as a theme, the penultimate chapter of this volume discusses what Alpha has to say and the experience of gay people who have come into contact with the course.

Another related area that this volume seeks to address is the consequence of mass-producing a world-wide programme which bills itself as an introduction to Christianity. This is particularly important in relation to Alpha's apparent inflexibility. For those running the course there would seem to be little room for innovation or discretion. It is, in theory, the same programme, the same themes, and the same structure the world over. This obviously has implications for the growing influence of the church that put Alpha together – Holy Trinity, Brompton. In short, one church has exported its standard version of Christianity across the globe. Sociologically speaking, this allows us to engage with debates concerning cultural, economic and technological change in the modern world and its implications for religious faith. It encourages us to explore themes such as that of 'McDonaldization' – a concept first devised by the sociologist George Ritzer (1996). Through this concept Ritzer considered the implications of standardized products in a shrinking global market, as typified by McDonalds the fast-food chain. McDonaldization, according to Ritzer, has come to impact every aspect of life. By applying Ritzer's theoretical framework we might suggest that religion too, with its discernible and distinct 'marketplace', is not immune from such developments. Not only is Alpha a particular type of Christianity, it has also saturated the Christian market in a fairly standardized form and, as suggested throughout this book (and addressed squarely in Chapter 9), there are various wide-ranging implications and consequences.

Perhaps the greatest consideration, however, is the experiences both negative and positive of those who have been through the Alpha programme. It addresses probably the single most important question: is Alpha working? Does it do what it claims to do in advancing an introduction to Christianity? Is it making converts and setting people off on a spiritual road? This is related to another principal question: who signs up for an Alpha course? Other chapters in this book consider the various categories of people who join up and their experiences of Alpha, including those who have been converted, those who left early, and those who saw out the programme but have decided that Christianity was not for them. A further chapter is dedicated to variations of the Alpha course directed deliberately to appeal to distinct social groups. This includes Student Alpha – a customized variety of the course which is aimed at students in universities and other institutes of higher education, and Prison Alpha – the variety of the course run in penal institutions.

Finally, I have been encouraged to move forward with more research by many Christians running the Alpha course (even by Holy Trinity, Brompton, if tentatively) and by others who do not. I hope that the volume is constructive in its approach. I am grateful to those churches and individuals who have participated in the research upon which this book is founded. While every effort has been made to produce a balanced volume it invariably once again falls between the twin stools of sociological enquiry on the one hand and the sensitivity of religious belief on the other. On the plus side we all have something to learn from Alpha, both from within the churches and academia and, from the Alpha guest's point of view, to discover a new rendition of the age-old and unchanging gospel.

Notes

1   *Alpha News*, November 1999–January 2000, p. 4. *Alpha News* is published three times a year by Holy Trinity, Brompton.
2   *Baptist Times*, March 2001, p. 9.
3   *Alpha News*, November 1999–January 2000, p. 6.
4   Gyles Brandeth, *The Sunday Telegraph*, 14 March 2001.
5   Julie Llewellyn Smith, *The Times*, 23 April 2002.

Chapter 1

Alpha: Developments So Far

The Reach of Alpha

Alpha has to be put in historical perspective. As an evangelizing enterprise it proved to be a rather late contribution to the so-called 'Decade of Evangelism' of the 1990s. As the century closed, Alpha was regarded by many church leaders in the UK as the most important initiative of its time. The Decade of Evangelism initially amounted to a large-scale evangelizing effort by UK churches and was perhaps most noteworthy because of its monumental failure to win the converts that it sought and hence to reverse the decline of the churches and restore their fortunes lost in the post-war years. Yet the UK initiative was spurred not only by declining church attendance, but also by an appeal for a global mission from wider quarters. The call for world-wide 'evangelization' had first been ventured by Pope John Paul as part of a dedication to the Christian mission and commitment leading up to the second millennial celebration of Christ's birth. The Decade of Evangelism was the Christian response in the UK. Tentatively supported by the Archbishop of Canterbury and enthusiastically validated by Protestant evangelicals (perhaps wishing to match the efforts of the Catholic church), the Decade of Evangelism attempted to combat but also constructively engage with the secular forces of the contemporary world.

Most of the previous outreach programmes (largely based on leafleting and poster campaigns) put together during the 1990s as part of the Decade of Evangelism, were ill-conceived and ineffectual. They often embraced only one method of evangelism, and conspicuously failed to understand the nature of society today – its level of disbelief, secularity, plurality, and prevailing cultural trajectories. Alpha followed a number of these other rather unsuccessful evangelizing initiatives that surfaced in the early/mid-1990s. Probably the two most noteworthy endeavours were Minus to Plus, whose title clearly recognized church attendance decline, and Jesus in Me (JIM) instigated by the Pentecostal denominations Elim and the Assemblies of God. Despite the effort and finances poured into them, such evangelistic forays into the disbelieving world appeared marginal and inept.

Rather ironically, it was two leading personalities of the Pentecostal churches who instigated these initiatives by departing from the narcissistic preoccupation with the pentecostal experience and all things related to the charisma that had dominated evangelical life since the 1980s. In doing so, they also turned their backs on the much-vaunted evangelizing formula of the soul-winning crusade. Wyn Lewis of the Elim denomination headed up JIM. It cost several million pounds to initiate and underscored the fact that large-scale evangelizing outreaches require money and plenty of it, but its posters and pictures proved too enigmatic and the language too archaic to impact upon the secular world.

The second initiative, Minus to Plus, was the brain-child of the South African evangelist, Reinhard Bonnke. Minus to Plus involved the distribution of a booklet which was posted through the letterboxes of millions of householders in the UK and subsequently to other countries in Western Europe. It was Christian tract, but clearly contemporary Christian tract. However, without 'the human touch' of contact through a church, it largely proved to be a failure – certainly in terms of winning converts. It is noteworthy, nonetheless, that Minus to Plus, with its designated aim of increasing church attendance, was also locked in several prophecies emerging from a number of leading neo-Pentecostal churches, at least from their leaders or self-designated prophets. These prophecies spoke of an impending world revival, which would commence in the UK and then spread to all other nations. Bonnke had uttered such prophecies himself and they were made known as he led a number of crusading conventions in Western Europe to launch Minus to Plus. In the UK he shared a platform in the autumn of 1994 at the Central Methodist Hall, London, with key figures in the charismatic churches – both from the mainline denominations and the so-called 'New Churches'. There was much talk of revival, of possibly the last revival before the Second Coming of Christ. This hope born in Christian eschatology might seem very remote from the more realistic and sober language of much of the Alpha programme but there is a certain continuity, as we shall explore below.

Minus to Plus aimed at winning 250,000 converts. In the event only some 20,000 souls were won over, many of whom were believed to be those returning to the faith rather than discovering it for the first time. It goes without saying that this failure scotched the erroneous prediction of a coming revival, but this was not the end of the efforts of the evangelical constituency. Enter Alpha, fully endorsed by the Evangelical Alliance – the umbrella organization for the majority of evangelical (mostly charismatic) churches in the UK. It promised much towards the end of the 1990s with its fresh approach and simple design and was prepared to learn from the mistakes of the earlier evangelizing initiative. It also had a fair amount of financial support and that other vital ingredient for the evangelizing effort, an abundance of soul-winning enthusiasm.

In September 1998, over 4,000 churches came together to launch the first £1 million so-called national Alpha initiative. This was some three years after the churches were first encouraged to adopt the Alpha programme by its founders at Holy Trinity, Brompton. Towards the end of 1998 nearly 2,000 billboards were posted in towns and cities nationwide, while advertising space was taken out in hundreds of national and local newspapers. As far as publicity was concerned, this was the turning point for Alpha. Given the high profile, it was undoubtedly a success in that the non-churched increasingly became aware of Alpha's existence even if they had not signed up in any great number.

Alpha's Appeal

Alpha's appeal has also proved to be universal. Over 7,000 churches in the UK now sponsor the programme. In addition, there are allegedly nearly 20,000 courses running world-wide in approximately 130 countries. On a global scale Alpha is believed to have attracted almost 3 million people to its programme, the figure provided by *Alpha News*.[1] The same edition stated that 4 million people in the UK 'have either done the course or know someone who has'. These are estimates and rounding off statistics in an upward direction obviously forges good impressions.

Despite such tendencies of self-aggrandisement, the growth of Alpha since 1998 has undoubtedly been phenomenal. If Christ had given the command for the gospel to be preached all over the world, then Alpha was seen as a major vehicle for doing so – a unique package of evangelism exported on a global basis. Hence, Alpha courses steadily proliferated from the mere four ran at Holy Trinity in 1991, to 200 in 1993, rising to 2,500 in 1995, and advancing to 10,500 as a result of the national initiative in 1998.[2] Interestingly, however, in November 2001 *Alpha News* stated that 7,300 courses were running in the UK. This might suggest that the 1998 national initiative marked the height of Alpha's impact in the churches.

Alpha has unquestionably developed rapidly over the last few years. The first national initiative of 1998 was aimed at bringing the programme to saturation point in order to enhance a greater public awareness of what it had to offer. Those who put Alpha together were well aware that people outside of social networks which fed into the churches through friends, relatives, neighbours and work associates, were not being contacted. This meant that a fair proportion of the population were failing to be reached with the gospel

Table 1.1   Number of Alpha courses in the UK

1991	4
1992	5
1993	200
1994	740
1995	2,500
1996	5,000
1997	6,700
1998	10,500

Source: Alpha: God Changing Lives, published by
Holy Trinity, Brompton

message and that those who knew of Alpha did so mostly through association with people already in the church. The national initiative of Alpha therefore marked an attempt to supplement personal contacts, as valued as they were, with saturation advertising in order to reach those previously untouched. The newly-established aim was to develop large-scale advertising through high-street posters and the comprehensive leafleting of homes and, in doing so, it was hoped to reach a wider section of the population. By supporting the rather vague messages that the posters carried, every house in the UK was meant to be leafleted in order to provide more details about Alpha and stipulate points of contact. The latter did not quite come to fruition. Nonetheless, many national initiatives since 1998 have carried the same strategy of media saturation.

UK churches have certainly tried hard to promote Alpha and sustain its high profile. In September 1998, over 4,000 churches (all supposedly contributing £100 to the campaign) of the major denominations came together at London's Docklands Arena to launch the first £1 million national initiative. In the weeks which followed more than 1,700 large posters were displayed nationwide, while smaller posters were placed on church notice-boards. Approximately 5,500 poster sites in total were set up. At the same time, 4.5 million invitations to attend Alpha courses were distributed in the form of leaflets through letter boxes, supplemented by advertisements in 850 local newspapers across the country in addition to those in several national newspapers. Free nationwide publicity was also given to the campaign by television and radio stations in the UK. ITV's flagship news programme 'News at Ten' carried the Alpha national initiative as a major news item, and BBC1 devoted an entire edition of 'Songs of Praise' to its launch.

Although the campaigns associated with the Decade of Evangelism had failed spectacularly to return people to the churches, Alpha at least offered the promise of human contact and gave them something to 'jump off onto' rather than mere media advertising. The problem was that there was no contact address displayed on the large billboards: 'The Alpha course. Starting at a church near you' was (and remains) as close as things got to specifics. The initiative then appeared to lay with the 'customer' – or what Alpha refers to as the 'guest'. Yet the poster campaign epitomized a fresh strategy since it marked a new way of thinking about communicating with the public. Posters did not include quotations of biblical text. There was no call to repentance. Rather they were deliberately designed to be eye-catching, challenging and tended to be rather zany. Local and national newspapers also carried other provocative inducements to discover the Christian faith:

Job, Flat, Car, Girlfriend, Season ticket to United. Still not Satisfied?

You're born. You live. You die. End of story?

An Opportunity to Explore the Meaning to Life.

Christianity: Boring, Untrue and Irrelevant?

Alpha into the Twenty-first Century

In September 2001 the fourth annual 'Alpha Initiative' was launched. It was the first in which no voluntary contribution was requested from the 7,000 or so churches that subscribed to Alpha in the UK. Instead, the money had been raised from the 'Alpha Partners', a group of private donors, churches and trusts. Holy Trinity, Brompton, itself contributed £2 million towards the running costs. As part of the new national campaign hundreds of churches also took part in the nationwide so-called Alpha Supper Prayer Initiative, when over 300 meetings were organized.

The 2001 national Alpha Initiative amounted to the largest ever poster campaign. The face of black Alpha course leader Ade Adebajo was chosen as the main image this time. Pictured with his head thrown back and laughing, Adebajo appeared on 1,500 major billboard sites in the UK, 75 London underground stations, 3,000 buses, hundreds of thousands of leaflets and brochures. Other images showed a happy group of people of various ages and this undoubtedly was meant to indicate that all were welcomed and that Alpha had a broad appeal to every section of society, the old and young, all ethnic groups, men and women, people in different occupations, and the less well off alongside the more affluent.

The 2001 initiative was also expected to be boosted by the 10-week national television documentary on the independent channel which began in July of that year – 'Alpha: Will it Change Their Lives?' – hosted by the well-known and respected personality Sir David Frost. It proved to be a non-critical, mostly highly favourable approach that was programmed extremely late on Sunday evenings and therefore had relatively low viewing figures. Around 2.3 million people switched on to the first programme which was succinctly described by Frost as 'Big Brother meets the New Testament'. Viewing figures settled down at under one million – allegedly, according to *Alpha News*, because of the late scheduling.[3] Undoubtedly its late coverage ultimately said something, perhaps most obviously that the television company anticipated Alpha would have a very limited appeal. This did not prevent *Alpha News* from claiming that the ten young people who had taken the televised course were so inspired by Alpha as to either become committed Christians, embarked on a spiritual journey, or simply that participation 'changed their attitude to life'.[4]

The impact of Alpha is by no means restricted to churches in the UK. Even before the launch of the 1998 national campaign, the programme had taken on global dimensions and was soon running in 75 countries by the end of that year. In mid-1999, its organizers claimed that there were 11,430 Alpha courses established internationally; in total over one million people across the world had passed through the programme since 1995, a further half a million by 1999, doubling to 3 million by 2002.[5] By the end of 2003 the figure of those graduating through Alpha may well have been nearer 4 million.

Outside of the UK, Alpha courses have been set up in Eastern Europe including Albania, Romania, and other former Soviet bloc nations which were starved of religious expression under decades of communist rule. Far-flung places such as Australia, Latin America, the Far East, and sometimes more remote regions of the world, have also embraced Alpha. Where it has performed especially well however is, perhaps predictably, in the USA. Thousands of Alpha courses have been set up, thus establishing North America as the major growth area for the programme in recent years. At first its spread was largely through the highly successful global network of USA churches, the Association of Vineyard Churches with which Holy Trinity, Brompton, and other major evangelical churches in the UK had developed a close contact since the early 1980s. Indeed, Vineyard as a 'movement' had in its own right impacted powerfully on the charismatic 'scene' for nearly two decades. Its closeness to charismatic Anglican circles in particular had further developed with the renowned evangelical, the late David Watson, who was befriended by Vineyard's then leader John Wimber. The dissemination of Vineyard's teachings and practice followed the influential Third Wave conference at Methodist Central in 1983 – an event which attracted national denominational representation.

More recently Alpha, through the active work of Holy Trinity and its associates, has expanded to thousands of other churches in the USA. Over 3,500 American churches were registered in early 2002 as running Alpha courses compared to 2,300 in September 2001. According to the Alpha website this had risen to 5,000 churches by the end of 2003, with over a million people having graduated through the programme. Something of an Alpha craze has struck America and, as with most else in the country, Alpha is on a bigger scale. The largest-ever Alpha conference with 1,500 church leaders gathered in Boston. It was just one of the 40 Alpha conferences taking place throughout America during 2001.[6] These are early days for the USA as far as Alpha is concerned and despite its apparent ready acceptance the course remains fairly limited to the Vineyard churches and their fellow passengers, as well as mainline churches of a typically charismatic orientation. Many other churches, however, including those of a more traditional fundamentalist persuasion, remain largely outside of its influence. Nevertheless, according to the Alpha website, leaders of some of the largest churches and ministries in the USA, along with respected theologians, are increasingly endorsing Alpha and the site boasts complimentary quotes from a variety of Christian celebrities including Bill Hybels, J.I. Packer, Luis Palau and Jack Hayford.

Indicative of Alpha's international appeal is its sale of books and other material supporting the course. Most have been written by Nicky Gumbel who heads the Alpha initiative and has largely devised it. *Questions of Life* (Kingsway Publications), Gumbel's first and best-selling book on the Alpha course, has been on sale since July 2001 in high-street mainstream bookshops as well as the usual Christian outlets. The book has sold more than 500,000 copies (150,000 in the USA) around the world since it was originally published in 1993. It was voted 'Christian Book of the Year' in 1994 and has been consistently in the top-selling Christian volumes in the UK ever since. It is now translated into 28 languages including Romanian, Chinese, Russian, Japanese, Korean, Arabic, and Welsh, and can be bought in 55 countries.

More than a million copies of the half a dozen other books written by Nicky Gumbel have also been sold, including 300,000 of *Searching Issues* and more than 60,000 of the millennium edition of *Why Jesus?* These are booklets which address two of the questions most asked by 'guests' on Alpha courses: 'What about other religions?' and 'Why does God allow suffering?' Another sign of its international dimension is that the Alpha course booklet and other accompanying literature has been published in at least 17 languages. There are also Alpha brochures, a poster pack, sweatshirts and car stickers, the *Alpha Cookbook*, and more paraphernalia besides – all of which add to Alpha's ever-expanding commercial industry.

The Significance of Holy Trinity, Brompton

As we have already noted, the centre of Alpha activity is Holy Trinity, Brompton, London. A large poster outside the church proudly announces 'HTB – the Home of Alpha'. The first impression is of an inconspicuous-looking parish church positioned just off Brompton Road. It is by no means easy to locate, hidden away behind the far grander and more impressive Roman Catholic Oratory of St Philip Neri, next to the Victoria and Albert Museum in Kensington. HTB's modest structure belies its national, indeed international, importance in evangelical circles.

HTB's lack-lustre exterior, however, does little justice to the size of the interior and hive of activities that are carried out within its walls. In addition to all the usual aspects of church life, it caters for hundreds of 'guests' on Alpha courses and thousands of people attending regular international conferences related to the programme. It is a bustling church which never appears to close and never stops. Every moment and every square foot of space is given optimum use in the evangelizing initiative. There are well-furnished conference rooms and a basement coffee shop. There is also a bookshop which stocks the complete range of Alpha accessories and further offerings of Christian literature and teaching material, besides the obligatory compact disks and audio and video tapes that are now such a familiar part of the contemporary Christian scene. Today, HTB is the wealthiest Anglican church in England with an annual income of £3 million. A good part of this income obviously originates from the sale of evangelizing materials, not least of all from Alpha. A total of £400,000 is derived from the sale of tapes, pamphlets and books. The income is also partly donated from the church's well-heeled parishioners who are drawn from the affluent community of Kensington and its neighbourhoods. Added to this Alpha receives around £1 million in donations from its own congregation and £1.7 million from other gifts, trusts and benefactors.

Alpha is undoubtedly HTB's invention. The beginnings of the course can perhaps be traced back to late 1969 with the publication of the book *Questions of Life* that was initially conceived as a four-week introduction into the basics of Christianity at HTB. However, Alpha commenced in earnest in 1977 when Charles Marnham, a clergyman at the church, sought a means of presenting the fundamental principles of the Christian faith in a relaxed and informal setting. To start with, Alpha was aimed at educating new converts into the rudiments of the faith and only later was it extended to non-church-goers when course leaders noticed that people were bringing along their unconverted friends and associates. John Irvine took over in 1981; he lengthened it to ten weeks and added a weekend on the theme of the person and work of the Holy Spirit. When Nicky Lee assumed command in 1985 there were about thirty-five people on each course held exclusively at HTB. Under his leadership the figure grew to over one hundred.

By the time Nicky Gumbel took the helm, in 1990, Alpha was a central feature of HTB's church life. It was then substantially developed by Gumbel in 1992 and has evolved ever since. Under his tutelage the course has become longer in length and more informal in its working philosophy. HTB has continued to refine Alpha by sending questionnaires to those who have completed the course and by welcoming comments by the churches involved. The general idea has been to find out what matters relating to the Christian faith truly interested people. Gumbel has also modified an important element of the course – the near-compulsory and controversial weekend away with its emphasis on the teachings of the Holy Spirit which now includes the important and controversial element of 'Ministry Time' (see Chapter 14).

Gumbel is the key figure in Alpha. As an ex-barrister and old Etonian, he is very much representative of the congregation at HTB. Having given up a lucrative career in order to become an Anglican clergyman, he has matured into his leading role. In his forties, Gumbel is an impeccable and lively Christian personality. There are no controversies surrounding his private life, although my own view of the man in my short meeting with him is that he is something of an enigma. I sense that he is a far more complex character than the straightforward and uncomplicated personality often portrayed in his video presentations at the heart of the Alpha programme. Feelings towards him are, as I have discovered, rather mixed among Alpha course leaders, ranging from a dislike of his cultural nuances to great laudation of his personal role in developing the programme. Regarding the latter appraisal, Gumbel was described to me by one Baptist minister whose church subscribed to Alpha as 'an earnest professional, a good communicator, and the most important evangelist since Billy Graham'. A recommendation indeed.

There are a number of stories associated with Gumbel and his link to Alpha which have become almost a mythology. To the fore is that which relates that he was, to use charismatic jargon, 'empowered' by the 'anointing' of the late healing evangelist and leader of the Vineyard movement, John Wimber, in the mid-1990s to take Alpha nationally. Gumbel's mission then, is a special one, legitimated by one of the most influential evangelists in recent times. It is also this kind of anecdote which more than suggests the continuity of Alpha with broader developments in the charismatic movement over the years. This is a continuity that cannot be over-stressed and which will be detailed in Chapter 3. What can be said at this point, however, is that the growing success of Alpha would appear to fulfil a distinct prophecy related to HTB. This relates to one male member of the congregation, who for many years prayed for God to perform something special at HTB. This was some thirty years ago when pews and choir boys could be found at the church – both now long gone. Alpha would seem to have answered this man's prayers. Anecdotes such as this have added to the range of charismatic myths that surround HTB and, indirectly, Alpha.

Today, Alpha at HTB is extremely impressive in terms of its scale and who attends. The church itself claims that most of those who sign up are not committed to the faith but are earnest seekers wishing to know more about Christianity. It may well be that HTB is rather atypical – possibly because it has been running Alpha for far longer than other churches, and has therefore perfected its strategy and established wide networks of individuals who potentially constitute Alpha fodder. Alpha courses at HTB are the ones which generally attract media attention. They are well-attended, effectively organized, glossy, and highly publicized affairs. In many other churches, I will suggest later in this volume, Alpha may tell a very different story.

For several years at HTB almost 1,000 people had attended one of two courses. Today, on Wednesday evenings, some 900 people are involved (of which 200 are leaders and helpers). A standard talk on a subject related to basic Christianity is given in the main part of the church – often by Gumbel himself (failing that, a selection of guest speakers). This large assembly of Alpha initiates is then broken up into groups of ideally 10–12 people sitting around in a circle to discuss what has been said. For those who cannot attend the evening course an alternative is run one morning every week (about 50–100 people attend). HTB also has 5–6 church 'plants' within a few miles' radius, often in once declining parish churches. Each one has adopted an Alpha course and, indeed, most of these 'plants' were initially established or have grown by running Alpha.

The images to be found in the interior of HTB in which the Alpha course takes place tell a story. A glance at the elaborate decoration in the main part of the church, of Christ, the Madonna, of the saints, gives away the fact that HTB was once of Anglican High church tradition. Today, like other churches of its ilk, most of the visual clues to its former allegiances are now hidden by all the trappings of contemporary worship – drums, guitars and the screens upon which the lyrics of state-of-the-art Christian songs of worship are projected during services. The fading religious pictures are almost obscured by these screens. The pews have been replaced by chairs which have increased its seating arrangements – to 'pack 'em in' – or can be removed to one side as the claimed 'power' of the Holy Spirit causes people to collapse to the floor. The Sunday services are frequented by nearly 2,000 people. It is not just a congregation that is distinctly upper middle-class, but one that is charismatic in orientation where singing in tongues is frequently evident. In all these respects, HTB presents itself as a role model for other churches that might seek to aspire to success and adopt the cultural baggage of the charismatic movement.

Sited where it is, HTB is able to attract media-profile celebrities, largely through the Alpha course itself. Among the notables who have graced Alpha courses at HTB are ex-page 3 topless model Sam Fox who had a fleeting involvement and, more recently, former Spice Girl Geri Halliwell claims to have found a measure of spiritual enlightenment by attending. The attraction of such celebrities has served to highlight the public profile of Alpha, especially through the popular press.[7]

The culture and ethos of HTB is upper middle-class and at times this is very evident. Victoria Moore, in her article in the *Daily Mail* detailing her experiences and impressions of Alpha on the first night of the programme she attended, wrote:

> Shiny BMW follows shiny Porsche into the car park, delivering chattering leather jacket and designer jean-clad people into the reception marquee pitched outside. It feels, for all the world, as though I'm going to a rather posh wedding.[8]

HTB is one of the most influential churches in the UK and has an increasing international reputation. Today it is the core of an evangelical movement with an elaborate system of church networks stretching from the USA to South America to Australia. This impact is not merely due to the profile afforded it by Alpha. Rather, the church has for years been well enmeshed in the cultural milieu of the charismatic movement and is one of a cluster of high-profile, influential 'mega' charismatic churches that have grown up in the last two decades or so, many of which are based in the capital. Prominent leaders at HTB, including Sandy Millar and Nicky Gumbel, were recognizable figures within the wider movement, both nationally and internationally, before Alpha launched them to further fame.

To help spread the programme and cater for the needs of the course, a one hundred-member full-time team runs the Alpha project from HTB and this includes organizing approximately 50 international conferences every year. At HTB there are also 50 pastorate groups with around 30–40 people in each. In 2001, 14 pastorates sent teams to support churches all over the UK as part of their Alpha training days and regional events. At the churches' request, these pastorates supported training, gave talks, led worship, and otherwise helped with Sunday services. In this way HTB, its teaching, practices and culture penetrate thousands of churches in the UK and beyond.

Summary

This opening chapter has been concerned with outlining the significance of Alpha, its origins and growth among UK churches and then globally. It has also emphasized the role of HTB in organizing and developing the course and extending charismatic theology and culture. This orientation should not be underestimated and its relevance will be explored in more detail in Chapter 3.

The view of HTB towards outside research of Alpha also needs to be noted. Personally, I have had little dealing with HTB. Before initiating my research for *Anyone for Alpha?*, I contacted the church offering a co-operative venture. This was refused. However, when the book surfaced I was approached by HTB, and then with Gumbel and HTB's publicity officer, I was suitably wined and dined. The church is now more open and accessible, the possibility of joint research was mooted by both sides. Gumbel seemed to have been particularly interested in finding out why churches in the same neighbourhood often appeared to have different rates of success when running Alpha courses. I was struck by this interest since it seemed to suggest that HTB might be seeking to strengthen its hold on how Alpha is run at the local level. As far as the research is concerned I have opted to go it alone for a second time, partly so as not to be entangled with the vested interest of HTB. It was also partly because Nicky Gumbel told me that he had bought my first book on Alpha, read half of it, and then had 'permanently misplaced it'.

Notes

1 *Alpha News*, November 2001–February 2002.
2 Ibid., November 1998–February 1999, p. 1.
3 Ibid., November 2001–February 2002, p. 2.
4 Ibid., p. 1.
5 Ibid., November 1998–February 1999, p. 17; March–June 1999, p. 1.
6 The largest Alpha conferences prior to this were held in Johannesburg with 1,300 delegates and one for 1,200 delegates hosted by the Roman Catholic churches in Vancouver in 2000.
7 *Daily Mirror*, 3 December 2000.
8 *Daily Mail*, 1 January 2001.

Chapter 2

Alpha: Towards a Sociological Framework

We have embarked on a new decade – a decade all the churches are calling a 'Decade of Evangelism'. Let us make no mistake about it, this decade could conceivably be one of the most critical in the history of Christianity. Why is this so? Well, look around and see the advances of secularism, the invasion of new forms of paganism and the insurgence of Islam and other faiths. Christianity no longer has a monopoly in our land; we are in the market place of religions and no faiths and in a real way our back is up against the wall.

So: despair? No, never! Rather there is a wonderful opportunity for the church of Jesus Christ really to be his church; open, alive, radiant with faith and hope. I know that churches can grow and my expectation is that we shall.

Former Archbishop of Canterbury, George Carey[1]

The Religious Marketplace – a Theoretical Overview

There is much which is significant about the above quote. Writing at the beginning of the 1990s, the words of the former archbishop have proved to be both pertinent and prophetic given the emergence of the Alpha programme. While the precise content and outline of Alpha will be overviewed in Chapter 4, broad questions can be raised at this stage as to its relevance in terms of contemporary religion generally, and the future of Christianity in particular.

Firstly, the programme should be put in perspective in terms of its relevance in the contemporary religious 'scene'. Undoubtedly Alpha is interesting because of its apparent popular success throughout a wide range of denominations from mainline churches, to Pentecostal and independent evangelical churches. It draws attention because of the number of converts that it claims; reversing the fortunes of Christianity in Western society. This it attempts to do by 'winning souls' to a distinct belief system and returning people to the institution of the church, or at least set them off on a spiritual journey. Alpha is also fascinating because of the strategies it uses, its underlying theories, and culturally accommodating aspects. In this way Alpha typifies various views of religion today, namely its increasing commodification and methods embraced to win converts by attempting to be relevant to people's lives. Finally, it is of sociological relevance because, while acknowledging that it is thoroughly modern, it also arguably carries a strong fundamentalist element albeit with a charismatic gloss. This admixture, I will argue below, accounts for its appeal and relative success. I use the term 'relative' because I believe that its achievements are very much limited, despite all the hullabaloo that surrounds the programme.

Religion in Post-modernity

A number of recent approaches have been developed in the sociology of religion which might provide a framework for understanding the nature and growth of Alpha. Of course, such approaches are not only useful as a starting point in analysing the programme per se, but in throwing light upon the nature of contemporary Christian evangelism in particular and some of the dilemmas that it is presented with. The most obvious framework to locate such a study is perhaps that of post-modernity – a paradigm that is gaining increasing respectability within the sociology of religion, although as I shall argue here, it is not one without its difficulties.

Theories of post-modernity generally, and of contemporary religion more specifically, are predicated on the belief that Western societies have moved beyond what was previously understood as modernization and industrialization and most of what these overarching transformations entailed. However, establishing a precise definition of post-modernity and identifying its key features is by no means an easy exercise and it remains a heavily contested concept. One consequence of a certain ambiguity within this paradigm is that religion in post-modernity is frequently discussed in a contradictory way and the theoretical trajectories taken have varied considerably. Yet despite the complexities, post-modernism has become an increasingly fashionable approach in academic circles.

Notwithstanding the different accounts offered by sociologists of the nature of post-modernity, there are some commonly grounded assumptions.[2] Most of the commentators who have developed theoretical frameworks tend to agree that with the process of post-modernization a new world view is gradually replacing the outlook that has dominated the developed societies of the West since the Industrial Revolution. Thus post-modernity transforms the core norms circumventing politics, economic life in production and especially consumption, the family, values, morality and religion. As far as the latter is concerned, many post-modernist writers would identify the growth of particular forms of religiosity. In this respect the notion of post-modernity suggests that the Enlightenment, and the modernity to which it was intrinsically linked, has been overtaken by new cultural developments that have repercussions for religion as with other aspects of social life. Theories related to post-modernity therefore tend to abandon 'classical' secularization and seek to find ways of explaining the perseverance of religion in some quarters and even the proliferation of unique forms of religion, as well as the decline of expressions of other types of religiosity in Western societies into the twenty-first century. There are, nonetheless, various directions of thought as to what the core processes are.

The French theorist Lyotard has argued that post-industrial society and post-modern culture began to develop in the mid-twentieth century, although the rate of development and the stage reached varied between and within countries. The transformations are essentially related to technology, science, and a number of social developments, but most importantly they are connected with changes in language and meta-narratives. According to Lyotard, meta-narratives of human emancipation and social progress are undermined by the advent of post-modernity. Everything becomes relative which, from one point of view, aims a critique at religious absolutes since there is a widespread willingness to abandon the search for overarching or triumphant myths, narratives or frameworks of knowledge (Lyotard 1984).

This latter theme is also taken up by Don Cupitt who sees the development of the post-Christian West as intrinsically linked to the emergence of post-modern society. Western culture is no longer dominated by the belief in progress and an optimistic view of history that once characterized modernity. Such ideas previously provided people with hope for the future and filled the world with significance. For Cupitt, this abrupt breakdown of the idea of a better future has also meant the disintegration of the idea of a legitimate past. In the West this suggests the decline of Christianity. Christian tradition is dying, the past has lost its old authority. What has occurred then, is that the Christian way of seeing the cosmos, history and reality as an objective 'truth', has disappeared and in terms of human meaning there now exists a cavernous vacuum. This includes the demise of an all-embracing Christian world view. From this perspective, new forms of religion, such as the New Age or feminist spirituality, arise in an increasingly fragmented culture where all cultural styles are deemed as equally 'valid' (Cupitt 1998).

Ironically, according to many post-modernist writers, a new vitality of religion results from the uncertainty of meaning produced by the post-modern condition. The collapse of all-embracing religious world views and traditions leaves an emptiness, a 'crisis of meaning'. This is not a new observation. Peter Berger (1970) earlier suggested that pluralism and secularity reminded individuals that their beliefs (and indeed non-beliefs) are a personal preference and a matter of choice. While Berger saw little possibility of a resurgence of religion, Bauman (1992), arguing from a post-modernist perspective, maintains that questions pertinent to religion endure and are likely to be satisfied mainly in the form of quasi-religious movements or types of religion which display a strong moral content. As far as the latter is concerned, the pursuit of meaning perhaps suggests, rather paradoxically, the perseverance of traditional forms of religiosity which may give rise to expressions of fundamentalism.

There is more to reflect upon concerning the tendencies of religiosity in post-modernity. The contributions of many commentators focus upon the observable commodification of religion which, in turn, is derived from the belief that a resurgence of religion in the contemporary world may also be derived from the fresh emphasis on culture and its dominant consumer ethic (Lyon 1996). Consumerism, with its preoccupation with taste and the accompanying aestheticization of social life, constitutes a new appreciation of the symbolic realm and a quest for transcendental meaning. The post-modern era is one where belief has become fragmented, a matter of personal preference and a commodity to be packaged for the spiritual marketplace. In this regard much will be linked, according to post-modernist thought, to spiritual considerations of identity and notions of the self and the body, all of which are cognate with choice and lifestyle.

For Paul Heelas (1998) the disintegration of the certainties of modernity has left a situation in which post-modern religion – particularly mystical or New Age spirituality and what he terms 'self-religions' – has emerged to fill a spiritual vacuum and satisfy the need for meaning. The emphasis on self in this context is particularly pertinent. Post-modernity brings a utilitarian selfhood – an expressive form of existence, an emphasis on 'experience' and an 'off-the shelf' image. It establishes the freedom for individuals to create and sustain the self-image of their choice. Hence, traditional forms of religion give way to those congruent with contemporary culture, above all, those which deal with largely this-worldly concerns.

Some of these developments inherent within post-modernity have also impacted contemporary expressions of Christianity and are cogently discussed in David Lyon's suitably entitled book *Jesus in Disneyland* (2000). While Lyon is not exclusively concerned with providing an account of Christianity, the implications for the faith are clear in his analysis. The arrival of post-modernity means partly an aestheticization of culture through playfulness, parody and pastiche. At the same time it denotes the growth of consumerism and the expansion of new communication and information technologies. His general conclusion is that the principles that govern Disney theme parks, that is, dedifferentiation of consumption, merchandising and emotional labour, are not incompatible with religious faith. Rather, they provide opportunities for it. Lyon's argument is a complex one and full justice cannot be done to it here. However, he does provide useful insights into the tendencies and possibilities which now confront Christianity even in its more traditional forms. Christianity is now in the entertainment business, it utilizes state-of-the art technologies, and is dominated by larger-than-life charismatic personalities in the form of church leaders and evangelists. It is a faith where image is more important than substance. Lyon's contribution to the post-modernist account is a useful one since he stresses, in his own style, the 'supply-side' of religiosity as exemplified by niche marketing. Not all people are attracted to Disneyland, but some will be. Not all people will be attracted to a religious version of Disneyland, but some will opt for it.

From the post-modernist perspective, those types of religion experiencing growth or emerging as new forms, other than those which bring a revalorization of tradition (largely through fundamentalism), frequently express individualistic religious 'experience' in line with the contemporary culture and its attraction of the fleeting dramatic, titillating, and exotic. Much then is concerned with entertainment. Such is the nature of Disneyland. This emphasis on experience may be at the expense of codified beliefs that informed traditional religion. As typified by the New Age movement (York 1996), we might expect not belief and stringent dogma to be important but that 'experience', through various forms of mysticism, will be to the fore.

The Resurgence of Religiosity?

At this junction I need to do more than pull together some of the theoretical frameworks discussed above. It is also necessary to disclose my own sociological inclinations and theoretical preferences since they will inform my analyses of the Alpha programme. Broadly my account refutes the claims of what might be termed the post-modernist 'revisionism' which conjectures that religion is enjoying something of a resurgence. I do not doubt that the decline of religion is extraordinarily complex and that this complexity has often been ignored or played down by earlier theorists. There are, it must be acknowledged, areas of stability if not resurgence, alongside observable decline.

Certainly, in the Western context religion may constitute a form of cultural defence. Perhaps above all and most observably, it is utilized by ethnic or national groups to protect their identity from external threats and, under certain conditions, acts as an enhancer of boundary maintenance (Bruce 1993, 1997). While obviously a very complex issue, a good deal of evidence does suggest that the long-term, if unequal, process of assimilation is occurring whereby ethnic religions adapt themselves to Western circumstances and even give way to secularity and disbelief. This may be difficult to argue given the high profile and often negative coverage that such religions are subject to, especially in the media, in relation to the perceived problem of religious fundamentalism. However, long-term developments cannot be ignored.[3]

At the same time, fundamentalism, or at least its Christian variety, has enjoyed something of a popularity and heightened profile, especially in the USA, although its impact has frequently been exaggerated (Bruce 1988). While gaining a high profile, it has failed to win over a great number of converts, or substantially influence legislation regarding issues such as abortion through its political wing that designates itself the 'Moral Majority'. Observably fundamentalism, or at least more conservative forms of religion, has been more successful where it has been prepared to adapt to the culture in order to generate a wider appeal. These expressions of religiosity, religion as an ethnic cultural defence and fundamentalism, both as largely expressed through neo-traditionalism, ultimately mark a response to the challenge of secularity, its rationalism and pluralism. They are not, I would suggest, indicative of a religious revival in Western societies.

Secondly, in weighing up the significance of contemporary so-called 'mainline' Christianity it is clear that its decline is an uneven one, especially at a global level. Certainly there is evidence of considerable variations in its demise in different Western societies. In terms of church attendance, decline appears more marked in the Protestant countries of Northern Europe than in the Catholic nations of the Mediterranean region (although they are speedily catching up). Church attendance is minimal in Scandinavia with countries such as Sweden displaying rates as low as 5 per cent. In the Benelux countries, declining attendance is something less of a straightforward process, while in Northern Ireland, for distinct historical reasons, church membership remains high at over 50 per cent. Also complicating the picture are developments in the USA – supposedly the most advanced industrial nation on earth. The *Yearbook of American Churches* states that from 1940 to 1957 church membership increased from 49 per cent of the population to 61 per cent, while average weekly attendance rose from 37 per cent to 40 per cent. Though there was a minor decline in attendance during the 1960s and early 1970s, today over 40 per cent of the population appear to attend church on average once a week.[4]

Thirdly, while stepping aside of the debate as to the level of true religiosity and world-accommodating inclinations of new expressions of religiosity such as the New Age, it is certainly true that their impact is relatively minor compared to the religious (Christian) revivals of past centuries. This is another complex development which cannot be considered here at length, yet I would argue that the alleged resurgence of new forms of religiosity must be put in historical perspective. Simultaneously, low church attendance rates, the increasing worldliness of the churches, decline in the political significance of religion, and the complexities of pluralism, all point to religion becoming little more than a choice for some people and of a declining social significance in general.

Finally, I would like to engage more broadly with some of the assumptions of post-modernist writers that there are discernible signs of a religious resurgence and in doing so concur with the analysis of Inglehart who suggests that post-modernity should be understood in its relationship to prosperity and security and this does *not* imply religious growth (Inglehart 1997). Post-modernity and the values that it engenders rests, above all, on a new stage of economic development – a rising sense of mass security and consumption. For one thing, there appears to be a near universal connection between increasing prosperity and a decline in conventional religion, which does not mean that there is not a search for meaning in the new cultural order. The key question is how *widespread* this religious searching is and the *depth* of its expression. Both, according to Inglehart, may be doubted. Moreover, the way that religion is expressed in post-modernity is through values linked to self-improvement, identity construct and therapeutic techniques – a very different form of religion from those with a strong supernaturalistic and moral element. Although there are a number of other criticisms of the post-modern paradigm, Ingelhart's will suffice in that it has at least relevance for the theoretical framework that I would seek to develop in exploring the significance and impact of the Alpha programme.

Believing Without Belonging?

In arguing for the general demise of religion it is necessary to engage in another debate within the sociology of religion, one which also has an important implication for Alpha. A significant aspect of the current discussion about the extent of religiosity is the relevance of 'belief' and 'belonging'. In the sociology of religion a great deal has recently been made of the notion of 'believing without belonging', much derived from the recent work of Grace Davie (1994). However, this is far from a new observation. Thomas Luckmann, for example, argued almost forty years ago that institutional practice was declining but that religion endured through more individualistic expressions (Luckmann 1967).[5] This tendency would now appear to be perfectly consistent with developments in post-modernity.

'Believing without belonging' is at present something of a 'buzz' phrase in sociological circles. It suggests that a high level of religiosity or latent religiosity exists in Western societies, yet in a form that is no longer necessarily institutionalized. This development, if true, is perhaps not surprising. In a contemporary society that is essentially individualized and privatized in orientation, the level of belonging to collective groups, ranging from trade unions to the Boy Scouts, has declined. The demise of institutionalized religion is, therefore, just one aspect of this decline in 'belonging'.

Believing without belonging suggests that a high degree of often unspecified and weakly articulated religiosity or 'hidden' spirituality remains but not in a collectivist or institutionalized form. Some sociologists and theologians who have developed this approach argue that the supply-side of Christianity only needs to be re-oriented and its institutions reorganized in order to win new converts, tap a latent spirituality and, just as importantly, prevent people from leaving the church in order at least to address decline (Richter and Francis 1995).

What does the evidence suggest about this so-called belief without belonging, at least as far as Christianity is concerned? This is not an easy question to answer. The problem is ultimately the perennial one of measuring religiosity however that is defined. Certainly, measurement in terms of belief and belonging, by so-called hard empirical evidence, is a notoriously hazardous enterprise.

Belonging to a religious institution or collective is perhaps the most obvious and visible way of measuring the extent of religiosity. Leading 'classical' secularization theorists such as Bryan Wilson have in the past been influenced by what may appear to be the popular view that a religious individual is one who regularly attends church and displays other discernible outward expressions of religiosity (Wilson 1966). However, the empirical evidence of decline is difficult to substantiate and is tied up with the problem of measuring the extent of personal and private religiosity behind expressed religious practices. Even those measurements of personal faith that have been carefully constructed, such as those of Glock and Stark (1969) (including knowledge of one's faith, claims to a religious experience, and regularity of ritual observance), are impossible to apply in any meaningful sense to religious decline at the level of the nation-state.

Certainly a good deal of statistical evidence concerning religious practice does seem to point towards religious decline, despite the complexities of validity and reliability. Church membership and attendance figures are often provided as a measurement, as are the rates of the performance of special Christian ceremonies such as baptisms and marriages. In the UK, the immediate backdrop to the Alpha initiative, decline is evident.

By 1979, church attendance in England and Wales had dropped to 4 million adults, and throughout the 1980s there was a further decline to 3.7 million.[6] In 1989, only approximately 9.5 per cent of the population attended a church on Sunday.[7] In 2000, the figure was closer to 7 per cent, with the projected figure for 2020 approximating a mere 1 per cent.[8] While the Roman Catholic and Anglican churches have experienced the greatest decline, all denominations have suffered a severe dip in attendance including Methodists, Baptists, Congregationists, Seventh-Day Adventists, and Quakers.[9] Only a sizeable number of the older Pentecostal (including a new wave of black churches) and some charismatic churches have been able to hold their own.[10]

Opinion polls probably supply the simplest type of data related to religious belief. In the early 1980s, in the case of the UK, the European Systems Study Group found that some 58 per cent defined themselves as 'a religious person', 50 per cent claimed that God was important to them, and 45 per cent believed in existence after death.[11] At the same time, however, only 19 per cent admitted to a religious experience some time during their life. In addition, evidence from the UK suggests that the number of people who would describe themselves as atheists or agnostics remains fairly constant at just under 27 per cent.[12]

Clearly these statistics are very much open to interpretation. It might be suggested that a sizeable majority of the population of Western societies retain religious belief and, therefore, could be used as evidence against secularization even if only a minority attend religious institutions and perform religious ceremonies with any regularity. This kind of approach would seem to endorse Davie's conviction that a separation of belief and belonging has occurred. Widespread belief remains but it is not necessarily expressed by institutional allegiances.

Does a high level of Christian belief exist? The evidence suggests that belief in Christian teachings are not widespread, although arguably the evidence is again subject to interpretation. Findings produced by the European Values Survey (1981) show that in Europe at least, belief in traditional Christianity has been undermined over a number of decades, yet half those sampled purported that God was significant to them. At the same time, traditional Christianity is facing rivals in the pluralist society in the form of the new religions and the faiths of ethnic minorities whatever the significance we wish to ascribe to them.

Table 2.1 suggests that there has been a decline in traditional Christian beliefs. While a belief in God remains relatively steady at some 75 per cent, the validity of Christian morality and the belief in hell as a punishment for the wicked have declined. Accompanying the demise of such beliefs has been the corresponding emergence of non-Christian ones such as reincarnation.[13]

Why Alpha?

We may seem to have moved a long way from an analysis of the Alpha programme. While I have tried to avoid a trawl through the numerous theories and complexities of arguments regarding secularization a brief overview of the contemporary theorizing and evidence of the nature of contemporary religion is probably inevitable in moving towards an understanding of Alpha. Below, and through subsequent chapters, I will suggest how we can weave both theorizing and hard empirical data together into our understanding of Alpha. However, just as important is how the Alpha organizers see developments – as it were, the 'actors' point of view. Interestingly, while fired by the notion of an impending revival long carried by the charismatic movement (and the significance of this will be seen in the

Table 2.1 Erosion of the Christian tradition: international patterns of belief in God and in life after death

% who say they believe in (1981)	UK	Ireland	France	Denmark	Europe
God	76	95	62	58	75
A personal God	31	n.a.	n.a.	n.a.	32
Absolute guide-lines for telling good and evil	28	n.a.	n.a.	n.a.	26
Life after death	24	76	35	26	43
Heaven	57	83	27	17	40
Hell	27	54	15	8	23
Reincarnation	27	26	22	11	21
% definite atheists	9	2	19	21	11

Source: Based on the European Values Study data collected in 1981; Harding, Phillips and Fogarty (1986), pp. 46–7; Gerard (1985), pp. 60–61 (n.a. = not available)

next chapter), the decline of Christianity is readily acknowledged by Alpha's supporters. Many of the dilemmas have been summed up by Sandy Millar from Holy Trinity, Brompton, one of the key movers in the Alpha programme. Millar has maintained that a demand is 'out there'. The problem lies in the inability of the church to reach people with a meaningful message. As he has argued with a tone of abundant optimism:

> Questions about God have fascinated human beings since time began. Many men and women today experience a very real sense of spiritual hunger without having any contact with a church. One of the most frustrating aspects of church life, until recently, has been our ineffectiveness in reaching people with this hunger and getting them within the sound of the gospel. We have longed to find a way of enabling them to discover the liberating, life-changing power of God, revealed in His Son Jesus Christ through his Holy Spirit, in a way that allows them to explore in an unthreatening atmosphere of love and acceptance. Until recently they have been hard to interest.[14]

The previous Archbishop of Canterbury, George Carey (a great advocate of the Alpha course), who spent months arguing for a few Christian prayers to be included at London's Millennium Dome year-end celebration, put things in perspective at the time when he remarked that the UK had developed 'something of an allergy to religion'. Given the views of leading churchmen, a successful Christian evangelizing initiative might appear to be an imperative. Carey shared the conviction of many leading churchmen that there is a latent spirituality which could be tapped. He applauded the plans for the advertising initiative of Alpha and spelt out some of the difficulties facing the contemporary church:

> Many young people today have no experience of church. We have seen the country moving through materialism. Sometimes there has been exploration into the New Age movement or wherever. A lot of people are saying, 'These things didn't satisfy. I wonder if there may be something in historic, orthodox Christianity'. Churches are growing significantly as a result of people coming to a personal faith in Christ through one of these (Alpha) courses.[15]

Whether a latent spirituality is 'out there' is, of course, questionable. The key point, however, is that the leadership of many churches believe that there is and it charges their mission. At the same time the conviction that Christianity has been on the decline is also evident, not least of all in Alpha's major publications. This is clear in the following extract from Nicky Gumbel's book *Telling Others*:

> The vast majority of the population of the United Kingdom do not attend church, and of those who do, many only go at Christmas or Easter. Following in the wake of the decline in Christian belief, there has been a decline in the moral climate. The fabric of our society is unravelling. Every day in Britain at least 480 couples are divorced, 170 babies are born to teenage mothers and 470 babies are aborted. In addition, at least one new crime is committed every six minutes. Although there are 30,000

clergy of all types, there are more that 80,000 registered witches and fortune tellers.

(Gumbel 1994, p. 17)

Alpha: A New Approach?

It is tempting to approach Alpha with the application of theories related to post-modernity. This would be convenient and in line with state-of-the-art theorizing. Moreover, not infrequently this is the way in which contemporary clergymen also reflect. At times, in the sociology of religion, we are inclined to neglect and even insult the level of intelligence of those that we seek to observe and analyse. Clergymen, in the main, are well-educated and thinking people. Some have degrees in sociology or psychology. Many I have had communication with have been quick to discuss the implications of post-modernity for contemporary Christianity. In an interview, an Anglican minister explained to me the virtues of Alpha:

> In the secular world standing on the street corner preaching fire and brimstone does not work. Few people have any idea what you are talking about ... in the postmodern society people have no knowledge of church or the Bible. The church is a square peg in a rounded world – particularly in terms of its language. People have no church background and today is foreign to them with a foreign language. Alpha helps overcome some of these problems.

This last point was reiterated by another Anglican minister I interviewed who declared that 'sin' was a difficult concept to get people to appreciate. Nevertheless, it could be approached in terms of 'getting your life in a mess'. This was, he pointed out, Alpha's way of putting across some of the basics of Christianity. Other clergy interviewed saw the post-modern condition as something of an advantage for Alpha. The view was that in contemporary Western society people are increasingly open to ideas of the supernatural. In the competition between Christianity and other faiths it was this super-naturalist element which could be stressed with Alpha offering the forum, while the so-called 'Holy Spirit weekend' that is a principal part of the programme provided the necessary 'proof'. And, as yet another interviewed clergyman explained, 'Christianity had many advantages over the X-Files'.

The working philosophy of Alpha is to ease people into the faith in their own time and pace. Being relevant to the man and woman in the street is imperative. Alpha, perhaps above all, claims to take people how they find them and to repackage Christianity in order to bridge secular and church culture – a gap that is forever widening. The challenge to Christianity is to convince the spiritual searcher of its relevance to them and, moreover, to a rapidly changing society.

During the course of my pilot study, many clergy spoke of the nature of the post-modern society and the necessity to redirect evangelism accordingly. In short, their informed argument was that contemporary culture is one where ideological absolutes, including religion, were severely undermined in a world of relativism. No abstract, God-given morality held sway. In the realm of ideas and faith, 'all was up for grabs'. What one wishes to believe in, if one wants to believe at all, is now a matter of choice. Evangelizing in public with an antiquated vocabulary has limited appeal. A proselytizing programme for the new world was in order; one where people could ask the questions and slowly find their way forward. In the competition with other faiths Christianity could prove itself as the 'truth'.

Nicky Gumbel comes quite close to recognizing the advent of post-modernity in the following extract from his book *Telling Others*:

> Graham Cray, principal of Ridley Hall theological college in Cambridge, has spoken with great insight about the culture of the 1990s, which is in the process of shifting from an Enlightenment culture to a new and coming one. In the Enlightenment, reason reigned supreme and explanation led to experience. In the present culture with its 'pick and mix' worldview, in which the New Age movement is a potent strand, experiences lead to explanation ... Others coming from the New Age movement find that rational and historical explanations leave them cold, but at the (Alpha) weekend away they are on more familiar territory in experiencing the Spirit. Previously they will have been seeking experiences which have left them discontented and only in experiencing a relationship with God through Jesus Christ do they find their hunger satisfied.
>
> (Gumbel 1994, p. 17)

Such evidence suggests that Christian leaders are not only aware of religious decline, have a grasp of why decline is occurring, but have some suggestions as to how to rectify it.

So much for the viewpoint of those who head up Alpha. Where do I stand in terms of theoretical speculations? My reluctance to adopt a post-modernist framework wholeheartedly in attempting to address the Alpha programme results from the conviction that it does not provide a full understanding of religion in the contemporary world and that, as we have seen above, there are some telling criticisms. There is the danger however of throwing the baby out with the proverbial bath water. The post-modernist paradigm, as suggested, emphasizes aspects of contemporary religion frequently neglected by earlier theories and throws at least some light upon the nature of contemporary religiosity.

What is useful, to my mind at least, is the notion of a spiritual marketplace: of a 'supply-side' and 'consumer needs'.[16] It is my conviction that such a market has developed in Western societies in relation to religiosity. While there is a peril in pushing the concept too far, contemporary religion does tend towards the dynamics of a 'market'. The Alpha programme has come to exemplify the inclination for many forms of Christianity to adapt to 'market' forces. It is not unreasonable to suggest that the decline in religion in the West as indicated by the loss of status for the Christian churches, the separation of church from state, and the voluntary organizational status of religious participation, has meant that churches are now forced to see themselves as units in a market competing for the time, loyalty and money of a limited clientele. In this situation, they largely behave as secular, commercial units operating in their markets: with an eye to mass appeal, advertising, showing a sensitivity to competition and 'profit' innovation, and so forth.

There are several implications in this market orientation for the Christian church. Pressures towards ecumenism are, significantly, pressures to gain some measure of control over what might be termed 'the ecclesiastical cost/benefit ratio'. Whatever its theological rationale, the ecumenical movement among the various mainline denominations in recent decades, at least, can be interpreted as an effort to 'rationalize' in the competitive spiritual market. Alpha, with its universal application and 'basic Christianity' has enhanced the ecumenical effort in such a marketplace. The programme also addresses the nature of religious belonging and in doing so displays an astute sociological awareness. These observations can be explored at length.

It is rather glib to argue that Alpha parades different aspects of secularity and reacts in various ways to the spiritual marketplace, but it does so in often apparently contradictory ways. However, these evident contradictions do display a bundle of realistic responses to the contemporary world and the decline of Christianity within it. Although born in the anti-rational ethos of the charismatic movement, the Alpha programme has strong rationalizing tendencies built into its business enterprise strategies and in this respect it becomes world-accommodating. Indeed, it is compelled to do so in order to maximize its efficiency and compete with rivals in the spiritual marketplace. Commodification is evident, as we have seen, in the business empire that has built up around the programme and even its charismatic element is rationally and attractively packaged. At least as far as its supply-side is concerned, commodification amounts to the rational application to a spiritual market. It must be conceded that, by its nature, religion is perhaps the last aspect of social life to adapt to commodification and be subject to the culture of consumption. Nonetheless, in the competitive marketplace of religiosity Christianity is forced either to adapt or be marginalized in its more sectarian expressions. The contemporary world forces such adaptation. It is simply a matter of sink or swim.

One implication of this commodification is standardization and the aim to establish a monopoly. It is the inevitable outcome of the attempt to maximize the opportunity for 'profit' in the spiritual marketplace. At first glance it would appear that a fairly standardized Alpha package has been deliberately and systematically exported across the world by Holy Trinity, Brompton. Perhaps then, it is not too unreasonable to describe it as a form of 'evangelical McDonaldization' – a theme which will be developed in Chapter 9.

The supply-side of religion may also display other aspects of the economic market. One, in particular, is worth considering in the context of Alpha: over-production. One aspect of capitalism that is often ignored is waste. The question is: what happens to commodities that do not sell? They are either sold at knock-down prices, or they are simply disposed of accordingly. Of course, it is difficult to suggest that a religious supply-side operates in quite the same way, but it is possible to argue that the Alpha programme 'over-supplies'. In short, there is much hype about how many courses are running, yet there may be more than the demand requires or justifies. Many people may not be happy with what is on offer and opt out of the programme. In simple terms, the advertising image may not live up to reality. Also, an integral part of advertising is to convince people what they should want even if they hitherto had felt no need for the product. Posters asking the question 'Job, Flat, Car, Girlfriend, Season ticket to United. Still not Satisfied?' suggest that Alpha has this element.

The other dimension of the marketplace model is the 'customer'. In the case of churches this means the religious 'seeker'. How might we understand the significance of this, especially in relation to the scale of the supply-side? In recent years a great deal of sociological attention has been given to the nature of belonging to religious institutions in Western societies. Much has focused on what is frequently referred to as the 'new voluntarism'. This term implies that the basis of joining any sphere of social activity is purely a voluntary choice on the part of individuals and is clearly a consequence of relentless social and geographical mobility which has resulted in the breakdown of communities and primary group association. Free from community obliga-tions and conformity to group norms, the individual is uncompromisingly exposed to the values of an achievement-orientated culture and accompanied by purposeful, instrumental and self-advancement strategies that have come to encompass so many areas of social and economic life.

For a number of more recent sociologists the new voluntarism has spilled over into the religious sphere and marks a profound shift from 'collective-expressive' to 'individual-expressive' religious identity although, it is frequently argued, this by no means marks a decline of religion (Wuthnow 1993). It invariably accompanies the general erosion of religious commitment in cosmopolitan, multi-cultural Western societies. Indeed, religious activity can be said to be particularly challenged by contemporary transformations since both social and geographical mobility have undermined the 'religious culture' and the community where it has historically been embedded and thrived. The outcome is that there is little or no social pressure on the individual to convert to a faith through the proselytizing efforts of the religious collective since, ultimately, the momentum is derived from the religious 'seeker'. The new voluntarism also suggests that people are more likely to join a group for personal advantage and instrumental reasons, rather than collective concerns since the contemporary world heralds a more profound individualism and utilitarianism that influences the religious domain, whatever the form of religion preferred.

Sociologists in the USA such as Hammond (1988) suggest that today there is an increasing link between identity and voluntary religious belonging, as clarified by church membership. Previously people were largely influenced in their religious affiliation by primary group pressure such as the local community or the family. The membership of these primary groups has historically been involuntary. Today, however, secondary group membership is becoming more important in determining institutional membership. These voluntary associations perhaps include age, occupation and lifestyle preferences. Allegiance is freely chosen and is linked with the construction of personal identities.

Wade Roof (1994) similarly argues that religion only survives by accommodating cultural values and if it proves relevant to the experiences of individuals in this world. Hence the advance of achieved, or self-created, religious identity is primarily based upon personal lifestyles and tastes. This broadly reflects the modern market economy that has increasingly encouraged a culture of consumer choice and accompanies the fragmentation of occupational specialism and the pluralism of life-experiences. Mirroring cultural change, the sphere of religion tends to take on attributes of marketability. In short, a veritable 'spiritual marketplace' has emerged which encourages people to pick and choose until they find a religious identity best suited to their individual, rather than collective, experience – a freedom to seek a religious faith which reflects, endorses, and gives symbolic expressions to one's lifestyle and social experience. The contemporary religious environment therefore permits individuals the freedom to discover their own spiritual 'truths', their own 'reality', and their own 'experience' according to what is relevant to their lives.

Roof maintains that the 'individual-expressive' tendency of contemporary religion is not necessarily confined to 'privatized', introspective forms. It may still have communal dimensions. Indeed, people (especially through new expressions of religiosity) are now capable of combining individualistic religious exploration with a hunger for community. This conjecture has been supported by fairly recent empirical research in North America. The religious marketplace generates a quest for religious expressions of self-identity, yet the search for identity leads to the felt need to be with 'people more like myself' in terms of age, family composition, education, ethnicity and so on.

The importance of identity construction can be seen in the locus of religious belonging. Contemporary church congregations, for example, are becoming what Bibby (1993) refers to as 'homogeneous clubs'. People are increasingly opting to belong to religious groupings that are constituted by 'people like me' which enforce and sustain identity formation. Such developments are consistent with the market model of religion. Individuals 'buy into' a religious collective where they most feel at home. People may be on an individual spiritual journey, nevertheless they will converge on religious associations with the like-minded and those of a similar experience. Successful churches, and other religious organizations for that matter, are those which can establish a sense of belonging to a sub-culture composed of people of a similar social background and life experience, and who embrace corresponding religious aspirations and cultural ethos.

Notions of this 'new voluntarism' are, sociologically speaking, more articulated in academic discourse in the USA than on the other side of the Atlantic. This is perhaps not surprising given that the former has historically displayed a culture more conducive to belonging. Americans like to belong, and this cuts across their ethos of individualism. Nonetheless, the general orientation of the new voluntarism helps us understand the developing nature of religious adherence in Western Europe and elsewhere. Although not specifically stated, this basis of religious belonging is one that has been recognized by the largest churches in the UK and USA, especially those with a charismatic tendency. Many of these assumptions are built into the Alpha programme that has been embraced and developed by such churches, along with other discernible sociological and psychological assumptions as how to build congregations and engender church growth.

Alpha and the Mass Marketing of God

How can we apply these observable tendencies regarding spiritual consumerism and individualism to an understanding of the Alpha programme? One of the most obvious and key questions to ask about Alpha is why was it devised in the way that it was? Those who had run Alpha for some time had learned through years of experience that people who had signed up to a course did so largely as a result of personal contacts: friends, relatives, neighbours and work associates. Moreover, it was understood that these were the same channels through which individuals generally came to join a church. This process was to be heavily exploited by those who wished Alpha to expand as an introductory course throughout the churches as well as a broad strategy for church growth.

Although the refined Alpha course of today has its own history, it has also been influenced by other sources, not least of all by philosophies of church growth. Most are earlier evangelizing strategies that have helped forge Alpha into its present state. In some respects Alpha can be seen as a finely-honed accumulation of evangelizing techniques and theoretical developments in the field of missionology. Some of the most significant have impacted over three decades or more, especially in charismatic circles where the attraction of church-growth strategies fulfilled particular needs, not least of all the revival imperative. When considered at length, it is clear that these earlier initiatives are noteworthy because they have significant bearing on ideas about winning converts through networking and by crossing church–secular divides.

Alpha brought a recognition that the large-scale post-war proselytizing campaigns, typified by those of the American evangelist Billy Graham, were largely redundant. There was a time when such strategies appeared to work. Perhaps the most successful evangelistic campaign in the UK in the last century was Graham's Haringey Crusade of 1953. At least it was successful in terms of ecumenical backing, media coverage, and large numbers of people leaving their seats and going forward to the front 'to be saved'. Since his heyday of the 1950s Graham periodically visited the UK until his health dictated otherwise. Even as late as 1984 in Mission England he was able to fill stadiums and convention centres. Graham was to have several pretenders to his throne in later years. Eric Hutchings, a member of the Brethren church, was to enjoy minor success in the 1960s, and Luis Palau, the Argentinian evangelist, could claim a significant impact in the 1980s. Yet while some such as Morris Cerullo and his Mission to London might continue to have an attraction for black Caribbean and West African, largely Pentecostal, churches, these campaigns have declined in line with other communal events, religious or secular.

In appraising the new approach of evangelism we need to go further. A popular idea in church-growth thinking is that potential members are most likely to be won over to a church constituted by people similar to themselves. They have to be lured out of their former social allegiances and into new (Christian) ones. However, this transition could be eased if evangelism was conducted through social networks of people with similar backgrounds.

The initial influence for this kind of thinking came from the USA. In the late 1970s an early founder of the so-called 'church-growth' school, Peter Wagner (from Fuller Seminary) advanced the view that the best way of 'making disciples of all nations', as commanded by Christ, was to use secular methods of business and organizational growth, alongside the insights presented by sociology and psychology. The strategies of Wagner and other church-growth advocates have had considerable impact in the USA and UK church circles over the last two or three decades.

Today, the basis of church belonging is very different compared to the past and this recognition is now part and parcel of teachings on church growth in seminaries and Christian evangelical conferences. In the contemporary world, where there is a great deal more social and geographical mobility, people tend to seek out churches consisting of people like themselves and where they feel comfortable. This 'seekership' is based on personal choice rather than as a result of social pressures.

Church growth founded on the notion that 'like attracts like' was developed as a fine art in the strategies of the late John Wimber who had considerable impact on the charismatic movement in the UK throughout the 1980s and 90s. His theory of the 'homogeneous unit principle' had, for several years, underscored popular strategies of evangelism and church growth.

Alpha marks an explicit acceptance of the viability of these church-growth tactics and the profound social changes which have taken place over the last few decades. This is certainly true of the notion that 'like attracts like'. It is typified not only by Youth and Student Alpha, but also by Daytime Alpha, first run at HTB, which is directed at other distinct social groups – those who are most likely to be free during the day to attend the course: young mothers, women's groups, the unemployed, elderly, and shift workers. Nicky Gumbel puts it this way:

> We try to put people of a similar age together and possibly those who live near to each other. We find that mothers enjoy being with others who have children of a similar age, as it means they all have similar joys and problems.
>
>   (Gumbel 1994, p. 153)

Church members from these groups are encouraged to bring along their family members, friends and work associates. The problem, however, is that at a general and localized level, the culture of Alpha, as already noted, remains largely middle-class and thus sets limits to its attraction.

Another aspect of contemporary evangelical thinking has impacted upon Alpha. Potential converts have to be seen as religious consumers with specific needs. Over the recent decades UK churches, particularly of a charismatic perspective, have argued that there were certain secrets to successful evangelism. The archetypal model for this radical way of thinking was frequently said to be offered by Willow Creek Community Church in Illinois, USA. With a successful fellowship of thousands it claims to have the secret of bridging church and secular culture. At Willow Creek it is imperative that people feel comfortable with Christianity and the church as an institution. Being comfortable is not limited to avoiding certain unattractive doctrines such as hell and eternal damnation. It is the promise of heaven and the practical and positive aspects of Christianity for the believer in the here and now which enjoy the greater emphasis. This is only part of a package which also sees the church offering 'seeker services' before gravitation to the services that are explicitly more 'religious' for convinced Christians. There is also a shopping mall for the thousands of people who attend so that church can be merged with buying life's necessities.

According to Willow Creek the church experience should be intimate, safe and friendly – as familiar and welcoming as a person's home environment. This thinking has led to Alpha courses being held at someone's house rather than the alienating environment of the local church. Thus the potential convert is, at least in theory, eased into church culture over a period of time. In addition, the church has different evangelizing ministries to interact with people at various stages of spiritual development and various social backgrounds.

One of the aims of the Alpha programme is to put the needs of the 'customer' first. The principal rationale behind the initiative is to encourage people to raise issues about the Christian faith: it is meant to be about exploration. For this reason HTB has spent several years attempting to find out what matters and interests people, what kind of issues are relevant, and what questions are most frequently asked about Christianity. In previous years questionnaires have been used to explore objections and reservations in detail. Controversial topics such as sexuality (particularly homosexuality), why God allows suffering, and the apparent contradiction between science and faith, are at the top of the list for most non-believers before joining an Alpha course. Many of these topics are built into the Alpha programme.

Hence, the tendency for HTB to be rather dictatorial and dominate from the top-down is consciously tempered by the need to satisfy consumer demand and provide the answers for the erstwhile spiritual 'seeker'.

It is clear that Alpha is well-designed for a secular age. Its function, for the church, as we shall see in the following chapters, is very much in line with the challenges of secularity and in doing so it displays contradictory elements. However, these apparent contradictions do forge a package of realistic responses to the contemporary world and the decline of Christianity within it. It is neither largely experiential in nature (although its supernaturalist element is certainly there to be observed) nor is it lacking in its codified beliefs, 'its basic Christianity'. Alpha is fundamentalist up to a point – seeking to defend the faith at the same time that it puts forward an attractive programme. Yet there is more to the equation; a recognition of the development and experiences of the wider charismatic movement in which it is located. This is the subject of the next chapter and will allow an appreciation of the fuller picture of where Alpha fits in.

Summary

Has the Alpha programme with all its attractions in the religious marketplace succeeded in its aims? I will argue in the chapters to come that the charismatic movement (in which Alpha is essentially rooted) can claim to be as vibrant as any over the last three decades or so. Nonetheless it has largely failed to regalvanize the religious scene and has done little to reduce the increasing marginalization of the Christian faith which had, for centuries, dominated social life in the Western world. Moreover, I will contend that many of the developments in the charismatic movement provide good indices of the relentless, if uneven, march of secularity. Although it has robustly responded to challenges from secular forces, and attempted to win new converts and retain members within its own ranks, the movement has displayed many of the dynamics of the classically accepted processes of secularization. While accepting that something akin to a religious marketplace has recently developed and that the charismatic movement has adapted itself relatively well to such a transformation, it is apparent that this accommodation is a sign of weakness rather than strength. Indeed, marketability has done little to reverse either the demise of the movement or, more generally, the Christian faith as a whole.

Another point which must be raised at this juncture is concerned with the boundaries of the sociological enterprise. There are limits to this academic approach with its emphasis on the religious 'marketplace' whatever conclusions might be drawn. As stipulated above, it is the realm of religion among all social phenomena which is least likely to lend itself to notions of a marketplace. Religion, by its very nature, cannot be reduced entirely to sociological frameworks no matter how sophisticated they are. The difficulty lies in the significance of meaning, motivation, and the nature of belief systems which are dearly held by religious 'actors'. There is a tendency to ride roughshod over beliefs and conviction, the day-to-day calling to faith and earnest attempts to change lives. This is so with accounts of evangelical Christianity. For example, that it is difficult to speak of 'consumers' in the context of prisons, and that the zeal for evangelism and personal commitment of individuals constitute something as abstract as 'the supply-side' to strip the evangelizing gospel of any true meaning and the meaning of participants involved. Do we need a theoretical framework at all? Undoubtedly we do, yet it is important to recognize the limitations and boundaries.

Notes

1   Carey from the Foreword to his book, *The Church in the Marketplace* (1990).
2   For a discussion of contrasting theories of post-modernity, see Inglehart's *Modernization and Post-Modernization* (1997).
3   For example, in Germany only slightly over half of the 1.7 million Moslems living there actually practise Islam. Hence it would seem that even the strongest systems of belief and practice are besieged by the relentless forces of secularity. See Abdulla, *Muslim Minorities in the West* (1995).
4   Hadaway et al. (1993), however, suggest that such statistics are misleading because of the way they are calculated. As a result of the 'massaging' of figures among Roman Catholic and Protestant churches the attendance figures may be only 50 per cent of what they are commonly held to be.
5   See also Bellah (1964).
6   Brierley (1992), pp. 30–32.
7   Ibid., pp. 30–31.
8   Brierley (2000).
9   Brierley (1992), pp. 33 and 35. Another way of presenting the statistics is that the same number of people go to soccer matches as churches (Percy and Taylor 1997).
10 Brierley (1992), pp. 30–31.
11 Harding et al. (1985).
12 Brierley (1992), pp. 30–31.
13 In particular, Tony Walter (1999) suggests that a belief system based upon reincarnation seems to have increased over the last half a century, especially in recent years. He conjectures that it could be because people are encountering Eastern religions either through contact with ethnic groups or through music and the mass media, or through multi-faith teachings in schools. Whatever the origins of the increasing popularity of this belief, it is indicative of the rising alternative belief systems to the historical dominance of Christianity.
14 Millar (n.d.), *Alpha Changing Lives*.
15 George Carey quoted in an article by Dominic Kennedy in *The Times*, 9 September 1998.
16 It is important to recognize that notions of a 'supply-side' of a religious marketplace have been more central in the theorizing developed by sociologists of religion in the USA since the 1980s, but are more stringently linked to the

rational-choice paradigm. The rational-choice theories have a unique approach to secularization which do not directly engage with post-modernist frameworks, despite some obvious overlaps. According to Stark and Bainbridge (1980), secularization is a self-limiting process in that the scientific and rationally based society itself generates religiosity. Indeed, according to this view something of a new revival of religious consciousness is emerging, not merely because contemporary society brings its own emotional and psychological needs, but because 'ultimate questions' which religion has traditionally addressed still prevail: the meaning of life, the possibility of life after death, and issues related to suffering and the human condition. Principal evidence for this is the appearance of fresh and innovating cultist expressions of a religious 'supply-side' which, generally free of the deficiencies of the older religious traditions, are in line with the requirements of individuals in Western societies.

Stark et al. (1996) and Finke and Iannaccone (1993) maintain that, free of ecclesiastical 'monopolies' or state involvement in religion so evident in European history, the religious marketplace of today increases religious activity as consumers are now liberated to express their religious requirements in a variety of ways. For Stark and his co-writers religion is now increasingly 'marketed' and likewise 'consumed', and there subsequently exists the endless potential for religious growth in terms of satisfying personal spiritual, material, and psychological needs. The model therefore suggests that the individual exercises considerable volition, and makes rational choices, in subscribing to a particular religion. At the same time, a growth of the 'supply-side' of religion can be discerned whereby traditional religious structures adapt to the needs of religious 'consumers'.

Chapter 3

The Charismatic Movement and its Significance for Alpha

The Renewal Movement in the Churches

While the spiritual marketplace is a useful framework in which to discuss Alpha, its more immediate background in terms of contemporary Christianity should ideally also be taken into account when exploring its origins, growth, aims and orientations. In this respect Alpha's connection with the doctrines and praxis of the charismatic movement must be considered. Although the broader movement itself has developed within the marketplace of religiosity, it has also evolved over a period of years and has displayed its own dynamics within the Christian constituency. This chapter thus considers Alpha's relationship with the charismatic movement, tracing its significance after several decades of what amounts to a quite radical transformation.

The charismatic movement is otherwise known as neo-Pentecostalism, a designation which implies that it is a new version of an older religious manifestation. The earlier movement, with its legendary beginnings at the Azusa Street mission in San Francisco in 1906, and its counterpart on the other side of the Atlantic largely through the Welsh Revival, is now typically referred to as 'classical' Pentecostalism. In time-honoured tradition it was a sectarian movement which set its face against the established Christian denominations of the period and eschewed institutionalized ecclesiastical arrangements. By way of contrast, neo-Pentecostalism emerged in the mid-1960s in the form of a renewal movement *within* the mainline churches, while inspiring the creation of numerous independent fellowships. In its new guise, neo-Pentecostalism displayed many of the characteristic features of the earlier movement and turned out to be a second, and in many respects, more dynamic and consequential wave of the same phenomenon.

On a global level the Pentecostal movement has proved to be of considerable significance. Classical Pentecostalism had disseminated itself across the world, revitalizing churches and establishing its own with an earnest missionary endeavour. The more contemporary movement continued the self-assigned world mission with considerable success – one that has been attributed not only to its powerful spirituality, but also to its theological flexibility which has engendered substantial enculturation in different global contexts.[1] By the end of the twentieth century the two movements had become virtually indistinguishable with a constant interaction of dogma, practice and personnel.

Today the scale of Pentecostalism is impressive. With some justification one of the leading apologists of the movement, Peter Wagner (1992), has argued that on a global scale Pentecostalism is the most significant non-political and non-military social movement in the latter half of the twentieth century. Its appeal in Third World countries has been interpreted by the prominent sociologist of religion, David Martin, as largely a result of its ability to offer a popularized form of (mostly) Protestant Christianity which provides for the needs of the impoverished masses. In short, it furnishes means of social and psychological survival by offering a 'substitute society' (Martin 1990, p. 258). While in the West Pentecostalism has proved attractive to particular social groups, its appearance in the form of the charismatic movement was initially associated as more of a response to the long-term decline of the Christian churches.

Renewal movements in the Christian church are far from new. For example, by the end of the eighteenth century practically all Christian denominations throughout the Western world, including Orthodox, Catholic and Protestant churches, had experienced revivalization alongside the emergence of new movements ranging from the Wesleyan revival in the UK, to the New England 'Great Awakenings'. Like its predecessors, the renewal movement in the middle of the twentieth century confronted increasing secularization, rationalism, disbelief and pluralism and this it sought to do by bringing new life to the established churches at a time of a steady reduction in church attendance.

In a similar way to the earlier renewal movements, mid-twentieth century neo-Pentecostalism in both Roman Catholic and Protestant churches advocated the return to the pristine condition of the first-century church in order to reverse decline. For those involved in the movement this meant a spiritual renewal and experience of the charismata (glossolalia, prophecy, healing, and so on) and where the terms 'revival', 'awakening', or the 'outpouring of the Holy Spirit' were frequently used to designate the Pentecostal experiences of early Christianity as an attempt to counter the growing perceived worldliness and general demise of the churches.

Clearly, the charismatic movement of today is not the same movement that it was in the mid-1960s. Beginning with the aim of renewal and revival, often appearing to be sectarian and elitist in form, it has undergone a process of considerable transformation. Although 'fundamentalist' inclinations are still observable they have been adapted to contemporary cultural themes and rendered increasingly attractive to religious 'consumers'. More recently, a weakened movement has moved towards a greater unity, sometimes displaying a homogeneity on an international scale, in order to maximize its opportunities in the spiritual marketplace. The constant variable during this time has been the imperative to expand its membership. Evangelical in orientation and driven by the desire to win converts, the charismatic movement has recently put much emphasis on marketing techniques and thus presents itself as a credible test case for the conjecture that the spiritual marketplace invariably means the growth of religion.

Has the renewal movement succeeded in reversing decline in the churches and provided a viable and stimulating form of Christianity? We may make some general observations in the UK by way of example. In the last two decades there have been few surveys of church attendance and membership. The most significant is probably the 1989 Church Census. The findings were published in *Christian England* (Brierley 1992) and those related to church attendance and membership have been overviewed in Chapter 2 (p. 28). The census indicated the general pattern that while their mainstream non-charismatic evangelical cousins were declining, many charismatic Anglican and Free Churches (Baptists, Methodists, and so on) were at least holding their own in terms of church membership, but that there was little sustained growth (Brierley 1992, p. 116). Similar conclusion can also be drawn regarding the fortune of the movement in many countries in Western Europe. The situation in the USA is, however, rather more complex since the charismatic movement has tended to have been eclipsed by other variants of conservative Christianity.

The fortunes of these mainstream churches were related to the fate of the charismatic churches as a whole. In fact, in just over a decade the renewal movement in the established denominations had ground to a halt. As early as 1977 the Fountain Trust, the umbrella organization for mainline charismatic churches, raised the question 'The Renewal is it Stuck?'.[2] In the 1980s and 1990s it had made little further headway. Nonetheless, the principal elements of the charismatic movement, albeit diluted, dominated many churches in the UK and its appeal to the more evangelically-oriented churches was undeniable. Indeed, it is probably true to say that from the 1960s to the close of the twentieth century a preoccupation with religious experience and happy sing-along songs associated with the charismatic movement has dominated the evangelical world. Of the million or more believers that the Evangelical Alliance has claimed to represent since the late 1980s, almost 65 per cent could be characterised as charismatic or neo-Pentecostal, yet the movement which emerged out of the 1990s was not the same as that which had its origins three decades earlier.

The so-called supernatural 'gifts of the Spirit', along with the doctrine of 'the Baptism in the Spirit', were the core elements of the charismatic movement. They were often understood by its adherents to be the features which separated 'true' believers from the rest of Christendom and, in turn, indicated its elitist inclinations. For Steve Bruce this supernaturalistic nature of all things charismatic denoted a certain sectarianism, not so much because it offered a more satisfying form of faith but because it was a shroud to core fundamentalist beliefs (Bruce 1998, p. 288).

By the late 1970s the cultural and liturgical trappings of renewal had spread widely through the established churches, but very often the substance and dogma, the charismata and its supernaturalistic element, were less and less discernible. This supernaturalist component began to fade as the movement impacted churches hitherto untouched by renewal. While much can be attributed to the relentless process of the routinization of charisma in the sense that a spiritual revolution was becoming more ritualized, its watering down was also in order to widen its appeal and, in essence, increase its 'marketability'. By the mid-1980s supernaturalism had been rediscovered with the impact of the USA-based Vineyard movement in the UK and its distinct theology and praxis that was typified a decade later by the so-called 'Toronto Blessing'.

The Cultural Trappings of Renewal

While the charismatic movement has clearly attempted to revitalize Christianity it has, from the very beginning, also constituted part of a wider cultural milieu. The movement rapidly moved from sectarian to more world-accommodating forms typified by a whole battery of therapeutic healing techniques. This apparent transformation has belied the broader picture that the movement had always displayed the inclination to follow, in many respects, the contours of Western culture. Roy Wallis (1984) identified this tendency in the movement at an early stage and designated it as 'world-accommodating' in two overlapping regards – firstly, by way of its attitude to this world and, secondly, in terms of the types of people that it appealed to, namely a fairly affluent middle-class constituency.

The first tendency towards accommodation was that neo-Pentecostalism seemed to exemplify the predilection of evangelicalism to adapt to cultural changes in order to survive in a largely secular society (Bebbington 1998, pp. 272–3). Even at the time of its emergence in the mid-1960s, the movement seemed to display a number of similarities with other emerging forms of religiosity. It is hardly surprising, then, that Eileen Barker, a leading sociologist of religion, placed it under the rubric of a New Religious Movement since it shared many attributes of rival NRMs – offering human potential and fulfilment, community, creativity and the endeavour to build a kingdom of God on earth (Barker 1999, pp. 25–51). Throughout the 1980s and 90s a number of contemporary themes were accentuated by the charismatic movement albeit given a veneer of spiritual growth and the cultivation of the charismata: the constant pursuit of self-improvement and self-expression and, in some quarters at least, the emphasis on health and prosperity and this-worldly success that was inspired by the so-called Faith ministries from the USA.

At the same time that it endorsed cultural attributes, neo-Pentecostalism, unlike its 'classical' predecessor, continued to attract a fairly distinctive middle-class clientele. Key leaders of the charismatic movement in the UK frequently complained that it had, in an appreciatively short period of time, degenerated into a static, inward-looking, seemingly affluent lifestyle and, as a movement of renewal, rarely transcended beyond its middle-class enclaves (McBain 1978). The reason for this is complex and various sociological accounts have been offered. Roy Wallis (1984) and David Martin (1990) have both concluded that movements such as neo-Pentecostalism provided a form of escapism and helped followers to cope with their negative worldly experiences and compensate for the difficulties thrown up by the modern world, notably rationalization, social isolation and, especially for the middle-classes, the increasing bureaucratization and alienation of professional life. Whatever the precise explanation however, the tendency for the charismatic movement to appeal to the middle-classes appeared to fulfil the market model in that particular types of religion suited specific social groups and addressed their needs, be they material, psychological, or spiritual.

Designer Christianity

David Martin has observed that the significance of Pentecostalism in the West can be seen within the broader context of the willingness to adapt to a pluralist culture. While not approaching anything like the thoroughgoing application of the economic model of the North American theorists, Martin (1990, p. 52) maintains that the principal means through which this has been conducted is via mass consumption in a 'free spiritual market'. Pentecostalism, whose global appeal could be explained partly at least through its enculturation, impacted in the West by way of adaptation to the spiritual marketplace. In advanced industrial societies, however, this proved to be indicative of its weakness rather than its strength, a speculation that needs to be substantiated.

There are various ways in which the increasing market appeal of the charismatic movement might be considered and appraised. To some degree it is confirmed in the growing desire to be more user-friendly, less sectarian and 'fundamentalist' in order to retain its members and to win over new converts. This might seem to run counter to the claim of the North American 'supply-side' theories that 'buying into' fundamentalist-sectarian forms of religion was more than a viable option for some religious consumers (Warner 1993, p. 1068). While this remains a possibility, the evidence suggests otherwise – even in the USA. Empirical studies indicate that the most successful forms of Christianity are those which could offer an authentic form of (often uncompromising) religious belief and experience without insisting on strictness or commitment synonymous with sectarianism (Mauss and Perrin 1992). Moreover, it appeared to be the case that the more successful churches were those which expressed a form of religiosity that was congruent with lifestyle preferences and which avoided, or at least lessened, the painful transition from secular to more fundamentalist expressions of a Christian subculture. There were churches, typified by the Vineyard movement, that provided meaning, 'significance and purpose' – all dressed in an attractive cultural package.

The findings of sociologists in the USA are far from irrelevant to the UK church context, although cultural differences need to be appreciated. Perhaps more obviously, the Vineyard movement influenced the charismatic churches in the 1980s and 90s. At the same time, the so-called 'New Churches' in the UK offered many of the same attractions. They have increasingly diluted their 'strictness' to bring mass appeal. In a very few years these churches had become less exclusive and more ecumenical (for example, weakening their controversial 'shepherding' practices of spiritual guidance) since the 1980s.

Significantly setting the tone for the adaptation of charismatic Christianity to the spiritual marketplace in the UK, the New Churches had undergone significant transformations. Initially, they represented a more thoroughgoing sectarian expression of neo-Pentecostalism. Running concurrently, or even predating the charismatic movement in the established churches, was the Restorationism movement (sometimes misleadingly referred to as the 'Housechurch movement') which also embraced the characteristic features of Pentecostalism. Andrew Walker, a leading commentator of the movement, asserted that Restorationism was 'the most significant religious formation to emerge in Great Britain for over a century' (Walker 1998, p. 28).

It was unique in that it sought not just to bring spiritual renewal but to create ecclesiastical structures in line with the first-century church in order to restore God's kingdom and in doing so denounced the historical churches as 'the abomination of the denominations'. In their early stages the Restorationist churches, represented by those such as New Frontiers, the Pioneers, and the Bradford Community Church, were decidedly more elitist and displayed many of the typical characteristics of the sect identified by sociologists: voluntary association, high levels of lay participation, exclusiveness, personal perfection, hostility or indifference to outside society, a dualistic theology, and so on.

After a short period of time, while experiencing a relative decline or at least stagnation, many of the larger representatives of Restorationism have mutated into the New Churches (a self-designated term that was preferred for greater respectability). Such churches are of a new genre and ironically in many respects have, in time-honoured tradition, subsequently taken on denominational form (Wright 1996). During this period the New Churches increasingly endorsed aspects of today's culture and technological advances which could enhance the cause of winning souls. Contemporary dress and music, state-of-the-art church buildings, alongside aspects of commercialization (including Christian broadcasting) constituted what was rapidly forming part of a Christian consumer sub-culture as these churches increasingly inspired and even dictated the tone of the rest of the charismatic movement with which they now had ecumenical connections. The New Churches were, in short, becoming more marketable. While still clinging to what might be regarded as a number of fundamentalist dogmas, the Restorationist movement had, both literally and metaphorically, sold itself out. There was much evidence to suggest that they were evolving into what Harvey Cox calls 'designer churches' that wish to be judged by the speed of growth of their congregations, funds available, attractive buildings and other hallmarks of success which reflected the wider enterprise culture (Cox 1994, p. 272).

This apparent endeavour to forge a wider appeal however, had limited success. The *Christian England* publication noted the 'significant growth' of charismatic independent churches (Brierley 1992, pp. 32–4) and that these New Churches displayed an 'increasing dominance' over the decade (Brierley 2000, p. 44). In the early 1990s they constituted some 14 per cent of all churches in the UK. Again this growth has proved to be only a relative one. The reality was that the New Churches probably peaked in terms of membership in the mid-1980s and have continued to decline (Walker 1998, pp. 301, 342, 405). At the same time this only apparently vibrant wing of the charismatic movement was displaying a membership dynamic which suggested 'the circulation of the saints'. In other words, the membership of the New Churches was largely derived from 'church switching' in the restricted Christian marketplace. This was not to say that new converts were not being won, but as Walker has suggested some 90 per cent of the membership were already Christian and were defecting from other churches – some already charismatic in persuasion (Walker 1998, p. 228).

There was nothing new to be observed in these developments. Most of the large Restorationist churches had begun as house churches constituted by those who had left the mainline denominations – even those in the renewal movement. The major development, however, was that by the early 1990s neither the New Churches nor their denominational counterparts could claim any significant growth. In fact the movement had reached what might be understood as a point of 'critical mass' in terms of its membership in the spiritual marketplace. Increasingly, it was not solely concerned with winning over new converts and this 'supply-side' of charismatic Christianity became preoccupied with retaining the membership that it already had.

Despite enculturation, the endorsement of marketing techniques, and its appeal to a fairly demarcated clientele, the broad charismatic movement in the UK failed to simulate the Christian constituency and the religious sector in general in the closing decade of the twentieth century. Although every effort had been made to win converts with the best of management and organization techniques, and the attempt to 'flog its wares' in the spiritual marketplace, the movement's process of growth, consolidation and decline had occurred at an extraordinarily rapid rate. In desperation, since the 1980s, it has diversified and fragmented, with various strands offering different attractions, some majoring on prosperity, others on healing, still others on prophecy. These attractions however, frequently seemed more oriented to sustaining the interests of its own constituency rather than winning converts.

To this attractive package was also adjoined some more familiar themes. After the outbreak of Pentecostal revival at Azusa Street in California in 1906, some evangelistic crusades added 'signs and wonders', such as healings and prophecies, to the preaching of the gospel. These signs and wonders had their place in the renewal movement of the 1960s. As renewal stagnated so did the 'signs'. By the early 1980s they were imperative in both reifying the belief of the already converted and winning over more converts. This emphasis on the evidence of the supernatural, particularly spiritual warfare and deliverance, was epitomized by the strategies and theology of the late John Wimber. His cultural package strongly appealed to the white middle-class expression of the charismatic movement in Western Europe. Wimber's influence in the UK in particular was impressive, especially since he opened up close contacts with many charismatic leaders including influentials at Holy Trinity, Brompton.

Wimber believed that supernatural phenomena could be manifest if God was given room to act via the faith of believers. It was 'a theology of power' which was furnished with a practical expression through 'power evangelism'. Accompanying this was the notion of 'the divine appointment' which meant the appointed time at which God reveals His power to an individual or group through the spiritual gifts or other supernatural phenomena. The Holy Spirit, Wimber taught, could bring signs and wonders, healings, miracles and other manifestations if people were open to them. The secret therefore, was to create the right psychological environment for the Holy Spirit to work. At times quite remarkable esoteric phenomena were to be observed: shaking, shrieking, 'falling in the spirit', and what appeared to be the deliverance of evil spirits.

This kind of ministry advanced by Vineyard became very popular in many UK charismatic churches during the 1980s. It also informed much of what went on during the so-called Toronto Blessing in the mid-1990s. While the emphasis upon 'power evangelism' and signs and wonders has declined considerably, the pastoral and emotionally healing element remains. So has the practice of evoking the Holy Spirit in which God is asked to minister to those gathered in his name. It is a practice which engenders a great degree of suggestibility and anticipation and it is one, as we shall see, that is woven into the Alpha weekend away which constitutes, in many respects, the crowning point of the programme.

The emphasis on signs and wonders that was expected to bring church growth (as its exponents believed was the case in the first century of the Christian church), proved to be part of a self-limiting process. Healings, especially of the physical kind, are seemingly rare. They are, moreover, controversial if attributed to miraculous intervention. The practices of the deliverance of evil spirits has been subject to damaging criticism from within and outside of the church. The so-called prophetic movement that emerged in the decade before the symbolic date of the year 2000 and frequently predicted a mass revival (although the date itself was played down as having a great millenarian significance) burned out in a very short space of time. Neo-Pentecostalism, in all its guises, seemed to be increasingly a movement without a rudder.

The Toronto Blessing and All That Stuff

Claims to visions and prophecies may be regarded as essential aspects of charismatic church life. Hysterical laughter, barking and other animal noises, shaking, trembling, twitching, probably less so. However, from the early 1990s these were the identifiable characteristics of the so-called 'Toronto Blessing' which did its rounds not only in the charismatic churches in the UK and the USA, but tens of thousands of others on a global scale. The 'Blessing', as it was more popularly known, became associated with distinct forms of ecstatic and esoteric phenomena. The peculiar manifestations temporarily amused or bewildered the UK media, with an article in one popular national newspaper posing the question 'What in God's name is going on?'.[3]

To some extent the Toronto Blessing, at least in my assessment, resulted from the psychological pressures built up by the prolonged hope for revival (Hunt 1995) – a hope, as noted above, that was to be observed from the very beginning of the charismatic movement. It was also arguably the effective signs and wonders, the 'rumour of angels' (to use Peter Berger's phrase) of a marginalized religious community in an age of disbelief (Berger 1972). From another perspective the phenomenon expressed a freshly discovered unity. The Toronto Blessing constituted an ecumenical movement of sorts in that charismatic churches of different persuasions were involved. However, this tendency towards a new-found unity exposed an inherent fragility. Integral to the renewal movement in the 1960s had been a sense of unity implicit in the belief that denominations were artificial constructs and that even the Protestant–Roman Catholic divide could be breached since all were brothers and sisters 'in the Spirit'. Such an inclination can also be interpreted as an extension of earlier ecumenical initiatives, and ecumenicalism, as Bryan Wilson (1968) has argued, is indicative of an underlying weakness of contemporary Christianity rather than a sign of its strength and endurance. This point has been advanced within an economic-supply framework in recognizing some of the dynamics of the Toronto Blessing.

Andrew Walker noted the significance of the Toronto Blessing in establishing a unity in terms of the spiritual marketplace. He is worth quoting at length:

> What I think is of particular interest in the British context is that by 1990 the charismatic scene had become not only a more co-operative movement, but also an increasingly integrated Christian market. A small group of powerful producers were supplying the spiritual (and shopping needs) of large numbers of religious consumers. So much so, that we can usefully talk of the development of a Protestant charismatic monopoly (Catholic renewalists had little stake in this enterprise economy, except as occasional consumers) ... (There are) interconnected rings of charismatic influence and somewhat incestuous (wheels within wheels) (which) had reached religious consumers at significant arenas of consumption throughout the country ... I am not suggesting, for a moment, that

> this Christian market was either a total or a planned monopoly. However,
> its existence partly explains how, when it broke in 1995, the Toronto
> Blessing was able to spread so quickly ...
>
>   (Walker 1998, p. 129).

Other sociological reductions of the Toronto Blessing seemed to be conducive to the broad framework of a spiritual marketplace. Exploring this tendency was Philip Richter's (1995) work which emphasized the supply-side of the charismatic movement. Richter argued that there was room for charismatics to invest in a new enterprise for their share of a relatively static religious market, or at least to safeguard the gains which had been made in terms of numerical growth. There was, he maintained, space to give the customer another dimension of the ecstatic market, or what Roy Wallis once termed 'the further transcendentalizing of one's product' or the phenomenon which attracted the faithful in the first place (Wallis 1984, p. 101). Moreover, the various streams of the charismatic movement had come to regard themselves less as competitors, and more of a unified group with a comparable product and the similar cause of church growth (Richter 1995, p. 20). An attractive package of ecstatic manifestations disseminated itself globally. It was accomplished by thoroughly contemporary means: electronic communications, videos, evangelical magazines, and popular paperbacks.

The Toronto Blessing had run its course by 1997. The need to repair cognitive dissonance by its supporters has meant that it has come to be interpreted as one of God's periodic blessings on his people, rather than as sign of imminent revival. For the most part however, it has been forgotten as rapidly as yesterday's news headlines. There has since followed a more measured and systematic attempt to win converts. Thus, charismatic churches (and a not insignificant number of non-charismatic churches) have embraced the Alpha programme. Alpha amounts to a large-scale evangelizing campaign initiated by churches previously involved in the Toronto Blessing in the UK, but subsequently embraced by others across the globe. In one respect it marks an attempt to 'get back to basics' since it is an initiative which seeks to win converts through what amounts to a series of Bible studies. More importantly however, it is an endeavour to market Christianity in what its instigators recognize as a largely secular society.

New Directions: From Esotericism to Bible Study

The Alpha initiative became the fresh focus of interest for many charismatic churches in the late 1990s. The timing is significant. Indeed, Alpha is entrenched in the experiences of the charismatic movement of recent years. Initially it may have given more than a few people something to do after all the excitement of the Toronto Blessing with its array of ecstatic phenomena.[4] At the very least it must be acknowleged that the Alpha national initiative was set in operation in 1998 as the Toronto Blessing petered out and was propagated by one of the major players in the exportation of its accompanying phenomena from Canada to the UK, namely Holy Trinity, Brompton. The situation has been put succinctly by Andrew Walker:

> Think of Wimber and 'Toronto' and you think of HTB. And yet it is from this church, renowned for its theandrical therapy rather than for its theology, that a highly structured evangelistic process has been successfully launched which has confounded its critics.
>
> (Walker 2001, p. xi)

To be sure, the great majority of other 'mega' charismatic churches in the UK were involved in 'the Blessing', including St Andrew's, Chorleywood, and Queen's Road Baptist Church, Wimbledon. However, it was HTB that was the principal 'carrier'. It put the church on the map. It became the focus of both church and secular media attention. It boosted HTB's church service attendance for several months with very long queues of people waiting to witness the phenomena.

Since its disappearance in the late 1990s there has been the need (although there is a reluctance to mention it in charismatic circles today) to explain what the Toronto Blessing was all about. Many construed it as one of God's periodic blessings on His people, rather than of great eschatological significance. Others saw it as heralding revival. At one time it was suggested that it was God preparing his people for evangelism – a prophecy which Alpha would seem to verify. However, it is a mark of religion today that major movements within the churches are quickly embraced and more than quickly forgotten, easily consumed and easily dispensed with. While, for the most part, the Toronto Blessing has been rapidly resigned to church history along with its characteristic manifestations (some have chosen not to remember it at all) there has now followed a more measured and systematic attempt to win converts and this is what Alpha is essentially about.

The Alpha programme was partly born of the enduring hope of revival. It may be interpreted, if one wishes to speculate, as forcing the expected revival and fulfilling prophecy. Throughout the 1990s, as we have already noted, there was much talk of a predicted revival, including a prophecy that there would be a revival among the most marginalized groups of society such as those in prison and 'on the streets'. It is evident that those subscribing to Alpha (both churches and their Alpha guests) are to some extent, whether they know it or not, inheritors of the Toronto Blessing and this is most evident in the so-called Holy Spirit weekend which is a significant part of the Alpha programme. Alpha amounts to a return to Bible-study, without the 'signs and wonders', although some of this is evident in the so-called Holy Spirit weekend.

Clearly Alpha brings the attraction of 'strength' without the strictness. The charismatic and evangelical dimension is supported by a number of fundamentalist elements but also provides an attractive cultural package that is simultaneously rationalist and supernaturalist. It is this admixture which potentially makes it so attractive. Alpha tones down the traditional evangelical language. In today's world there seems to be little room for insensitive, sometimes incomprehensible vocabulary associated with the call for repentance, the awaiting punishment of hell, or old fashioned terms like 'salvation', which all appeared to be increasingly irrelevant in a secular and ever-changing society. New terminology was necessary, one with greater appeal and relevance. Then there was the recognition that church environment has become a distant and alienated one for many people. The problem was the culture generated by the churches themselves in that they frequently seemed, at least to outsiders, to offer little more than a dry, ritualized and spiritless Christianity. The difficulty, to some extent, was that of image. A new image had to be forged which sported a wide popular appeal and this image was built upon all things charismatic.

It almost goes without saying that Alpha's rather charismatic slant is attractive to those already of a charismatic orientation. There are, in total, some 24,200 churches in the UK from the various denominations. About one in six have taken Alpha under its wing. It might be drawing too much of a conclusion, but approximately 4,000 churches were originally involved in Alpha at the time of the first national initiative in 1998. The question may be legitimately asked, does this constituency represent a kind of charismatic nucleus? Certainly, it is interesting to note that about the same number of churches were said to be involved in the Toronto Blessing at its height in the mid-1990s and by far the greater bulk of these were, or became, of charismatic persuasion. If it is true that these churches are charismatic in orientation they have, over the period in which the national initiative has been launched, been joined by more than 2,000 others who have been persuaded as to the advantage of Alpha.

Summary

The more informed reader may have found this trawl through the recent history of the charismatic movement rather tedious, however it has been necessary to chart developments as they pertain to Alpha. Let me conclude this chapter, then, by putting the charismatic influence on Alpha in perspective. I will argue throughout this volume that Alpha's net effect is in extending charismatic Christianity, albeit in diluted form, to the churches including those previously untouched by the Renewal movement. According to the interviews and questionnaires upon which the findings of this book are based, it is apparently the charismatic element that has provided a deeper expression of the faith for many already in the church. Charismatic Christianity therefore continues, for good or for bad, to carry on the same function that it has for nearly four decades in spiritually reinvigorating those already in the churches. This has been by far its major achievement. Yet this is not to say that it has failed to meet with other accomplishments and some of these will be discussed in subsequent chapters. It has met with a degree of criticism too, which will also be taken into account. We proceed in the next chapter, however, with a detailed outline of the Alpha programme, providing both a vindication of the theoretical background developed so far and an indication of where the charismatic movement has now arrived. It will also provide the framework by which such themes as its possible fundamentalist tendencies, its attractions and weaknesses, and its cultural inclinations might be discussed.

Notes

1 For an account of the global impact of neo-Pentecostalism see David Martin (1990) and Harvey Cox (1994). Good accounts of the charismatic movement in the UK include Peter Hocken (1994) and Andrew Walker (1998).
2 Agenda of the Fountain Trust Consultative Council Meeting, May, 1977.
3 *Daily Mail*, 10 May 1994.
4 Post-Toronto Blessing, some esoteric phenomena briefly flourished. One craze in some charismatic churches in the late 1990s was of 'teeth-filling' – a belief that God was filling the teeth of believers with gold (see Andrew Walker 1999).

Chapter 4

The Alpha Programme

What precisely does Alpha entail and what might we make of the broad programme, or at least the one to be found in the official literature? At this juncture we can consider a fairly detailed outline of a typical evening on the Alpha course and briefly explore the contents of the Holy Spirit weekend. We can also raise a few pertinent points, some of which will be developed in subsequent chapters. In passing we shall note a number of Alpha's strengths and weaknesses, at least according to the experiences of a sample of 'guests' who have passed through the course. More importantly, we shall see how it is designed to be 'user friendly', providing an attractive package in the spiritual marketplace. Whether this is, in effect, achieved in any substantial way provides another consideration for this chapter and those to come.

The structure of the Alpha programme is fairly standard by way of both a typical Alpha meeting and the content of the topics taught. Alpha evenings (sometimes the course may be arranged during the daytime) are run for some two hours over a duration of eleven weeks (including the beginning or end-of-course meal). Ideally it is hoped that the course will be at the house of a church member, hence creating a conducive and less threatening environment. As Nicky Gumbel puts it:

> The ideal venue is a home. For many years the Alpha course at Holy Trinity was run in a home. We had considerable hesitation about moving from a home because such an environment is unthreatening for those who do not go to church. We only did so eventually because of the increasing size of the course. When the course outgrows the home, a venue needs to be found with a welcoming atmosphere.
>
> (Gumbel 1994, p. 47)

In reality, few people are prepared to open their homes to complete strangers, among whom will occasionally be a few difficult characters, while invariably those who do offer such hospitality end up doing much of the work entailed themselves including the often laborious job of catering and clearing up. Thus many Alpha evenings will probably be in the hall of the church which is organizing the programme and where responsibilities can be shared between church members or, where churches come together, members of different congregations. There may be alternative venues too, such as the local community hall. In the Alpha courses that I have attended I experienced all these variations and would identify minuses and pluses in all of them. The church environment can be problematic. Some guests find it quite threatening since the immediate surroundings hardly breach the gap between non-church and church culture. It is part of the reality of Alpha 'on the ground' that the local church context does not live up to the glossy image, slick professionalism and razzmatazz of Holy Trinity, Brompton. A drafty and cold church hall may be the experience for many Alpha guests.

A typical evening on the Alpha course, based on Nicky Gumbel's recommendations, is generally followed by the great majority of churches – even the precise timetable and the time of year they may run (Gumbel 1994, p. 48). This stringent acceptance of the course structure obviously enhances the standardization of the Alpha product. The itinerary for an Alpha course is laid out in the literature as follows:

6.15 pm	Leaders and helpers meet to pray
7.00 pm	Supper is served
7.40 pm	Welcome
7.50 pm	Songs of worship
8.00 pm	Talk
8.50 pm	Coffee
9.00 pm	Small Groups
9.45 pm	Finish

The Alpha Supper

The overall three-hour weekly programme and its components are of interest since they have been set out to create a specific environment and to produce calculated effects. The Alpha evening begins with a meal although there is considerable variation in churches as to what this constitutes. The 'meal' can range from a three-course arrangement at some churches, a buffet meal, to tea and biscuits at others. A more generous three-course menu that was intended to be an end-of-course banquet at a Baptist church I attended was quite an impressive affair.

A great deal of emphasis is placed on the meal. It is clearly an act of hospitality in good Christian tradition, while the communal meal has long had considerable significance throughout church history, from the Last Supper onwards. For those who put the Alpha programme together the meal is considerably more than its historical value. It is seen very much in terms of group dynamics and one of the principal means by which the Alpha guests and course leaders can gel and is believed to be conducive to creating a relaxed and cordial atmosphere. A kind of implicit cost-return is involved here in that on being fed (although a small donation for the cost of the meal is expected) there is a certain obligation for guests to accept, be open to, or at least tolerate what follows on a typical Alpha programme evening.

Before or at the end of each ten-week Alpha course a meal, sometimes quite an elaborate one, will be laid on. It is a special event and a great deal of work will generally go into organizing what is regarded as the most important social occasion: a time when a farewell is said to those guests that have stayed for the duration of the previous course, and to welcome prospecting guests for the next time around. Those who have taken the course, along with members of the congregation, are encouraged to invite friends to attend and, presumably, as a result of one of the national initiatives, there will be at least some who have contacted the church as a result of poster advertising or leafleting. These guests it is hoped will, after being suitably wined and dined, become the raw recruits for the next Alpha course. At such functions a number of people are usually invited to stand up and give a positive appraisal of their experiences of an Alpha course. The newly-won convert, it goes without saying, has prime focus.

The Alpha course meal, like other social eating events within and outside the religious context, has significance in terms of both its symbolic representations and group dynamics. Anthropologically speaking, food for special events and for collective eating is of great importance in many societies. Cross-culturally, communal eating can reflect social status, particularly by way of dictating whom eats with whom. Such occasions have a distinct etiquette with different seating arrangements around the table according to status and role, while bringing a symbolic expression of a variety of social sentiments and in marking the significance of special events (Leach 1976). Even drinking has heightened symbolic relevance as a 'marker' of social relations, including class ranking and structured gender divisions, roles and status (Douglas 1978). Conversely, collective eating, especially where food is shared can display an egalitarian ethos and bring a levelling social effect (Leacock 1981).

In its symbolic respects, the Alpha meal can be impressive. It is capable of breaking down social boundaries and status since all share the same table and the same menu (although there may be a buffet arrangement which can create a different set of dynamics in terms of a broader arena of interaction). Problems may arise however. The conversation which surrounds the meal can be awkward if people – guests and leaders – are of a different social background and feel obliged to make small talk. The responses of people in this situation vary and some may find it an awkward time. In my experience, while some guests have warmed to this strategy, others have been rather alienated from it largely because of their unfamiliarity with eating in public (especially in the contrived environment of the church hall), or even with anyone else. Also, it can be observed that a feeling of being obliged to engage in conversation with strangers brings a sense of intimidation and may be one of the reasons why people leave an Alpha course in the early weeks after enrolment.

The function of eating in the context of contemporary culture of the West is, from a historical perspective, a unique development: it is a private and individual experience for many. The decline of the family meal, the meal for special occasions, and the tendency for people to eat 'on the hoof' or in fast-food restaurants, not to mention the 'TV supper', has eroded the experience of collective eating and the norms that were once expected to surround it.

This means that the Alpha meal, especially in the first few weeks, can be rather intimidating and what is purposefully geared to enhance a cordial event may rapidly be transformed into a negative experience. At one end-of-course Alpha meal that I attended the evening was set up to create a suitable ambience with candlelight and waiters (young males from the church youth group) in smart suits akin to those in an expensive restaurant. The less cultured guests found themselves searching for the correct cutlery. Indeed, the whole situation was fraught with embarrassment and ambiguity for many people. Concerned with such problems of etiquette, one local Alpha leader remarked to me in an interview that he was wary of meals becoming so lavish to the point that evangelism became a mere side issue.

Several other difficulties arise when offering a meal at such a public event. One obvious quandary is what kind of food to serve. It has to be recognized that, in the wider social context of Western culture, food has become a subject of much debate and concern, especially as to what constitutes healthy food. Most societies have classifications of what can or cannot be eaten, but food is one area where it is hard to accept other people's customs – what food is favoured and how it is prepared, arranged and served (Delamont 1984).

In Western societies today there is a certain distrust of food and no reliable consensus or guidelines appear to exist. This creates a great deal of confusion and anxiety (Sellerberg 1991). To a large extent fashion plays a role in forging norms regarding food – or standards of good taste – by guiding the modern eater in the perplexing task of selecting proper meals and deciding what constitutes socially acceptable food and drink. Notions of what amounts to good taste are constantly changing (Campbell 1987). Certainly, food has become part of the general health fad in contemporary society (Gronow 1997), while selection and intake are increasingly a matter of individual, not social, preference. 'Ethical eating' has developed with its link to alternative lifestyles and values, and it has even been suggested that there is an implied religiosity involved (Sellerberg 1991). The Alpha meal makes few allowances for taste or cultural likes or dislikes, apart from vegetarian dishes. It is obviously at the discretion of the local church, even with the availability of the *Alpha Cookbook*. Meals tend to be oriented to the common denominator – what is assumed to be widely acceptable tastes. Hence, pizzas, pastas and simple curries are to be found in abundance on the average Alpha course.

After-dinner Business

While the meal is not without its difficulties, the worship which follows creates its own actual or potential range of problems. As the meal ends and conversations die down a short period of worship is generally arranged. Of this time Nicky Gumbel states:

> I have found that although many (guests) find the singing the most difficult part of the course to begin with, and some are even hostile

towards it, by the end they often find it the part they most value. For many, such singing is their first experience of communicating with God. It also helps people to make a step from Alpha to the church ...

(Gumbel 1994, p. 51)

Not all Alpha groups partake in worship, especially if the group tends to be small. At one course I attended, despite the fact that the leader could claim to be a professional musician and his wife a 'worship leader' in their church, worship was omitted entirely. Nonetheless, contemporary Christian audio-tapes were played for some forty minutes as background music before the video commenced.

During its time of worship, Alpha may again give away its charismatic credentials despite the recommendation by Gumbel that familiar hymns are included, alongside the new 'choruses' that have become part and parcel of church life for some time. A group of church members may reach for their guitars and flutes. Words may be projected onto a screen. This preference for screens rather than song handbooks has long been accepted in charismatic-style churches since it allows the hands to be outstretched in expressive worship and permits the body to sway or be free to dance to the music.

Much of this expressive worship is likely to be toned down in the company of unconverted guests, while singing in tongues will almost certainly be absent in even the most charismatic of churches. Prayers may be left out in the first two or three weeks of the Alpha programme as guests are slowly acclimatized to notions of communication with the divine. By the end of the course, however, they may be asked if they wish to pray in public. In making recommendations about 'worship time' (itself charismatic jargon) with Alpha, terms like 'worship leader' – common parlance in charismatic circles – are used frequently by Gumbel in the relevant literature, thus assuming a certain cultural familiarity by the readership within the churches subscribing to the course (Gumbel 1994, p. 50).

Specific words and phrases associated with charismatic renewal will acclimatize the guest to a particular brand of Christianity, one which suggests the immanence of a powerful and personal God, of the activity of the Holy Spirit, of close relationship with the divine and, not infrequently, personal healing of an emotional kind. This emphasis may be unbalanced and enculturated, nevertheless the attraction of such themes for believers and perhaps non-believers is potentially strong. Yet, despite Gumbel's claims, worship time can be difficult for many unchurched guests. Finding themselves in the unfamiliar environment of the local church, guests are expected to become involved in worship and follow the choruses, often with unfamiliar terminology, especially that which is charismatic-oriented and refers to the presence of the Holy Spirit. Because of contrasting expectations and cultural unfamiliarities, there may be a mismatch of course design and implementation on the one hand, and the needs of the spiritual 'searcher'. One guest I interviewed described his experiences of worship time:

> It was all rather curious. You were expected to join in a world that was entirely alien to you. I can't sing, and found myself either miming the words or remaining silent and looking around me at people swaying about and their hands outstretched, thinking they are all rather a strange lot really or what on earth am I doing here?

For others, worship in this environment can bring back unwelcome memories:

> It was church as I remembered it. I suddenly recalled why I stopped going in the first place.

In the early stages most 'true' guests (as distinct from church members) do survive worship time and acclimatize themselves quite well to the environment – they are prepared to give the course, and all it entails, a chance to prove its viability.

The Video

The meal and worship time are followed by a forty-minute video presentation. The video is not only the central feature of Alpha but also one of its most standardized products. While not insisted upon, most churches running the course will opt for the video since it is a ready-packaged visual medium. Those subscribing to Alpha will show the video relevant to the theme of that week. It is the same kind of cultural image and distinct Christian message week in, week out. This does tend to test the concentration span of some guests and a reduction in length of the video is one of the strong recommendation made by local churches to Holy Trinity, Brompton. As one of the very human points of Alpha, I found in my field research that it was not uncommon for those who had experienced a hard day at the office or factory to wilt a little before the video presentation had finished. At the very least, the video did test the concentration span of many guests. As one interviewee admitted to me:

> The video tapes, apparently a shortened version, were far too long. I found myself falling asleep after twenty minutes and missing the last half hour. I was then expected to be part of the discussion of what had been said. All a bit gruelling.

Despite these difficulties, in a culture dominated by television, film and the visual image in general, the video presentation can be a powerful tool in propagating Alpha: it is a polished and carefully contrived production.

Nicky Gumbel plays the pivotal role in the video – adding personality to the visual medium. It is a role which has made him something of a celebrity in church circles, not to mention establishing almost a cult following among older ladies. Some undertake a pilgrimage to Holy Trinity just to see him in the flesh. One lady I interviewed told me that meeting him was one of the greatest days of her life.

If, as David Lyon (2002) suggests, contemporary Christianity in the post-modern world is tending towards providing 'entertainment', then this aspect of Alpha would seem to verify his statement. The weekly message is a simple one and the 'hard' parts of Christian teaching tend to be played down. At the same time Gumbel represents the 'celebrity' part of Alpha's entertainment dimension. The notion of the Christian leader as a charismatic (in a Weberian sense) celebrity is part of the dynamic aspect of contemporary Christianity. The celebrity component adds to the authority of Gumbel as 'the face' of Alpha and the legitimacy of his message. Like many celebrities in the wider media of entertainment however, some Alpha guests warm to him, others do not. One way or another, such a celebrity is undoubtedly a key requirement of the Alpha package.

Each weekly video is watched by the Alpha group in conjunction with the relevant section of the *Alpha Manual* which every guest will be following (along with the pertinent biblical quotations). Sometimes the helpers on the course will sit next to the guest with an open Bible. More often than not, the Bibles will only make an appearance after a few weeks. At one course I attended it was put across as something controversial – almost as if reading the Bible was a little subversive. The course leader asked those assembled to shout out the number of the page for a particular reference for those who did not 'know their Bibles'. Some of the unchurched guests found this a difficult enterprise.

Guests are encouraged to make notes in the manual as they go along, either for their personal edification or to emphasize points to talk about in the discussion groups which follow. Again, this ploy can meet with a mixed reception. Many people are won over by Gumbel's warm and approachable manner. Others, feeling uncomfortable, find the video dull and fumble through the pages of scripture with a great uncertainty. Course leaders often expect a rudimentary knowledge, for example that St John's Gospel is to be found in the New, not the Old, Testament. Unfortunately, 'true' guests have rarely had the experience of even Sunday School classes to fulfil a foundation for such assumed knowledge. While Alpha has been described in positive terms as 'John Wesley's class meeting rediscovered',[1] few Alpha guests, outsiders to the church environment, are likely to be working with the taken-for-granted knowledge of their earlier Methodist counterparts.

Each Alpha video shows Gumbel speaking to a large and appreciative gathering of church members at HTB – a sea of smiling and laughing faces. He comes across as friendly and polite and with all the virtues of a good Christian. Generally he is seen standing at a rostrum with his notes and Bible open. Behind him is a large and colourful display of flowers. Throughout the videos Gumbel is portrayed as a 'laid back' but well-groomed, mature believer; articulate and accessible. It is a professional and refined act displaying the sincerity and seriousness of an evangelist with a sense of urgency, while he punctuates his talks with anecdotes, jokes, and the all-important human touch. Humour is an important component of Gumbel's repertoire.[2] It seems to take the edge off of the underlying serious message of the repentance of sin and salvation. For instance, on the first night Gumbel offers an anecdote about his best friend at university who once told him that he and his girlfriend had become Christians. Gumbel recollects his thoughts at the time:

> I was horrified by this because they were such nice people. I thought: 'Oh, no, the Moonies have got them! I must rescue them from this fate worse than death.'

Humour is a clever ploy since it no doubt defuses the fears that many people have today about the dryness of Christianity and perhaps the serious evangelical nature of the Alpha course in particular.

As Gumbel speaks, the camera scans the audience of HTB church members who are snappily dressed, well-groomed and display their wealth with designer clothes, smart hair-dos and accompanying expensive jewellery. The audience is appreciative and in tune with Gumbel's gospel, cultural nuances and middle-class accent. It is broadly the same image and format for ten weeks. Each talk systematically attempts to answer the topical question for the evening. In that sense, the video very much sets the agenda for the discussion which follows. In accordance with the constant monitoring of the programme, HTB are now seriously looking at the possibility of changing this format.

Some churches forgo the video, replacing it with a talk by the minister or Alpha course leader. More often than not, the talk is carefully choreographed. It is amusing that many speakers will mimic Gumbel's act to the point of including the same jokes and anecdotes, and even adopting the same posture and mannerisms as the man from HTB. Most guests do warm to the video, although more negative comments expressed by some guests interviewed will be considered in Chapter 11.

The Discussion

A discussion follows the video presentation. This usually takes place in small groups of half a dozen to a dozen people, with a recommended ratio of one church helper to every two guests. Since there is a tendency for church members to subscribe as guests on Alpha courses, it is quite likely that the average group will be stacked with those already converted. 'True' guests may find themselves heavily outnumbered. The discussion takes up most of the rest of the evening, lasting for somewhere between thirty to forty minutes. It is expected that the discussion will focus on the topic considered in the video for that week – for example, 'Christianity: Boring, Untrue and Irrelevant?' is the theme for discussion on the first evening. Guests may be encouraged to open the conversation with questions or comments, although course leaders are advised in the Alpha supportive literature to set the agenda sometimes by posing 'provocative questions' themselves. It is my observation that most follow this recommendation, yet the questions are generally far from provocative.

In my experience the discussion, much like the video, sometimes works and sometimes does not. Much may depend on the topic for any particular week, the ability of the course leaders, and the dynamics and composition of the group of guests – their disposition, level of education, experience and knowledge of the faith, and many other variables. This mixed success of the discussion groups will also be considered in more detail in Chapter 7. We may observe here, however, that each week has a self-contained programme which includes the subject for a particular session.

There is generally little room to reflect on what has been taught or discussed in previous weeks. A few guests that I interviewed identified this as a weakness:

> There was not always enough time at the beginning of each session to discuss important issues that may have arisen from over previous weeks.

> Not enough time for discussion and not having the scope to ask questions regarding issues which have come up in earlier weeks was one of the main problems of the course.

Course leaders, suitably trained at HTB conferences, are recommended not to be argumentative, certainly not confrontational or intimidating in the discussion groups, but to encourage discussion. They should ideally be unobtrusive and low key, and tolerant of the views of their guests. If individuals become angry and aggressive, if questioning is hostile, antagonists are not to be encountered by course leaders at a personal level. Polite responses such as 'thank you for your opinion' or 'I have never thought of that' are frequently to be heard.

Alpha training tapes are seemingly convinced in the optimistic view that the truth will prevail and that people will over time change their beliefs and values. Leaders are advised not to criticize people, especially in the early stages. They are not to condemn such sin as premarital cohabitation or homosexuality. Guests, it is maintained, will be convicted of sin by the Holy Spirit and will hopefully mend their ways, especially if conversion occurs.

If answers are not known to questions, leaders are encouraged to admit that this is the case or say that they will make a note and bring the answer along for the following week (Gumbel 1994, p. 94). There can certainly be uneasy occasions as admitted by one course leader that I interviewed:

> I think that it must happen regularly that people ask questions in hope that someone will enlighten them, but they remain none the wiser. This happens with us. It can sometimes be a bit like the blind leading the blind!

In such circumstances a variety of coping mechanisms come into play. The most obvious is to change subject as rapidly as possible, another is to have an uninformed stab at the answer. More frequently, the group leader will admit ignorance. This may be regularly appreciated by guests who value the human aspect of not knowing all the answers or that Christianity does not necessarily have them. Sometimes, as on the subject of women's ordination, it is honestly explained that the Christian church is divided in its attitude. Nonetheless, the more dogmatic group leader will have a doctrinaire opinion on just about every subject.

Beyond enhancing the broad aim of Alpha in winning converts, the discussion group is said to have 'six subsidiary aims':[3]

- To discuss the video presentation and issues arising out of the talk – giving the opportunity for people to be heard and ask questions.
- To study the Bible passages quoted, their meaning, context and relevance.
- To encourage open prayer without embarrassment.
- To develop lasting friendships within the body of Christ.
- To learn to minister to others through the gifts of the Spirit.
- To train others to lead (especially to lead Alpha courses).

The *Alpha Team Training Manual* recommends a number of themes to encourage discussion so, for example, in week 2, Who Is Jesus?, the following themes are likely to be covered:

- The guests' previous concepts of Jesus.
- What do other people think of Jesus?
- The question 'If you had the chance to meet him how would you feel?'[4]

These recommendations are, more often than not, taken on board by participating churches, further ensuring that the same package is exported in the fashion of the processes of McDonaldization (which we will consider further in Chapter 9). The themes, moreover, appear to be almost compulsory. The implications of this can be far-reaching – in some instances issues which are open to interpretation are put across in quite dogmatic style. For instance, week 7, 'How Can I Resist Evil?' insists that Satan is the personification of evil. There is no dimension to the debate which takes into account alternative interpretations of Satan as a metaphor for evil or any other exposition. The discussion is recommended to include the following questions:

- Do you believe in the supernatural/black magic/the occult?
- Do you have a concept of the devil?
- Have you ever thought about the existence of evil?
- Do you see the mess in the world as a result of ... evil power?

Weekly Topics

Fifteen basic topics have been selected by HTB to be taught over a period of ten consecutive weeks on the standard Alpha course. Each topic has supplementary reading indicated in the *Alpha Manual*, ranging from C.S. Lewis's *Mere Christianity* to the popular pentecostal work *The Cross and the Switchblade* by David Wilkerson. Added to these works are many of Gumbel's own writings.

The fifteen-topic framework is expected to be rigidly adhered to and constitutes the basics of Christianity. The topics, presented in the form of questions, are as follows:

1 Christianity: boring, untrue and irrelevant?
   An introduction to the course which seeks to engage the interest of the guests by relating little known historical facts about the faith and its relevance to today's world including the family, relationships, and money.[5] Christianity presents all the answers to a troubled and what is perceived as an increasingly evil world.

2 Who is Jesus?
   The historical evidence for the existence of Jesus and what the Bible has to say about who he is and what Jesus has to say about himself.

3 Why did Jesus die?
   The content here expounds a fairly traditional evangelical teaching on salvation and the atonement.

4 How can I be sure of my faith?
   Included at this point is a discussion of the significance of faith in the Christian tradition, and the relevance of the Bible, the experience of the Holy Spirit, and spiritual regeneration.

5 Why and how should I read the Bible?
   The importance of the Bible for Christian living, followed by an overview of what the Bible comprises and the link between the Bible and prayer.

6 Why and how do I pray?
   How to pray and the significance of prayer, followed by the question as to why prayers might not be answered.

7 How does God guide us?
   The believer's relationship with God and what He expects of the converted is linked at this point to the importance of the Holy Spirit.

8 Who is the Holy Spirit?
   The first of a number of teachings on the Holy Spirit: His part in the Trinity.

9 What does the Holy Spirit do?
   The nature and function of the Holy Spirit in the life of the believer leads to a consideration of the 'spiritual gifts' (charismata).

10 How can I be filled with the Spirit?
   Significantly, here we find the teachings related to the Holy Spirit which

are clearly pentecostal/charismatic in orientation with an emphasis on speaking in tongues.

11   How can I resist evil?
     The nature of the demonic and how to resist it: Satan's strategies and spiritual warfare.

12   Why and how should we tell others?
     These themes are concerned with evangelism: spreading the gospel and the means for doing so.

13   Does God heal today?
     Teachings of healing which are popular within the charismatic movement and its function as a spiritual gift. This is all accepted as important elements of basic Christianity.

14   What about the Church?
     The history of the church and some discussion of various traditions. The church as an institution.

15   How can I make the most of the rest of my life?
     The programme finishes with an elaboration of what the Christian life and spiritual development entails.

The significance of these topics and how they are taught should not be underestimated. All churches embracing Alpha are by no means charismatic in orientation but, to one degree or another, many involved in the programme appear to be. Those which are not initially charismatic will find themselves exposed to the beliefs and practices of the charismatic movement – perhaps for the first time. The significance of this is that, given the number of churches involved, the extensive use of Alpha is partly a measurement of the impact and spread of charismatic Christianity. The distinct dogma characterized by the speaking in tongues, prophecy, healing, and baptism in the Spirit, are the charismatic hallmarks which are stamped all over the basic Christianity of the Alpha programme. One example is the emphasis on healing, a topic which takes up one entire week of the course: healing physically, emotionally, psychologically and, of course, spiritually. *Alpha News* and other accompanying literature supports such themes. These publications are full of people's claims. 'My knee has been completely healed' is not an unfamiliar headline in *Alpha News* and accompanies a confession of conversion after one man had taken the Alpha course.[6]

In the discussions, especially those related to the Holy Spirit, the charismata is to the fore. Gumbel (2001a) clearly spells out his attitude to the charismata by stipulating that it is part of the 'normal' Christian experience:

> Nowhere in the New Testament does it say that these spiritual gifts will cease at the end of the apostolic age. (p. 27)

> We should expect today to see the supernatural display of the power of
> the Holy Spirit as part of his kingdom activity and as an authentication of
> the good news. (p. 53)

Those who compile Alpha are aware of the theological controversies which
surround the inclusion of all things charismatic. The supporting literature
seeks to placate those who might be opposed to the inclusion of the dogma on
an Alpha course. Nonetheless, following a discussion of the work of the
famous evangelist R.A. Torry (1856–1928), Gumbel writes in such a way as to
castigate critics of charismatic theology:

> Some of our readers may take exception to Dr Torrey's use of the term
> 'baptism with the Holy Ghost'. Perhaps if Dr Torrey lived in our day and
> saw some of the wildfire in connection with that expression, he would use
> some other phrase. But let no one quibble about an experience as
> important as the filling of the Spirit. In (his book) Dr Torrey quotes Mr
> Moody as saying, 'Oh, why will they split hairs? Why don't they see that
> this is just the one thing that they themselves need?'
>
> (Gumbel 1994, p. 120)

The Holy Spirit Weekend

Approximately one-third to halfway through the Alpha course guests will
usually be invited away on what amounts to a weekend retreat. This Holy
Spirit weekend is expected to occur after the talk on prayer but before the talk
on healing and for very good reasons. The weekend is held in the company of
leaders and guests on the course and anyone else who wants to go along
(usually members of the church that is organizing it). It is not a compulsory
part of the programme, although it will usually be offered to Alpha guests. It
is certainly very strongly recommended.

The weekend away is partly an attempt to create a conducive ambience – a
'laid back' environment geared to further enhance the relationships between
guests and course leaders:

> We have found that friendships are formed on a weekend much more
> easily than on a single day. As people travel together, have meals
> together, go for walks, enjoy the evening entertainments and receive Holy
> Communion together on Sunday morning, there is a cementing of
> friendships which have begun to form in the early weeks … It is in this
> relaxed environment that people unwind and some of the barriers begin to
> come down. I have found many make as much progress spiritually during
> the weekend away as in the rest of the course put together.
>
> (Gumbel 1994, p. 123)

A fairly stringent programme is recommended for the weekend away.

Weekend Timetable for the Holy Spirit Weekend (as suggested in *Telling Others*)

Friday
6.30 pm onwards	Arrive
8.00–9.45	Supper
9.45	Epilogue – a short introduction to the weekend

Saturday
8.45 am	Breakfast
9.30	Worship and talk 1: 'Who is the Holy Spirit?'
10.45	Coffee
11.45	Talk 2: 'What does the Holy Spirit do?'
12.00 pm	Groups
1.00	Lunch
	Afternoon free
4.00	Tea – optional!
4.30	Worship and talk 3: 'How can I be filled with the Holy Spirit?'
7.00	Supper
9.00	Revue – if you would like to contribute a song, sketch or anything? Come prepared (participation voluntary)

Sunday
9.00 am	Breakfast
9.45	Groups
10.30	Holy Communion and talk 4: 'How can I make most of Life?'
1.00 pm	Lunch

Afternoon free – but see you at the 6.30 church service.

An analysis of the theory behind the Holy Spirit weekend, the experience of guests, and my personal observations will be considered in detail in Chapter 14.

After Alpha

As an exploration into the Christian faith, Alpha clearly sets out not to pressurize. Those who are interested are encouraged not to sign up for an entire course, but only for one week at a time. If they do enlist, guests are eased into the course with a gentle touch. Alpha's softly, softly approach means that if anyone leaves the course they are not usually contacted or persuaded to rejoin, although in practice this may happen. People are not to be put on the spot about making a commitment to the faith at any point.

During and after the course there is no undue pressure to either convert or attend church. In most cases, a response is awaited by the church running the course.

The Alpha course is a self-contained, off-the-peg programme. People join, undertake ten weeks of study and then leave. For many years there was little follow-up by way of supplementary courses or further material offered to the guest who had completed the course. Today it is still not entirely clear what precisely is supposed to happen after an Alpha course. Those guests who see it through to the end have various options. They may wish to convert and join a church (and this, I will suggest later, is relatively rare), or they may go away and think about what Christianity has to offer and even consider conversion. Alternatively, they may decide that Christianity and church life is not for them and will never be heard of again.

Very little is said by HTB about what should occur after Alpha (Gumbel's *Telling Others* includes merely three brief paragraphs, mostly directed to follow-up material). There are however numerous post-Alpha videos and books which add to the ever-expanding Alpha industry: for example, Michael Green (an adviser in evangelism to the Archbishops of Canterbury and York), *After Alpha*, Kingsway 1998, and similar publications that outline the spiritual growth of the Christian life.

Holy Trinity, Brompton has recently given more thought to what happens after Alpha. For a while the nine-week course *A Life Worth Living* (based on the Book of Philippians), which utilizes a number of follow-up materials to the initial course, seemed to be in vogue. The book is regarded as good material for those having been through the Alpha programme (this has been my experience of post-Alpha). The operative word is 'new': new purpose, attitude, friendships, ambitions and so on. In other words, a new lifestyle. Such thorough instruction into the life of faith is itself interesting since it marks an attempt to create a unique Christian sub-culture in a largely faithless society.

Alternatively, the guest may opt to take Alpha for a second time or sign up for Beta or some variety of subsequent course. The Beta course (which seems to assume conversion) addresses such issues as helping people grow in their faith, discipline in prayer, how to read the Bible, and how to develop spiritual gifts. There are issues of worship, Christian living, the influence of society and the evils of the world, and how to manage personal finances.

Those who are less convinced about Christianity may wish, post-Alpha, to enrol on a Searching Issues course which seeks to expand on a number of the difficult questions which have arisen from Alpha and constitute something of a stumbling block: for example, 'Why does God allow suffering?' or 'What is the Christian attitude towards homosexuality?' *Searching Issues* (based, according to HTB, on the seven most common objections to the Christian faith, see Chapter 8) is also available in book form. Another book, *Challenging Lifestyles* (19 studies based on the Sermon on the Mount), deals with issues such as 'How to have an influence on society'. It is billed as a 'book (that) demonstrates how Jesus' teaching not only challenges our contemporary lifestyle but presents us with a radical alternative that is in every sense an "ultimate challenge" ' (Gumbel 1994, p. 24).

In 2001, the need for follow-up material led Gumbel to put together a two-year programme of adult Christian education. The programme has a reading list which currently includes *Question of Life, A Life Worth Living, Searching Issues, Challenging Lifestyles*, and *The Heart of Revival*. This package seems to represent the most comprehensive attempt to produce a substantive programme of Christian education post-Alpha. At the same time a number of churches have set up their own unofficial post-Alpha courses which vary considerably in their length, content and rationale. Many course leaders are unhappy about the absence of anything officially recommended post-Alpha. One I spoke to put the problem this way:

> Alpha tends to leave people a bit high and dry. They take the course and don't know what to do then. Neither do we.

Nonetheless, she explained, it was a useful starting point for some individuals.

Summary

An outline of the Alpha programme has been included at this juncture because it clearly enforces many of the observations made in previous chapters concerning the nature and trajectory of contemporary evangelism. Similarly, an overview of the content highlights its charismatic orientation, especially within the context of the Holy Spirit weekend. Alpha then, can be seen as resulting from the experiences of the movement over some forty years and what it has learned about winning converts. Other key aspects of the programme are also identifiable and will be explored in more detail in the chapters to come, including the implications of the wide impact of a standardized product – whether it truly impacts in terms of the processes of so-called McDonaldization. More analysis will also be made of Alpha 'on the ground' – the experiences of those who run Alpha and the guests who have enrolled. This will include the importance of group dynamics. Chapter 5 considers some of the controversies that have arisen around the course and which help provide an understanding of Alpha in particular, and contemporary wider debates within Christianity generally.

Notes

1   Robert Frost, National Evangelist, Methodist Church, quoted by Nicky Gumbel in *Telling Others*, p. x.
2   Humour is also an important part of the literature accompanying the *Alpha* programme. The cartoon opposite, taken from *The Alpha Manual*, depicts the

commonly held view of evangelism meaning 'Bible-thumpers'. Diffusing such a view by making the subject light-hearted contributes to a 'safe' impression of Christianity.

3 *The Alpha Team Training Manual* (1998), HTB Publications, pp. 1–8.
4 Ibid., p. 22.
5 There seems to be something of a preoccupation with money throughout the course and literature. The underlying message appears to be not whether you have it or not, but what you do with it (managing finances in some of the literature focuses on thrift and a kind of Protestant work ethic).
6 *Alpha News*, November 2001–February 2002, pp. 5 and 8.

Chapter 5

Critical Views of Alpha

Alpha and its Critics

Alpha, as implied so far, has achieved a high level of popularity within the churches, yet it is not without its controversies. Since this survey endeavours to be impartial and balanced, a summary of the critiques of the programme must be included. I have opted to discuss them at this stage mainly because they follow an outline of the course; its content, rationale and working philosophy, as well as the alleged virtues of Alpha stipulated by church leaders that will be evident again in the next chapter.

Why some churches do not take to Alpha is as important a question as why many so readily do. The views of those who have their objections and doubts tell us something about the central theological disputes that Alpha raises, as well as debates concerning how evangelism should best be conducted. Hence, criticisms are not explored here in order to bring an undue negative tone or invite controversy but to examine briefly the thinking about Alpha within Christian circles. Further critiques will also be addressed in subsequent chapters as other issues present themselves. At this juncture I will outline the major objections to Alpha largely in terms of theological debate and will pay particular attention to the claim made that the programme advances an uncompromising form of Christian fundamentalism.

The organizers of Alpha do not court controversy and it is more or less assumed that their basic Christianity is palatable to all. Indeed, to be fair, the rather unreflective way in which Holy Trinity, Brompton, hopes that Alpha will be introduced is tempered by a more modest spirit. Nicky Gumbel (1994) writes:

> In saying that we believe Alpha is a work of God I am not for a moment suggesting that it is perfect. I'm sure that it is greatly marred by human error and frailty. (p. 23)

For the critics however, the problems with Alpha are far more of a concern and it is clear that by no means all churches or church leaders have warmed to the programme. While it has proved to be very attractive to some, it is strongly disliked by others or has at least been met with suspicion or profound reservations.

Perhaps above all it is the charismatic element which has attracted most criticism. Just as the charismatic movement divided many congregations in the 1960s and 70s, Alpha, mainly because of its doctrinal content, has not infrequently generated the same repercussions. Exemplifying this rather mixed reception of the programme were events in a Canadian church in 1996. One of the first major Alpha training conferences was held in Canada at St Paul's Anglican church in Toronto in September 2000, with 700 participants from a variety of denominations. It was the largest conference on evangelism ever organized by a parish church in Canada. The event created a sharp division in the congregation. Many church members were disturbed by the so-called manifestations of the Holy Spirit observed during the conference, including speaking in tongues and 'falling in the Spirit', and also about the way in which Alpha was introduced by a small faction within the church. Others were concerned with its perceived close ties, via Holy Trinity, Brompton, to the Toronto Airport Christian Fellowship, and the more questionable aspects of the Toronto Blessing that it promoted and which now seemed to be evident, albeit somewhat diluted, in the Alpha programme. This concern brought to the surface some disquiet that non-charismatics in particular felt about Alpha.

Who are the critics? The answer is fairly straightforward. In the attempt to be ecumenical and user-friendly Alpha has tended to antagonize conservatives and traditionalists on the one hand, and more liberal-minded Christians on the other. This was clear in my interviews with a number of prominent national church leaders, as well as clergymen at the local church level. While liberals tended to see Alpha as too fundamentalist in its orientation, the traditionalists and conservatives, especially Protestant evangelicals, Anglo-Catholics and the more conservative Roman Catholics feared its ecumenical stance and its role in bringing in all things charismatic 'by the backdoor'. At the local level Alpha's theology, praxis, and accompanying culture is not infrequently perceived as alien to the local church whichever one of these traditions is subscribed to.

It is the charismatic faction in a church, being frequently the more forceful and determined constituency, who may get their way in introducing Alpha. Those who are prepared to administer and promote an Alpha course generally tend to be among the most active in the daily running of the programme. It is a way in which they can assert themselves and their theology and culture within their immediate environment. Their opponents, so I discovered in my research, often had nothing to do with the course once instigated, or on occasion left their church in opposition. A certain elder at a United Reformed church confessed to me that over half his fellow elders were on the verge of resigning in protest at the adoption of Alpha, and that in several UR churches some had actually resigned.

This is not to say that all those of a charismatic persuasion are happy with Alpha. I conversed with one course leader who expressed some concern about what the Alpha supporting literature has to say. The problem came with being obliged to accept the Alpha course in its entirety. He cited how, in one publication, it was taken for granted that all Christians should speak in tongues as a necessary sign of conversion. In this particular example Nicky

Gumbel spoke of how it might be necessary to sit opposite someone in a prayer group who is unable to speak in tongues and provide an example of how to do so. The course leader took exception to this teaching, although he was prepared to overlook it, arguing that no introductory course in Christianity will have *all* doctrines necessarily correct.

The Conservative Critique

One element of the church most vehemently opposed to Alpha are the conservative Protestant evangelicals. This is probably entirely predictable. Many of their number have lamented the cultural concessions of Alpha in its search for a popular evangelistic programme. A general feeling is that it undermines the basic tenets of the gospel, plays down the significance of sin and guilt and the need for redemption in favour of a 'feel good' factor that is part of the general cultural drift of the churches today. Being relevant to modern man and engaging people 'where they are', the conservatives argue, fails to recognize the need for genuine repentance. The views of this quarter of Christendom are quite evident on various Alpha websites where there are constant complaints that Alpha has 'sold out' to contemporary culture.

Conservative Protestants in the UK, particularly of the evangelical variety (many being under the auspices of the Fellowship of Independent Evangelical Churches rather than the more charismatically-inclined Evangelical Alliance), have taken the theological high ground and used Alpha as an opportunity to savage some of their favourite foes, namely charismatics and Roman Catholics, not infrequently in the same breath. As it was put to me by one pastor who is a leading light in the FIEC:

> We find it (Alpha) over manipulative, man-centred, minimalizing the sin question and over-emphasizes the charismatic element, especially with the notorious Holy Spirit weekend. The fact that Roman Catholic churches can use it without any qualms demonstrates its dismal lack of doctrinal content.

That Alpha also appeals to Roman Catholics is a cause of lament for the conservative Protestant evangelicals. The self-assigned anti-cultist organization Reachout Trust has generated a debate about Alpha on its website. Many contributors have taken a negative tone (there is an undercurrent in the debate that Alpha has developed into something of a cult – a possibility considered in Chapter 14). Observers have lamented its appeal to Roman Catholics – one contributor to the Reachout Trust's site suggesting that the Alpha course may be profoundly ' ... moving Roman Catholics into a tighter embrace of Rome's falsehoods'.[1]

Another pastor of a large evangelical church that I had communication with displayed considerable theological reservation about Alpha. In a rather sophisticated sociological as well as theological argument, he insisted that those who had designed the content had little understanding of the nature of

God, Jesus or the atonement, or the purposes of the Holy Spirit. It was, he claimed, a course for the post-modern consumer society where practically any form of morality was acceptable. This was a society with no clear moral guidelines and thus subsequently reflected in Alpha since it placed little emphasis on sin and guilt, or altering one's lifestyle to a degree compatible with what the conversion experience ideally entails. Moreover, Alpha, he insisted 'presents "a give me now theology" of "I have been through the course, believe – so give me my reward"'. He concluded that it was well-intentioned but badly aimed and that:

> People are probably not really converted and don't change their lifestyle.
> Like much of the charismatic movement, it is based a lot on emotions.

A similar kind of reasoning aimed at the theological element of Alpha is advanced by the evangelical writer Chris Hand in his publication *Is Alpha Leading People Astray?*[2] 'Leading astray' amounts to teaching a distorted kind of Christianity that gives too many concessions to the contemporary world. He suggests in no uncertain terms that:

> The God of Alpha is not the God of the Bible, the plight of man in Alpha
> is not as serious as in the Bible, and the Jesus Christ of Alpha is not the
> Jesus Christ of the Bible.

There is further evidence of the view of the more traditional Protestant constituency. Very much within the Presbyterian tradition, a booklet has been produced by Colin Mercer called *The Alpha Course Examined*, with a foreword by Dr Ian Paisley (for many years the leader of the Ulster Unionist Party in Northern Ireland). It is an interesting document and offers perhaps the most resounding critique to date. The booklet has the following headings:

1　Alpha presents unbiblical theology
2　(Alpha's) Failure to highlight the depravity of man
3　Alpha practices an unscriptural ministry
4　The corrupt foundation of Alpha
5　The charismatic deception of Alpha
6　Alpha produces false security
7　Alpha emphasises self instead of saviour
8　Alpha emphasises feelings instead of faith
9　Alpha emphasises remorse instead of repentance
10　Alpha emphasises sensationalism instead of sanctification
11　Alpha promotes ecumenical activity
12　(Alpha) Fails to expose the errors of ecumenism
13　Alpha rejects the scriptural command of separation from ecumenism

For this conservative Protestant contingent, Alpha is frequently portrayed as another sign of apostasy, while its existence simultaneously and conveniently vindicates a pessimistic pre-millenarian worldview. Hence the perceived errors of the nominal Christian churches in embracing Alpha confirms its own rather elitist and exclusive stance. Despite their intense opposition, it is interesting to note, however, that the conservatives have been unable to develop a viable alternative to Alpha and, if one has been produced, it has not been effectively marketed. This is mainly because, I would suggest, of their inability to come up with a creative package able to attract modern 'seekers', which is both culturally appealing *and* evangelical. In that sense the designation 'conservative evangelical' becomes almost a contradiction in terms.

Alpha in the Catholic Churches: Advocates and Critics

Criticisms of Alpha do not stop with the conservative Protestant evangelicals. In some quarters of the Roman Catholic church there is equal concern but predictably for very different reasons. While the charismatic element is problematic for traditionalists, there are other aspects of Alpha which might be disliked. Although not particularly outspoken, a handful of bishops in the UK and the USA are believed to be quite seriously apprehensive about the use of Alpha in their diocese because it would seem to amount to a form of 'creeping Protestantism'. Even the Pope, according to some sources, is known to have misgivings because of its origins within a Protestant church, namely HTB.

Like the Protestant wing of the church, the impact of Alpha on Catholicism is far from straightforward. About 400 Roman Catholic parishes in the UK are running Alpha programmes. I frequently received the impression in my survey, however, that in many instances it was a reluctantly supported fringe programme. While some Catholic congregations boldly advertise Alpha on large billboards in front of their church, the majority have smaller adverts of an impending course which may be lost on notice boards inside the building alongside other 'coming attractions' and only observable to parishioners.

Leaders of Alpha in Catholic churches are often left to their own devices since the course tends to be swamped underneath numerous other church activities and rival programmes aimed at enhancing loyalty to Catholicism. This has the effect of restricting the impact of Alpha in Catholic circles. I have also found that Catholic Alpha leaders are more reluctant to 'go public' with the course and more apprehensive of dealing with guests who are not Catholic. My broad sense is that there is a general confusion or at least concerns about Alpha among some Roman Catholics. A lively debate can often be followed in parish or diocese newspapers. Group leaders that I interviewed frequently expressed the view that Alpha was a bit of an anathema to some in the local church and did not quite fit in with Catholic traditions.

In the course of my study, which included several Roman Catholic churches, one of the leaders in a parish church was concerned that the Head of Religious Formation (responsible for Roman Catholic teaching) in his diocese had grave reservations because it was not sufficiently Roman Catholic in its theological component. At the same time, leading Catholic figures involved in the charismatic movement are discernibly much more enthusiastic about Alpha and not infrequently contribute to the programme's wealth of literature. *Alpha News* also periodically carries articles on Alpha's impact in Catholic churches.[3]

In Catholic, as well as Protestant, churches it is the charismatic faction that may readily embrace and run Alpha and it is frequently the priest of this persuasion who instigates it. However, other priests may be adamantly opposed to its introduction. On some occasions lay people who are enthusiastic about Alpha may actually change parish church if it is not supported by the clergy in the one usually attended, while other parishioners may go about their lives oblivious to the fact that Alpha is running in their local church.

Although Protestant critics of Alpha frequently believe that the course is used to enforce Catholic beliefs, it is my experience that Catholics who have given some thought to running Alpha in their churches tend to play down the theology, history and cultural trappings of Catholicism in order to attract a wider audience. References to the Pope, Hail Mary, the Sacred Heart, and all things related to the Catholic tradition are deliberately reduced in the ecumenical venture of Alpha. The concerns of more traditional Roman Catholics are perhaps, then, understandable.

On the other hand, Alpha can advance the Catholic cause. I became aware that some priests only allowed Alpha to proceed because of its potential to reverse decline in Catholic church membership and to address traditional moral concerns such as sex before marriage and the virtues of family life. I interviewed one priest who unashamedly endorsed Alpha. He decided to press ahead after a meeting of representatives and other local priests from Catholic churches, explaining that he was keen on evangelistic enterprises, whatever their source, to bring people to faith in order to restore Christian values, especially Catholic values, back into society. Alpha, the priest explained, was an introduction 'into the foundations' and these 'foundations' were clearly those of Catholicism. Nevertheless, he did have some concerns. The role of Mary was ignored, and there was nothing on the Eucharist in the programme.

In other respects however, Alpha in Catholic churches does seem to consolidate a particular version of the faith. The Catholic church has produced the booklet 'How To Support Alpha for Roman Catholics'. The publication claims not to be a Catholic version of Alpha, rather it is directed towards answering the kind of questions that Catholics ask about the course. As it declares, it is aimed at 'allaying fears that Alpha is not doctrinally sound or is too evangelical'. The Catholic Alpha Office (established in 1996) has also produced two videos directed at Roman Catholics within the context of Alpha: 'Why should I listen to the Church?' and 'Why should I go to Mass?'. As I will suggest in subsequent chapters, most of those 'guests' attending

Alpha courses are already in the church. This is particularly the case in Catholic churches, and many do not 'go public' with their courses.

There appears to be a contradiction in Catholic churches, given the evidence of Alpha courses, that the priesthood is the ultimate arbiter as to whether it runs or not and that a parish priest is likely to agree only on the basis of advancing traditional Catholicism. However, on the ground – if left to parishioners to run – traditional aspects may be played down in favour of a more ecumenical and charismatic stance. It may follow, therefore, that the extent to which Alpha is advanced in Catholic churches in the future will depend on its perceived merit: should it advance traditional Catholicism or is it more an instrument in the cause of renewal and ecumenism? In Catholic circles the debate on Alpha's merit will also continue and it is likely that it will never enjoy a full acceptance.

The Liberal Critique

So much for the conservative critique, be it Catholic or Protestant. From the other end of the theological spectrum, liberal churchmen have criticized Alpha because it is viewed as essentially fundamentalist in orientation, or at least promotes only one variety of Christianity. A continuing complaint from this constituency is that the Alpha course uncompromisingly opposes homosexuality and abortion, promotes celibacy outside of marriage, and generally fails to deal adequately with what are clearly very sensitive issues. This infers that Alpha is selective in its 'basic Christianity' and that what is omitted is perhaps more noteworthy than what is included. The Alpha programme, so it is argued, has little to say in terms of a social gospel. There is scarce attention given to feeding and clothing the poor, in advancing social justice, of debates about unemployment, and the negative repercussions of globalization. While there is a moral condemnation of high divorce and abortion rates, the rising rate of unmarried mothers and the decline of the family, there is next to nothing said about mass unemployment, the evils of materialism, or Third World issues. Very little justice is done, so it is observed by the liberals, to the complexity of Christian ethics – the basis of a just war and similar issues. These themes may be discussed on an Alpha course if someone wishes to raise them, but are not straightaway offered as vital aspects of Christianity.

In terms of its content, some liberal critics complain that Alpha has nothing in it which approaches a social gospel. Perhaps the closest it comes to a social conscience is evident in Gumbel's book *Challenging Lifestyles* which includes the brief early chapter 'How to Have an Influence on Society'. The chapter is mostly based on the Sermon of the Mount and the social consequences on society of striving to be meek, pure in heart, righteous, and so on. However, much is implicit, vague, and over-simplified rather than a systematic treatment of important issues. There is no coherent programme – certainly nothing amounting to a clear political agenda.

Another failure (certainly for the liberal critics) is that the Alpha programme sets and answers its own questions. It tends to over-simplify thoughtful critiques of Christianity and then destroys them in a rather brutal and unsophisticated way. This is evident in the supporting literature. There is a broad discussion throughout the programme, but not sufficient to do justice to complicated issues. It is then, in its own way, hermetically fail safe.

A related criticism focuses on the question: what has led to particular topics being advanced as representing 'basic Christianity'? Who decides what is included under the rubric of each theme and what is left out? Who is the final arbiter? The answers are not straightforward. Firstly, to some extent the content is oriented to answering certain fundamental questions. HTB has conducted ongoing research over a number of years to find out what issues are important to Alpha guests. Hence we might assume that some topics on the course will take into account popular consumer demand (see Chapter 8). Secondly, given its ecumenical and all-embracing nature, Alpha is meant to be as broad and inclusive as possible. It is not denomination specific and is intended to be user-friendly to all Christian traditions, calculated not to offend Roman Catholics or Protestants of different persuasions. It is, for its advocates, a basic and simple introduction to the traditional faith.

Liberal critics have taken the course to task at this point, arguing that it is too simple and largely fundamentalist in tone. For the theologian and sociologist, Martyn Percy, the content of the course shows that Alpha amounts to a fairly crude form of evangelical fundamentalism (Percy 1998). He is concerned with what is *not* included in the course in terms of historical Christianity. The subjects discussed are not, crucially, the Trinity, baptism, communion or community which might, despite the claims of Alpha to be ecumenical, be more appropriate to the needs of some Christian traditions. Rather the core concerns are with the Holy Spirit, healing, and the powers of evil. Moreover, for Percy, Alpha projects Christianity as an uncontextual project that is 'learned' through an over-simplified course offering certain types of (charismatic) knowledge and experience. In essence, it is sold and marketed effectively but sometimes gives the impression of offering a cheap package deal or endeavours to provide 'a bargain-break weekend for two in eternity' (Percy 1998, p. 16).

There is a sense here that Alpha cannot win. There are those who maintain that it is not sufficiently 'basic' enough and assumes too much knowledge for non-believers. Critics taking the opposite approach argue that it is too simple and unsophisticated. This dilemma was evident in the interviews and questionnaire responses of the main survey of Alpha. Some respondents praised its simplicity:

> The advantage of Alpha is the plain and simple explanations about Jesus Christ and Christianity.

> The course teaches the basics and then you can ask any questions you like in a safe setting.

Others, however, thought that it was too simple:

> Alpha might be a bit lightweight and not in-depth enough for some tastes.

One course leader had some reservations, describing Alpha as so much 'fizz, bank and wallop', by which she meant that there was a great deal of froth without too much substance. It was, she argued, an attractive cultural package, yet lacked adequate theological depth.

Other interviewees considered that Alpha was not simple enough and assumed too much prior knowledge:

> Sometimes people need to do something pre-Alpha if they have never thought of Jesus at all.

> Maybe Alpha is too much, too intense.

Among those who run Alpha at a local level was a common view that it assumed a large degree of prior knowledge. While critics have lamented its lack of theological grounding, it was my observation of a number of discussion groups that those outside the faith (and some inside) often simply did not understand what was being put across. In this respect, so it was occasionally argued, too much could be expected of Alpha. An Anglican minister observed that those being introduced to the Bible for the first time were hesitant and that was often why some guests gave up in the first few weeks. He complained that:

> Initially people are confused and find it very difficult to understand since they have no experience of the Bible. The discussion groups look at the biblical references, but it is lost on people. We had someone on the last course who had never heard of St Paul. Why should he? He had never been to Sunday school.

Liberal critics are concerned not only with what Alpha sees as basic Christianity, but also with its general cultural orientation. In this respect, Martyn Percy has concentrated on the over-emphasis in the Alpha programme on the Holy Spirit and its link to healing and all-things therapeutic. While this alleged unbalance may result from charismatic theology, it is also, he deduces, because Alpha is a product of time and place:

> The Spirit on offer obviously arises from a personable, therapeutic, home-counties context that is concerned with the individual.
>
> (Percy 1998, p. 9)

According to Percy, this focus upon the individual as the receptacle of the Holy Spirit is at the cost of his wider work in creation, justice, peace and reconciliation. This is because, he asserts, those who put the course together reflect the elite, upper middle-class outlook of HTB which has also enculturated the gospel for the needs of a distinct clientele rather than for a wide audience. Alpha may attempt to be relevant to modern man but, as clearly seen in its theology of the Holy Spirit, it is anchored in a particular cultural environment and Christian milieu constituted largely by middle-class charismatics and is, theologically-speaking, far from ecumenical.

For Percy, Alpha does not generate a broad appeal. Its intellectual level, cultural trappings and general image is more likely to be suited to what he describes as 'middle-England' – the relatively well-educated and at least moderately affluent. The fact is that in as much as Alpha is making converts, it appears merely to add to the middle-class cohorts of the charismatic movement. If so, large segments of the population who are not middle-class are failing to be reached even by the state-of-the-art evangelism that Alpha claims to represent. This was evident in some of my research findings. One High church Anglican minister said that Alpha was run on one occasion in his parish three years before he took the position at his church. While asserting that he had a reasonable understanding of what it was all about, he felt no obligation to take it up. In his Anglican church, he argued, Alpha was 'in house' and attracted middle-class people. He complained that evangelism should be directed towards the local government housing area and the poor in his town but it was not doing so. Neither was Alpha because its cultural nuances remained essentially alienating.

Is Alpha Fundamentalist?

One particular issue, a feature of Alpha, troubles many critics. Is the Alpha programme fundamentalist in nature? Does it offer the attraction of an uncompromising, 'certain' belief system for those who subscribe to it either as organizers or guests. If so, what are the likely consequences for the church at large? There are, potentially, a number of dangers, and much may depend upon how Alpha is applied at the local level where there is evidence of at least some negative consequences.

Mary Robins, an assistant priest at St James's in Piccadilly, London, claims that her church has helped people who have been damaged by Alpha. 'Alpha (courses) are very black-and-white', she stated. 'For instance, I find them very rigid in their view of what it is like to be a woman.' In respect of the money spent on the national initiative in 1999, Robins has commented that 'if my church had £1million to spend we would use it to set up day centres and support the Jubilee 2000 campaign to get rid of Third World debt'.[4]

St James, situated in the centre of London, has for several years offered advice and counselling to people claiming to be adversely affected by religious fundamentalism generally. According to Robins, her church had heard from dozens of people who had mostly seen out the Alpha programme but had been damaged in one way or another. The major problem appeared to be that they were weighed down by a sense of guilt, sometimes several years after having taken an Alpha course. People were frequently advised to change their lifestyles where they were deemed by Alpha leaders not to be compatible with their view of Christianity and the standards expected by God.[5] On such evidence some critics believe that it is fundamentalist in orientation and that there are implicit perils. Yet whether Alpha is fundamentalist or not is far from easy to answer and must be put in a broader context.

Fundamentalism is clearly a contemporary concern. It has recently received a great deal of sociological interest, as well as public 'bad press'. The emergence of global fundamentalism and its impact as a political movement since the 1980s took many sociologists of religion by surprise. But what is fundamentalism? To be sure, it is a slippery term and is open to ideological, not to say theological, interpretations. The commonsense view, often resulting from simple observation of world events involving highly visible religious fundamentalist movements of various faiths – Christian, Muslim, Jewish, Hindu and Sikh – is that it amounts to an extreme and intolerant expression of religiosity. It is viewed at times as dangerous, and an ogre opposed to modernity and all that that entails: pluralism, secularity, permissive morals, and social and cultural transformation.

As a conservative form of religion, fundamentalism is frequently referred to by sociologists as an articulation of neo-traditionalism – not just defending religious principles but struggling against the perceived negative consequences of social change. Hence fundamentalism may be seen as a broader phenomenon denoting movements which appear preoccupied with self-consciously attempting to represent or reassert an authentic religious tradition in opposition to the modern world. In this respect it is typically seen within Christianity as primarily being concerned with the reclaiming of conventional moral and religious values, and in organizing protest against what it perceives as the detrimental social changes that have taken place. At this point an overview of developments within contemporary Christianity can be offered (even if its simplicity might prove a little nauseating to the seasoned theologian or church historian). Then perhaps Alpha's supposed fundamentalist credentials may be appraised.

Strictly speaking, the self-designated term 'fundamentalism' was allegedly first proudly proclaimed in the USA by Protestant conservatives who published a series of pamphlets between 1910 and 1915 entitled *The Fundamentals*. These works called for a return to what were held to be the core doctrines of the Christian faith which were under attack from outside and inside the church: from secular society and liberal theologians. This indicates that for some two centuries Christianity had produced a distinct form of fundamentalism that resulted from being the world faith that was first forced to confront and respond to modernity, its rationalism and pluralism. At the same time, the relationship between fundamentalism and Christianity is perhaps understandable since, like Islam, it is 'a religion of the book'. The moral imperatives of the one God are to be found in the Bible. God is the creator and divine mover throughout human history. However, the written word may be open to interpretation and fundamentalists bring their own exegesis even if they may disagree with each other.

Scripture, from the fundamentalist perspective, is given a literal interpretation with little or no room for the higher criticism associated with liberal theology which frequently focuses upon cultural and historical contexts. For example, that women should not speak in church and that homosexuality is sinful must be understood as prohibitions constructed in a particular time and place or that, for the liberals, biblical miracles are interpreted as metaphors or said to have some deeper moral significance. By contrast, for fundamentalists such themes as the prohibition of homosexuality are scriptural truths, absolute tenets of faith, and not open to interpretation or negotiation. In turn, such dogma has become a sign by which the fundamentalists distinguish between themselves as upholders of the faith and the liberals who they not infrequently label as apostates and even heretics. Having said that, biblical interpretation is a complex issue and it is clear that fundamentalists are selective in their 'fundamentals'; for instance, while condemning homosexuality they have next to nothing to say about usury.

Alpha Appraised

Is Alpha fundamentalist in orientation by any of the above criteria? The short answer is yes and no. Clearly the issue must be discussed with reference to the charismatic content of the programme and the attitudes of those leading church figures who put the course together and those who administer it at a local level.

For some of the organizers of Alpha courses in the local churches Alpha was seen as a way of 'getting back to basics' and was clearly regarded as a means of re-balancing liberal tendencies within the church. One Methodist Alpha leader I spoke to insisted that besides being a useful tool for evangelism, it was also good for those in the church since it returned to the 'foundations' of the faith. In this respect, she argued, Alpha countered much that is heard from the pulpit:

> These days people are taught not to believe. Liberal clergyman explain away the Bible; that Mary was not a virgin, that there was no bodily resurrection of Christ, or explain healing away. Christians today do not know how to use the Bible, Alpha teaches them how to do so.

Another interviewee however, was aware of the dangers of Alpha, particularly in the hands of certain course leaders at the local level:

> Alpha could be seen as fundamentalist and dogmatic if led by some people. It tends to promote only one form of Christianity.

The claim that Alpha is fundamentalist needs to be looked at carefully and the evidence thoughtfully weighed up. I will argue below that while there are certain fundamentalist inclinations, the alleged dangers of Alpha are minimal and that these fundamentalist elements are honed down by other aspects of the programme. An immediate observation, however, is that part of the problem of interpretation is that charismatics do not sit comfortably in the fundamentalist camp. Particularly in the USA they have not readily been accepted by the more traditional fundamentalists largely because of the pentecostal element – the dogma and praxis related to the emphasis and interpretation of the role of the Holy Spirit and the charismata.

There is more to consider, however, in the discussion of the fundamentalist nature of charismatic Christianity. Charismatics are not consistent biblical literalists. This is evident in the Alpha programme. On the one hand, as we have seen above, Alpha endorses the familiar charismatic teaching on healing, the powers of evil, and the nature of spiritual warfare. In fact, in this respect they seem to major on a theological minor. To put it succinctly, there is an insistence on certain 'basics' which are not regarded as central to the faith by all Christians. At the same time, like their conservative evangelical counterparts, they are rather selective of what they condemn on biblical grounds. As we shall see in Chapter 14, Alpha is hostile towards the homosexual act (although not as forthrightly condemning homosexual orientation as do many other fundamentalists).

Alpha may not be as fundamentalist as it first appears. It seems to have little problem with women in the ministry (even though it is not raised as an obvious issue). Similarly, charismatics have a pro-life attitude towards abortion and criticize the alleged decline of the family (most may not be concerned with the politics of permissive change and few are active regarding moral issues in quite the same way as the Christian Right in the USA), but there are not many who have problems with the remarriage of divorcees and they tend to be open-ended on the creationist issue. Like most fundamentalists (if that is what they are), charismatics pick and choose what aspects of modernity they are opposed to. They tend to be fairly liberal on some social issues. At the same time, while it can be recognized that all fundamentalists are selective of what they accept or reject of the modern world, charismatics are particularly prepared to enculturate themselves and this is self-evidently true of much of the working philosophy of Alpha.

There is another, perhaps more obvious, reason why Alpha is not stringently fundamentalist, because of its need to be ecumenical. Besides the core Christian doctrines such as the Trinity, the virgin birth, and the atonement which have been distinguishing features of the historical church (and of course the unique charismatic element with its emphasis on the Holy Spirit, healing, spiritual warfare and so on), Alpha is designed to appeal to Catholics and Protestants and is administered in mainline denominations and different traditions within them. It is hard to designate these traditions as fundamentalist by most criteria or suggest that churches are being hoodwinked into accepting a fundamentalist form of faith. Moreover, it would appear that Alpha leaders are prepared to leave at least some dogma and interpretation of aspects of scripture to those who administer the course locally. The interpretation of hell and eternal damnation, it seems, is open to negotiation, while child baptism is left to a matter of denominational preference.

The question of Alpha's fundamentalism does not stop there. Critics would also suggest that through Alpha, the basics of Christianity reveal themselves as the appeal to a largely inerrant Bible, a powerful Holy Spirit, and the expression of evangelical atonement doctrine. It is also possible that organizers of Alpha tend to see themselves as a kind of spiritual elite (note the rhetoric of the Toronto Blessing) or, to use charismatic-speak, 'are at the forefront of what God is doing'. While listening to comments about Alpha from the churches that subscribe to it, HTB is not fond of critics and is clearly unmoveable on some issues: Alpha is 'basic Christianity', HTB-style, and there must be little departure from it.

This view again needs to be balanced out. While the theology of the Alpha course undoubtedly has some fundamentalist aspects, it is tempered by the need, in evangelical jargon 'to be relevant to modern man'. The call to be relevant was once part of the liberal agenda. Throughout the nineteenth and early twentieth centuries a fundamentalist–modernist split, often articulated through conservative–liberal theological debates, was essentially stimulated by changes in the modern world and the challenges they offered to the faith. In the nineteenth century, theologically liberal churchmen foresaw the difficulties for the survival of Christianity posed especially by the separation of church and state. To retain cultural power and influence, Christian intellectuals embarked on a process of accommodation, engaging with newly emergent scientific and philosophical traditions. In many respects this marked what can be referred to as 'internal secularization' – an attempt to adapt to a rapidly changing and increasingly sceptical world. The imperative was to retain the basics of the faith whist reducing the supernaturalist element which was to be judged in the light of human reason.

While contemporary charismatics, including those that have forged Alpha, have retained a supernaturalist dimension, they are following good liberal tradition by attempting, albeit selectively, to be relevant to today's culture. It is this balance which has brought it a measure of success and, at the same time, has limited its fundamentalist inclinations. We have seen above (Chapter 3) that sociological research suggests that the more successful churches were those which expressed a form of religiosity that was congruent with lifestyle preferences and that avoided, or at least lessened, the painful transition from secular to the more conservative expressions of a Christian subculture. There are churches, typified by the Vineyard movement, that provide meaning, significance and purpose – all dressed in an attractive cultural package.

Summary

In this chapter we have overviewed some of the criticisms of Alpha from within the church; those who support Alpha and those who do not; conservatives and liberals, Protestants and Catholics. This is not to suggest that theologians and church people are always clearly divided in their attitudes regarding Alpha. While there may be polar extremes, most Christians will carry both liberal and conservative attitudes in their belief system. Many who subscribe to Alpha are not always happy with the entire package but are willing to work within the broad framework of the programme, even altering components if it is felt necessary.

Clearly from the above discussion it is possible to view Alpha as controversial, although it would be wrong to make too much of its more notorious elements. I have my own views of Alpha and it is no doubt proper to make them clear at this point. As an outsider, I am fairly well predisposed towards the programme. Having sat through the course on several occasions I can say that I did not experience intimidation or anything approaching brainwashing. I have never felt anything but welcomed by honest and earnest people who administered it within the safety of well-established denominations. Besides its obvious charismatic and evangelical element, the content of the course is recognizable as historical Christianity even if a great deal is missing in terms of a social gospel. Neither can its middle-class cultural baggage be doubted. Yet I do not believe that it has sufficiently departed from the historical faith and what has passed as contemporary Christianity in most mainline churches for some time. The danger is, however, how certain issues are dealt with at the local church level, where dogma and insensitivity may prove to be detrimental.

Notes

1   Reachout website (9 October 2002). The same site shows how keen some Roman Catholic cardinals and bishops are on the Alpha course.
2   Chris Hand (1990) *Is Alpha Leading People Astray?*, Alpha website.
3   One Catholic church in Texas has increased its congregation from 2,200 to 3,000 as a result of running Alpha (*Alpha News*, July–October 2003, p. 24).
4   Quoted in an article by Dominic Kennedy, *The Times*, 9 September 1998.
5   Interview with Mary Robins, 8 October 2001. Among the many letters she received about the negative aspects of Alpha was one from a woman in Scotland who was unable to have children. She was told by a church leader running an Alpha course that it was biblically sound to pray for a child and that this would be guaranteed. In time it became clear that she was still unable to conceive, and as a result she lost her Christian faith. In Robin's evaluation, while some Alpha guests may search for the assurance that a more fundamentalist interpretation of the faith brings, others were seeking a more liberal, human and tolerant approach, and a view of Christ who accepts people as they are, including their sexual orientation, straight or gay. (Robin's views on the way Alpha deals with the subject of homosexuality are to be found in Chapter 14.)

Chapter 6

The Survey in the Churches

The National Survey

The research findings upon which most of the observations in this book are based are derived from a survey of a number of churches subscribing to Alpha in England and Wales. Research was also conducted in a number of institutions specializing in a variation of Alpha courses: in prisons and establishments of higher education (see Chapter 12). The survey was conducted between the summer of 2001 and late 2002. It followed the earlier pilot study of 1999–2000 which focused on just four churches each representing a major denomination. Like all pilot studies it was small scale but produced useful preliminary findings and helped modify methodological research tools.

In the pilot study some 400 questionnaires were administered in these four churches (with a response rate of 76 per cent). In addition, I interviewed twenty clergy or leaders of Alpha courses from a wide variety of churches in the same locality. Forty interviews were also conducted of Alpha guests who came forward as a result of filling in a questionnaire. I spent many hours reading the relevant Alpha literature and conducting field work which largely involved attending three Alpha courses in different churches. The pilot study yielded some important observations and a few of them will be mentioned below. It is worth pointing out that the findings of the pilot study and the larger national one reflect the experiences of church leaders administering courses, church members who have helped, and those 'guests' who have enlisted on them, besides my own impressions. While such participation complements the hard data yielded by questionnaires and interviews, as well as allowing insights into the experiences of others, it is bound to include a more subjective element.

The larger survey upon which this book is based took in 31 churches drawn from the mainline denominations as well as a handful of independent churches. That so much attention is given to these churches in this survey is justified by the fact that the Alpha programme itself identifies the mainline denominations as its primary vehicle and the natural basis for an evangelizing enterprise. This chapter will overview the methods used in the larger survey, the types of churches involved, some observations as to how and why Alpha was adopted, and the view of Alpha course leaders on its merits or otherwise. It will prepare the ground for subsequent chapters, particularly those related to the question of who joins Alpha, and the broader issue as to whether the programme is working in any meaningful way.

Initially the churches asked to participate in the survey were taken from a random sample listed in *Alpha News* as participating in the Alpha course. These were whittled down to 31 churches on the grounds of those who could or could not provide an adequate sample of people who had passed through Alpha courses and those who were prepared to participate. The survey also allowed a reasonable sample of churches of different sizes, varying demographic features of their congregations, and contrasting geographical areas. Different denominations and church traditions were also able to participate (the real names of the churches are not disclosed and, for the most part, this was the wish of the majority participating). The range of churches included Roman Catholic, Anglican, Baptist, Methodist, Congregational, Salvation Army, Pentecostal, independent evangelical and charismatic churches, as well as those linked to networks of churches. The initial contact with each of the churches was either with the minister of the church or a leader of the Alpha course in the church. These 'gatekeepers' were the individuals who decided whether research would proceed. In most cases, either the clergy or leader of the Alpha course was interviewed to 'get a feel' of the programme in each church and to solicit their broad opinions about it.

At this juncture a detailed statement can be made concerning the research methods used in this larger survey. As an opening observation we can note two things which will be discussed in detail as this chapter progresses. Firstly, the methodological difficulties of dealing with religious movements (if Alpha indeed can be described as a 'movement'). No sociological survey is without its difficulties. Those related to the study of religion has its peculiar methodological problems and a number of these became evident in researching the Alpha programme. This was true not just of the churches, but of Alpha as applied to prisons, youth groups, and students. Secondly, in its attempt to establish a research method and in the findings generated, the survey exposed some of the unrealistic triumphantist propaganda of the national organizers of the Alpha programme: a self-laudation that is not always justified.

The national survey of Alpha built upon the methods utilized in the pilot study. The qualitative methods were based on questionnaire and semi-structured interviews. Some questions, those concerned with demographic features such as occupation, gender and ethnicity were closed, while those related to the course itself, were open-ended. A number of respondents had little to say on particular topics while others took the opportunity to write copious amounts which varied in their constructive contribution to the survey.

The responses to several of the questions asked of Alpha guests have already been utilized in the earlier chapters of this book, but something more should be said here about the function and distribution of the questionnaires. Fifteen hundred questionnaires were administered with 837 returned (a return rate of some 55 per cent.[1] The number of questionnaires administered at each church varied considerably and was determined by how many times the course had run, the number of people that had been through it, and the size of the church. Some of the returns from churches were quite small with the fewest collected being a mere 10, and the most 83. There is the danger that some of the smaller quotas might have distorted a portion of the data. However, these smaller returns did contribute towards the larger picture.

As with the pilot study, the questionnaire of the larger survey asked for volunteers to come forward to be interviewed – 113 people consented. I selected 50 of them on the grounds of representation of gender, age, social class, church background, as well as their experiences and attitudes towards Alpha. The great majority of them were interviewed by telephone. Since the survey was a national one, involving churches from different parts of the country, it was impractical to conduct face-to-face interviews as with the pilot study.

Questions on the questionnaire were mostly the same as those on the pilot study (with one or two minor alterations) and were largely concerned with an attitudinal understanding of those that had taken Alpha courses. Again, given the distances involved and the preferences of churches not to give out the names and addresses of those who had been on Alpha courses, most of the participating churches administered and collected questionnaires themselves. This did have the advantage of respondents being contacted by people in the church whom they mostly knew and trusted. Churches were asked to administer questionnaires to all those who had taken an Alpha course over the years that the programme had been running and this varied considerably. It included all those that had completed or not completed the course (where traceable), were members of a church or unchurched, or were previously converted or not to the Christian faith. Participant observation of Alpha courses was at the core of the quantitative methods. Most of this observation was based on participation through five Alpha courses in different churches over a five-year period (although not always in their entirety). I also attended Holy Spirit weekends, as well as one post-Alpha course and have remained with a church 'cell' (study group) that has continued to meet even as I write.

The difficulties of involving as many churches in the survey as possible highlighted the methodological problems of the sociological enterprise. Every fiftieth church of the first 7,000 listed as subscribing to Alpha in *Alpha News* were selected for contact regarding the possibility of being surveyed. Interestingly, 26 listed had not run the course for a period of time and in some cases several years, and felt unable to contribute. Four listed churches had never been involved with the programme. Twenty churches could not be contacted (neither by phone nor otherwise). Of those that were contactable, 40 (about one in six) were prepared to be involved in the survey. Having offered to participate, some churches later opted out – sometimes halfway through the research, or returned too few questionnaires as to warrant inclusion.

Some churches simply refused to participate without explanation. Others offered various reasons as to why they did not want to be involved. 'Not the sort of thing our pastor wishes to be concerned with', was a not untypical response. Simply not having the time to administer questionnaires was another reason. A third was that it was felt by some churches that the research would be too intrusive and add to the difficulties of retaining people on the course. Fourthly, that churches administered their own questionnaires and were loath to over-burden their Alpha guests with paperwork. Two churches that did not wish to be involved nevertheless sent on their findings and these are detailed in Chapter 11 and serve to supplement my own findings.

Several churches in the Bristol and south Wales areas were approached regarding the possibility of participant observation. These are areas close to the institution where I am based and conduct research. Some of these churches did not wish me to personally participate on an Alpha course. As a matter of ethical concern, I insisted that any participation would be overt and known to course guests. One course leader, considering the prospect, complained that the guests on her course would probably feel 'like fish in a fish bowl' being observed and conscious that they were being so. This was discerned as counter-productive to the aim of winning converts. I was politely asked not to participate. However, I did join courses offered by other churches.

As already mentioned, churches with very small numbers of Alpha guests on the course were omitted. Some could claim only one or two over a period of several years. Several churches, having run the course as a 'one off', subsequently decided not to offer Alpha again because to one degree or another it failed to work. As a general comment I have to say, at a local level, that Alpha appears to be small-scale in many cases. This is true of the larger charismatic community churches as well as some of the sparse congregations of the mainline churches.

Churches Participating

Church no. 1   St Barnabas is an Anglican church situated in a fairly large rural town. It regards itself as traditionalist in church life with no significant charismatic orientation although there is a discernible small faction inclined towards charismatic beliefs and practices. The vicar claimed that his church was unique since no other Anglican church of its ilk in the area was prepared to take Alpha on board. At the time of the survey the church had run the course for some three and a half years. Through Alpha it boasted one or two converts among the several dozen who had taken the course (number of returned questionnaires: 19).

Church no. 2   Pine Lane Community Church is an independent charismatic church that has been in existence for ten years. Situated in the east of London, the congregation of some 180 adults is a mixture of ethnic groups being roughly equally made up of Africans, Black Caribbeans and whites, with a small contingent of Asians. At the time of the survey the church had just introduced Alpha, the present course being only the second one offered, and a sizeable number of people had enrolled. Individuals had joined the course through contacts with friends in the church, although the pastor admitted to me that many of the guests were already numbered in the congregation. Nonetheless, there was an evident enthusiasm for the programme with the pastor envisaging Alpha as being a vital part of church life in the future and a cornerstone of its evangelizing strategy (number of returned questionnaires: 32).

Church no. 3   The City Community Church is located in a poor inner-city area of London. The person given responsibility for the Alpha course described it as a 'house church' that began in 1983, and which was 'charismatic and strongly evangelical' in orientation. Alpha was merely one evangelizing initiative but nevertheless it had become an integral part of church life (number of returned questionnaires: 13).

Church no. 4   St Giles is an Anglican church in a large Midlands town. The Alpha course leader described it as having 'evangelical-charismatic leanings'. The church has a congregation (including children) numbering 160. In terms of social composition it is largely middle-class with an age profile that is middle-aged to elderly. The course convener accounted for Alpha in very glowing terms and stated that the entire congregation was behind the programme. She admitted that there had been very few converts. Nonetheless, for those in the church Alpha offered 'a great refresher course' especially through the Holy Spirit weekend (number of returned questionnaires: 13).

Church no. 5   St Mary's is an Anglican church in the east Midlands. The vicar referred to it as being 'evangelical and lightly charismatic'. There are some 70 members and the church claims to be particularly attractive to young couples with children – consciously forging its own culture for a younger generation. The vicar said that most members of the church had been through the Alpha course. In this sense it was valuable because it had reminded people of the basics of the faith. However, he admitted that when it went truly public 'the numbers plummeted' (number of returned questionnaires: 14).

Church no. 6   St Joseph's is an Anglican church on Merseyside. Although listed in *Alpha News* as subscribing to the programme, it turned out not to have run Alpha for three years. On asking him why he thought his church was included on the official list of those subscribing to Alpha, the vicar suggested that 'HTB are good at marketing themselves. It pads out the list and looks impressive'. He explained that his church had run the course twice but that it proved largely unsuccessful in attracting guests. Thus he had decided not to continue with Alpha (number of returned questionnaires: 10).

Church no. 7   River of Life Community Church is a charismatic church in north-west England. It is part of Bryn Jones' Covenant Ministries and is comprised of four congregations with some 300 people. Questionnaires were administered at the larger 'mother' congregation. Alpha had been run at this particular church for three years, and on an annual basis. The programme had been accepted without reservation and was the major evangelizing initiative of a very evangelically-minded church. Like many churches, members of the congregation passed through the course before it went public (number of returned questionnaires: 33).

Church no. 8   In this part of the north-east of England the minister is responsible for a large Methodist congregational circuit and two churches. He admitted during an interview that there were general limits to evangelism in his time as a minister, explaining that clergy often neglect evangelism under the deluge of church meetings and bureaucracy. This failure was, he claimed, something that churches like his had to seriously address. A course such as Alpha, he maintained, should have been put together many years ago. Both of his churches had run Alpha for several years and had experienced their ups and downs with the courses. At the same time, they had found differing levels of success. One, with a slightly larger membership, was more outgoing. It had a fairly sizeable middle-age and middle-class congregation. The membership was also more evangelically-minded. The second congregation was smaller with a mainly elderly contingent but of more varied social mix. It was not really charismatic in disposition but a few members thought that Alpha had its appeal. The minister argued that since so many churches adopted Alpha, the programme 'must have something going for it'. Alpha at this second church was more 'in house' and had no notable success in drawing the non-churched into the course. The first church was able to do this largely through personal contacts (number of returned questionnaires: 18).

Church no. 9   Although an independent church situated in southern England, this congregation is associated with the Baptist Union and is mildly charismatic in orientation. It has a membership of around 100 initially of different church backgrounds. The minister himself has lead the Alpha programme. Originally he had attended an Alpha conference at HTB and became convinced of the merit of the course. The church had run courses on three occasions with about a dozen guests each time. This had tailed-off to about three. According to the minister this was probably because Alpha had reached a 'critical mass' of potential guests in the locality. The church laid claim to three or four converts over the period of running Alpha – not always at once but as part of spiritual journeying. A handful had been baptized and joined the church (number of returned questionnaires: 16).

Church no. 10 This church belongs to the Assemblies of God pentecostal denomination in the east Midlands. It is a city centre church with a Sunday attendance at services of some 200 people. Alpha is seen as an essential part of the communication of the gospel to the city and had been run on and off for six years. The congregation initially organized Alpha in the church, then in people's homes. Because of the commitment involved and a shortage of people prepared to participate, it has returned to the church under the auspices of a full-time leader as well as the perceived advantage of maximizing resources. Those involved in Alpha (leaders and guests) have varied over time from a handful of people to two dozen (number of returned questionnaires: 19).

Church no. 11 This is a small Methodist church in the north Midlands. It runs Alpha with the help of a number of other Methodist churches in the local circuit. It had undertaken the Alpha course twice. However, a new minister had come in who had unspecified objections about Alpha and discontinued it. There was no particular resistance to the unilateral decision in the churches to abandon it (number of returned questionnaires: 17).

Church no. 12 The minister of this Baptist church in Birmingham had only been in the post for one year and had instigated Alpha as a priority when she arrived. She had run it successfully at her previous church for several years. She described the congregation of her new church as 'average' at around 130 members and as evangelical but not particularly charismatic. While teachings on the Holy Spirit were to the fore, it was not especially strong on the charismata, even if a few people openly spoke in tongues. The attraction of Alpha for this minister was that it was a useful tool for evangelism. It had, she explained, a good balance between instruction (through the videos) and exploration (through discussion groups) (number of returned questionnaires: 12).

Church no. 13 This is a 200-strong Anglican congregation, described by the minister who had been in the post for two years as being of a distinctly local low church tradition and mildly evangelical. He further described it as 'traditional and sleepy' and had no reservation about taking it much more in an evangelical and charismatic direction. Alpha appeared to 'fit the bill'. The church had run three courses with some dozen guests attending each time (number of returned questionnaires: 15).

Church no. 14 This Anglican church was described by the course leader as 'a sleepy rural south Wales congregation'. Alpha had been tried twice over a period of five years under the auspices of two different ministers. The course was run in conjunction with a number of other local churches. It had not been successful in attracting guests either inside or outside the church. The present minister had no short-term plan for running the course again (number of returned questionnaires: 14).

Church no. 15 A Roman Catholic church situated in a medium-sized rural town. Typical of many Catholic churches subscribing to Alpha, it has a small active charismatic faction in the congregation that initially approached the priest for permission to run the course. After expressing some misgivings he allowed it to go ahead. Unlike other Catholic churches, however, the course was open to the public without the 'dry-run' first for the local congregation. The course was largely unsuccessful and attracted few outsiders. While not completely abandoning the programme, only two courses have ever been run with no future ones planned (number of returned questionnaires: 27).

Church no. 16 This is an Anglican church based in a large southern seaside town. The congregation had slowly declined over a number of years. The vicar, newly arrived, was keen to bring in younger people. Charismatically and evangelically minded, he believed that Alpha served this purpose. At the very least, he explained to me, it could be used to allow local people to explore the faith. While he did not expect too many converts, he maintained that in a secular society Alpha could start people off on a spiritual journey (number of returned questionnaires: 15).

Church no. 17 This is a fairly large Congregationalist church in a medium-sized town in north-east England. Alpha had been run twice, first with the congregation and then going public. The leader of the course proclaimed that the results were disappointing. Few outside of the church were interested in what Alpha had to offer, and there were no new converts. Whether the course would be run again was something that the church was seriously considering at the time of the survey. The minister and Alpha course leaders were keeping their options open and looking at other evangelizing packages (number of returned questionnaires: 73).

Church no. 18 This is a well-established and large evangelical church in a northern town. Since becoming more charismatic in orientation it had begun to attract younger people, especially those with young families. Alpha was tried, the minister admitted, because of the wish of many of those in the congregation and because it was something of a fad. However, he had been pleasantly surprised at the format, and saw the course as potentially useful as part of a wider evangelical endeavour (number of returned questionnaires: 55).

Church no. 19 This is an inner-city Anglican church located in the east Midlands. Although it had a small congregation, many members were attracted to Alpha which evolved to become one of the principal activities of the church. Several members were involved in running the course, especially the younger contingent. While the vicar was rather sceptical of Alpha's chances of success, and was not entirely happy about the theological content, he was prepared to 'give it a try' (number of returned questionnaires: 46).

Church no. 20 As an Anglican rural church on the borders of England and Wales, this congregation was rather elderly and traditionalist in outlook and was experiencing a steady decline in membership. Alpha was only introduced after a long debate in the church. Although attracting some interest locally, it had hardly proved a success and the vicar had decided not to run it for another year, if it was to be offered at all (number of returned questionnaires: 29).

Church no. 21 Much like the previous church, this Anglican rural congregation, once the centre of village life, was on the decline. While the church was once the centre of village life, the membership was now numerically small and rather elderly. Two of the more active members of the church had pushed for Alpha to be introduced and, after much debate, it was given a try (number of returned questionnaires: 21).

Church no. 22 This large Baptist church, situated in an affluent southern town, sees itself adopting Alpha as a natural part of its evangelizing endeavour. Strongly charismatic in orientation, it had run five courses with the number of guests attending peaking in the year 2000. Neither the pastor nor Alpha leaders were available for interview (number of returned questionnaires: 83).

Church no. 23 A small Methodist church in an inner-city area, the congregation is experiencing a numerical decline. While it had no particular charismatic orientation, Alpha is seen by the minister and many in the church as a promising tool for evangelism, particularly for a younger generation. However, only two courses had been run. There were no plans to offer another in the near future (number of returned questionnaires: 21).

Church no. 24 This is a large charismatic Anglican church in a suburban area in south-east England. According to the church leader, it regards the adoption of Alpha as a 'natural part of its evangelism'. The church had run four courses and intends to continue them as long as there is a demand inside and outside the congregation (number of returned questionnaires: 72).

Church no. 25 An urban Anglican church in the east Midlands, the congregation is charismatic in orientation and is keen on running Alpha courses. However, because of small demand from outside the church, it had administered only two courses between 1999 and 2000. At the time of the survey, it was unclear whether any future courses would be organized (number of returned questionnaires: 14).

Church no. 26 This is a Salvation Army citadel in south London. Initially, it was keen on running Alpha. Its congregation is rather elderly and the church leaders sought 'new blood'. A number of courses were run in the late 1990s.

Few guests attended. The citadel was closed in 2001, with members moving to another congregation (number of returned questionnaires: 19).

Church no. 27 This small Anglican church in north-east England had run Alpha only once, in the late 1990s. Although it had proved relatively successful on that occasion in attracting guests from outside of the church, no other courses were subsequently organized. Attempts to advertise a future course through displaying posters and leafleting had failed (number of returned questionnaires: 19).

Church no. 28 This is an Anglican church from a rural area on the outskirts of a fairly large town in southern England. The introduction of Alpha had caused some controversy in a High church with a traditional outlook. It had run only one course in 1999 without a great deal of success in attracting those outside of the congregation. A future course was being planned at the time of research (number of returned questionnaires: 24).

Church no. 29 At this Methodist church based in an urban neighbourhood in south-east England. Alpha had been run on two occasions in the late 1990s. The course leader stated that 'We thought that it was the sort of thing that we should be running since other churches in the area were organizing them'. However, Alpha had not attracted a great deal of attention outside of the church and no future courses were planned unless they could be organized in conjunction with other local churches (number of returned questionnaires: 33).

Church no. 30 This is a Roman Catholic church in a run-down suburban residential area in London with quite a high concentration of ethnic minorities. An active charismatic faction had organized the Alpha course. It was mostly attended by church members (number of returned questionnaires: 14).

Church no. 31 This is a small Anglican church in a market town in the west of England. Although the church is traditionalist in outlook, Alpha had been largely welcomed. While the minister believed that its chances as an instrument of evangelism were not particularly good in the locality, the course had been run on several occasions largely as social events to draw attention to the importance of the church as a centre of village life (number of returned questionnaires: 11).

Patterns of Adoption

Churches such as those mentioned above constitute the localized 'supply-side' of the Alpha programme. How precisely they came to adopt it and the reasons why are important issues in understanding the penetration of Alpha into local environments. The evidence suggests that there are various ways in which it has been adopted. For those in key positions in their churches Alpha often has a special appeal, evident in the participating churches overviewed above. Thus there is a top-down process involved in the acceptance of Alpha, although this is not to argue that it is anyway imposed.

In most cases it is the clergy, or other church leaders, who will take the initiative in establishing the course, alongside frequent consultation with church members. Much will depend on the authority structure of the church's denomination. It is also usual for leaders, according to my sample, to send a deputation to another church to find out what Alpha is all about and whether it could be seen as advantageous. Not infrequently, those who wish to introduce Alpha to their church have gone through the course themselves as 'guests', attended a conference at HTB, or invited representatives from HTB to come and speak to their church.

There is usually a trial run of Alpha involving a few church members. Then, once embraced, the course proper will commence. The means of attempting to enrol people is either through church networks or advertising, generally the former. The number of courses run, and how often, will depend on the size of the church as well as the local demand or requirements of its members. Sometimes all church members are asked to go through the Alpha course before it goes public.

Several of the churches surveyed decided for various reasons not to go public at all. I found that one Anglican church appeared to see Alpha more as a course in basic Christianity for church members than an out-and-out evangelizing initiative. Although public outreach was envisaged as the long-term aim it was never forthcoming. In another example derived from the pilot study, a Roman Catholic church had run the course for some three years, exclusively to its parishioners, and was unsure how to take it to non-church members. Posters were tentatively placed on the church noticeboard, rather than publically displayed. Indeed, course leaders felt that they did not have sufficient confidence or expertise to use it for public consumption, although inquisitive members of the public were not turned away.

The charismatic disposition of church and course leaders was often the determining factor for adopting Alpha. In enquiring about their charismatic allegiances as part of the pilot study, five of the twenty clergy or Alpha leaders that I interviewed unashamedly described themselves as 'out-and-out charismatics' or something very much like it. An Anglican curate, responsible for the course in one of these churches, was prepared to identify a strong John Wimber influence running throughout the Alpha course which, he believed, was to be welcomed. His church had previously been of a conservative evangelical tradition but had moved towards the charismatic wing with many members sympathetic to the cause. This has not been an uncommon trend in evangelical church life over nearly two decades. All of these tendencies were found to be present in the larger national survey.

Five church leaders I interviewed as part of the pilot study could claim an active charismatic element at their church, while a further three estimated that charismatics made up a large proportion of their congregation. Similar patterns began to emerge with the larger study. Another Anglican minister of an Anglo-Catholic church admitted to me that he was pressurized by the charismatic contingent in his congregation to take Alpha on board and would probably not have otherwise run it. He was by no means the only clergyman I interviewed who felt obliged to do so as a result of grass-root activity. In most cases these clergy were unhappy about its charismatic element and the possible implications for churches in terms of long-term changes and the danger of bringing divisions in the congregation between traditionalists and those who preferred all things contemporary.

While, as I discovered, one or two clergy who more willingly adopted Alpha complained that it was too charismatic, it was not infrequently the clergy who led something of an Alpha revolution precisely because of its charismatic orientation. More than one minister unashamedly explained that he wanted to take his congregation more in a charismatic direction and that involvement in Alpha enhanced this enterprise. Moreover, while not themselves charismatically inclined, a number of those interviewed were not opposed to the cause and saw it as a general step in the right direction.

One Anglican minister had no reservation in taking his traditional church much more in an evangelical and charismatic direction. He insisted that there were many church-goers in the congregation who 'knew little about the facts of Christianity, and no great grasp of the scriptures'. Alpha was a way of changing all this and taking the church forward. The course had been run on several occasions over two years. It was not advertised to the public but was deliberately in-house. He felt that church life was improving and that Alpha had gained an unequivocal positive response.

The vicar of church no. 1, who described himself as an Anglo-Catholic, explained that while he was not personally keen on the course, he was open to new ideas and to the wishes of his parishioners. Thus, in taking Alpha, he explained, he bowed to popular pressure and allowed the course to proceed. This was not without some difficulty. The congregation had become split on the decision whether or not to endorse Alpha. The vicar explain that there were 'the usual fears expressed by some that Alpha is too evangelical'.

The generally charismatic orientation was one of the most frequent explanations put forward by church leaders for adopting Alpha. Nonetheless, there were a number of others which were often cited as significant and provided a barometer of contemporary evangelical thinking. Perhaps the most commonly expressed view of leaders was that Alpha is user-friendly for several reasons. Firstly, it was commended for not being heavily theological and advanced just 'the basics'. Hence, it was non-threatening to the 'just-looking'. Church no. 3 had run Alpha for several years. According to the course leader, it fitted well into the structure of church life. The leadership had long put a great emphasis on church growth and for that reason encouraged members of the congregation to bring along family members and friends to services. Indeed, one service each Sunday was run more like a 'seeker service' – allowing a 'safe' atmosphere for those who were unchurched and wished to explore the faith. The policy of the church was to encourage people to come to this service before taking up an Alpha course. In fact, some 50 per cent of those on the current course had taken this opportunity and thus had some familiarity with the church before they arrived.

Related to the belief that Alpha is ideal for religious 'seekers' is the conviction in many churches that it creates a constructive environment for evangelism and works through social networks and continues to build on relationships. In doing so, it is frequently believed, Alpha accesses a range of individuals not usually met by other evangelizing techniques and provides people with the opportunity to respond to thought-provoking issues without being especially demanding. As it was put by a Baptist minister I interviewed:

> It only needs one evening per week so does not amount to very much commitment. It's non-intimidating, and not instructed by clergy.

Another perceived advantage was the way that Alpha broke down secular culture. In the words of one representative of an independent charismatic church:

> We think that there is a spiritual demand out there. The church is now irrelevant for many. There is the difficulty in persuading people that the church is the answer. There is a huge cultural gap. Alpha is just one vehicle of communication.

Alpha was also applauded for breaking down denomination divides. As frequently accounted to me, it allows 'the realization of the Christian community'. In doing so it has strengthened church unity at a local level, both intra- and inter-denominationally, and at the same time has ensured that the influence of charismatic Christianity continues to spread through networks of clergy and church representatives.

Finally, there was the obvious argument that Alpha wins converts. In talking to church ministers such a conviction was mentioned most often in the context of Alpha. This is perhaps not too surprising given that there is the vested interest in boasting a thriving congregation and perhaps one can forgive the preoccupation with church growth when confronted with the statistical evidence of church attendance decline.

With reference to winning converts, some interviewees, in true charismatic movement style, had interpreted Alpha as a 'genuine move of the Holy Spirit'. After all, the revival that had been witnessed in Third World countries was now on its way to the West. Alpha then, as one minister declared, 'shows what God is doing today'. Alternatively, in a less excitable vein, some perceived Alpha tapping a latent spirituality. It could allow people to explore the possibility that God exists – thus it was part of a personal quest for some.

At the very least, Alpha was believed to kick-start people on a spiritual journey or, as it was explained to me by the pastor of a Methodist church:

> The aim is to set people on a spiritual road. It is particularly applicable to the post-modern society and provides key morality where beliefs and values are that of the supermarket and a society of choice according to how we feel. Christianity offers certainty in a world of uncertainty.

Some Limitations

In the interviews with ministers and leaders of the Alpha course it was clear that there were perceived limitations, even dangers, that they were well aware of. Some of these insights add to the criticisms of the programme considered in the previous chapter, although they are perhaps best regarded as observations made by those who have readily embraced Alpha. The gravest danger, as some clergy confided, came through the likelihood of resistance to the instigation of the course in a congregation to the point of potential splits and the possibility of some members leaving the church. There might be objections to the programme when first put before church members. This is not always an easy process and it is at this point that church division may occur since members will become aware of what it entails. In one church I surveyed, seven church members joined the first time Alpha was run, although half a dozen left, complaining bitterly of its charismatic content. It was the beginning of a short period of dissent in the congregation.

The vicar at church no. 6 called an end to the course partly for theological reasons in that he disliked the charismatic element and partly because Alpha had caused divisions within his church. A small group in the congregation had been prepared to organize and teach Alpha, but the majority of church members opposed its introduction. The vicar, who had just arrived at the church at that time, found an atmosphere of some discord. He admitted to me that he had 'a feeling of déjà vu'. Exactly the same thing had happened at his previous church. In short, Alpha had met with very different responses among his new congregation.

Church no. 14 had come across the same problem. The vicar was convinced that quite a few Anglican churches had given up Alpha for the same reasons: 'It is', he asserted, 'more trouble than it's worth' since it divided the congregation. However, being personally fairly evangelically-minded, he had now adopted Emmaus, which he found to be a more balanced programme, broader in scope, and providing more of a constructive introduction to the faith. Alpha, he maintained, was unbalanced because of the charismatic element and teaching on the Holy Spirit, healing, the charismata, and so on.

One of the major problems with Alpha, as the minister of church no. 12 explained, was its cultural baggage. It was oriented towards the middle-classes and attractive to those on the fringes of the church or had church networks open. It assumed a degree of knowledge that some do not have. For a person on the street, she explained, 'the content of Alpha may come as something as a cultural shock'. This, she suggested, is why people often leave within the first few weeks. Moreover, 'many of those who do drop out early can't stand Gumbel'. There were other reasons too, although because contacts were prohibited, it was difficult to discern them (see Chapter 11). This same minister argued that different forms of evangelism may be necessary for those with no knowledge, no church background, or are not middle-class.

Summary

There may be those who might argue that thirty churches does not constitute a sufficient number to survey given the scope and spread of Alpha. However, it remains a fairly representative sample in terms of denominational background, traditions and geographical dispersion, not to mention the experiences of different churches with the course. At the same time these churches also generated a good quota of interview and questionnaire responses which I will rely upon in many of the chapters to come. These are, of course, only the experiences of churches in the UK. The opportunity remains for surveys to be conducted in other cultural settings. At the same time, the experiences of these churches are only one dimension of the impact of Alpha. The programme's implementation in prisons and among youth and students, as well as those who organize the courses at grass-root level add to the much broader picture.

Note

1   This low return rate of questionnaires compared to the pilot study is probably due to not being able, given the geographical dispersion, to work closely with the churches, in other words lack of the personal touch. The return rate did vary between churches but not significantly.

Chapter 7

The Group Dynamics of Alpha

Small-group Evangelism

One of the familiar features of modern evangelism is that it frequently takes place in an orchestrated collective setting. Over previous decades this has evolved to the large-scale event, ranging from 'tent evangelism' to crusades held in vast sports grounds or similar venues. Of course, there is nothing new in this and, arguably, the big event can be traced back to the Wesleyan and similar revivals of the eighteenth century. Throughout the nineteenth and early twentieth centuries they were a familiar part of revivalism, especially in the USA. Since the days of Billy Graham in the 1950s, the strategy of the high-profile, charismatic evangelist relaying his message to thousands of people continued to prove popular. Today, thousands of people can still be reached, perhaps more readily through the medium of terrestrial and satellite television, or what is commonly known as tele-evangelism.

There were various reasons for the utilization of the collective setting for proselytization besides the obvious endeavour to win souls. One was to bring an economy of effort in that the message of the great man of God, the evangelist, was put across to a large number of people gathered in the same place. This had the added attraction of bringing pressures to bear through group conformity. Much is typified by the call to 'go up front and receive Christ'; to be convicted of sin and be 'saved'. When one sees hundreds of hands go up and people flocking to the front of the assembled to 'give their life to Christ' one may feel compelled by both the emotive message and collective pressures to do the same. Yet, as we shall see in Chapter 11, very few converts, at least in the long term, are gained by this strategy. There is, then, nothing deterministic about the result of such an enterprise.

Alpha marks a move away from the orchestrated large-scale setting to focus on the needs of the individual, the 'customer' (this individual approach is perhaps most clearly seen today in tele-evangelism which brings a particular form of face-to-face contact). For some ten weeks the Alpha programme operates in the arena of the small, rather personalized group. While this obviously brings its own economy of effort in that time is not utilized on a one-to-one interaction of learning and discussion, as typified by the home Bible study used by Jehovah's Witnesses in their evangelizing efforts, the group has been calculated to have certain advantages in the cause of winning souls. Group conformity is one obvious dynamic, although this is not specifically mentioned by the Alpha in-house publications. Nonetheless, the

107

benefits of the group setting is recognized over other forms of evangelism. Nicky Gumbel has this to say with reference to Alpha:

> The overall purpose of the small group, along with the course as a whole, is to help bring people into a relationship with Jesus Christ ... We have found that a group of about twelve is the ideal size. I do not think that it is a coincidence that Jesus chose a group of twelve.
>
> (Gumbel 1994, p. 903)

Little is said about the significance of the small group in the Alpha literature beyond the aims of the programme (detailed below), although there are certainly implicit assumptions related to the findings of major studies conducted by sociologists and social psychologists and now utilized in so many areas of social life. We have noted in Chapter 4 that those who put the Alpha programme together see the meal and other components very much in terms of group dynamics and one of the principal means by which the guests and course leaders can gel. There is also the HTB-produced *Alpha Team Training* audio tape where Nicky Gumbel expounds the relevance of group dynamics – how people naturally relate together in the Alpha setting and how, within the context of the course, relationships should 'develop naturally'. People are encouraged to talk in company, 'be themselves', and find new friends. Hence, a principal aim of Alpha is to integrate people into a small group and ultimately, it is hoped, into church life.

Given the importance highlighted by Alpha organizers to the dynamics of small groups, this chapter seeks to understand their general significance for the programme. In doing so I will move beyond the stipulated aims of the Alpha course itself, as far as the small group is concerned, to consider some of the dynamics generated in this environment. A number of them are easily discernible, others less so. Some enhance the positive aims of the Alpha programme, others work against it in a negative way. By briefly considering these dynamics we can come to a greater understanding of the Alpha programme and appreciate to what extent they contribute towards its success or failure.

We begin our task with an acknowledgement of the growth of academic accounts of group dynamics and processes which have become a popular field of study for well over fifty years, owing largely to the initial impetus provided by Kurt Lewin (1953) and his students. The importance of this pioneering work has been amplified by a general cultural concern with group processes. People everywhere are interested in groups, perhaps because we spend so much time in them during the course of our lives. In professional circles the social psychologist is interested in groups because they epitomize social situations and behaviour. Clinical psychologists are obliged to know about groups because so many personal problems are rooted in the individual's interaction with others. Knowledge about group processes also has a practical side in that many other fields such as education and business organizations utilize important research findings in achieving their goals.

Much has been written on various aspects of group dynamics and processes and much could be referred to within the context of the Alpha initiative. There is no attempt here to trawl through the vast amount of literature that has been produced especially in recent years, or to discuss in detail the rival theories of group behaviour and dynamics. Neither is there an endeavour to apply the great wealth of theories, and experimental and empirical findings on group interaction in any considerable depth since this would take up a book in its own right. I seek, therefore, merely to outline a broad structure in order to highlight the important processes that take place in the context of Alpha groups. The discussion will be limited to the following themes: organizational characteristics; the importance of individual motivation within the group setting; tasks and roles; physical, social, and personal environments; issues related to leadership; learning processes, group morale, and group pressures.

Formal Organizational Structures

The emphasis on the organizational or structural characteristics of small groups occurs most commonly in the sociological literature and that branch of the discipline traditionally referred to as 'structuralism' (an approach now somewhat out of vogue). This is perhaps understandable in view of the greater interest of sociology in the group as the unit of analysis in contrast to the psychologist's concern for the individual member and his/her psychological disposition, and so on. Here, for the sociologist, organizational goals become the major focus since specified goals are the raison d'être of any group, large or small.

The structuralist approach towards small groups is not merely concerned with goals however. There is also a consideration of subservient structural properties of individuals that are derived from these group goals, such as statuses, roles, and norms, and communication networks between individuals. In focusing on these elements there is the tendency for structuralist approaches to see the group as if it operates rather like a small community and that all group members function for the benefit and stipulated goals of the group itself. Early commentators on group processes stressed the importance of interdependency between group members, which was assumed to be largely based on the common goals which bring individuals together in the first place and that the activities of the group are directed towards the maintenance of the group itself.

In conceptualizing important group organization elements, structuralist sociologists refer to formal structure and role structure each of which consists of two elements. Formal structure includes functions and status, whereas role structure includes responsibility and the distribution of authority. These formal structures result from the predictable patterns of interaction in the group which lead to differentiated positions. In the organized group, the structure involves a predictable pattern of action, plus a system of mutually reinforced expectations. Status and function adhere in these differentiated positions in the group structure. Thus, status is a hierarchical relationship between two or more persons and defines the degree of freedom that the occupant has in initiating and maintaining goal direction. The function of the positions specifies the nature of the contribution that the occupant is expected to make to the group enterprise (Shaw 1971, p. 276).

Norms and rules of conduct established by the members of the group maintain behavioural consistency. If each member of the group decided individually how to behave on each interaction, no one would be able to predict the behaviour of any member, and the group would cease to function. Norms, for structuralist sociologists, provide a basis for predicting the behaviour of others and thus enable the individual to anticipate the action of others and prepare an appropriate response.

While for structuralists, status, roles and so on are a predictable element of small groups, no group is in a total state of positive functioning or 'equilibrium': there is an ongoing process and evidence of micro-dynamics suggesting that group formation does not stop with the affiliation of members. Indeed, the group develops over a long time and probably never reaches a completely stable state (Shaw 1971, p. 101). Development proceeds rapidly at first, with much structuring and organization occurring in the first minutes or hours of the assembling of the group. However, the establishment of the social structure of the group, the formation of status and role relations, norms, and power relations, can take a fairly long time.

A group forms and continues its existence for some purpose; when this purpose no longer exists, the group disintegrates unless a new purpose can be established. For experts in group dynamics the purpose is generally referred to as the 'group task' or 'group goal'. The task may often be to achieve a subgroup that must be attained in order to reach the ultimate goals of the group.

How might we apply some of this structuralist theorizing to Alpha? To some degree Alpha course groups do have very distinct goals or aims and individuals are brought together for a distinct enterprise. The primary long-term aim of Alpha is to win souls in the tradition of Christian evangelism. The short-term goal is to inform and educate people and encourage them to consider the possibility of following a spiritual path: to allow discussion and exploration. To put it succinctly, it is a crash course in Christianity for beginners, the unchurched, the faithless, and even those already convinced but who wish to refresh their faith or who want to go further in their Christian commitment. These very broad aims are not always clearly spelt out on Alpha courses at the local church level. One could suggest, then, that status, norms, and roles are also rather vague. It might be argued that in the informal setting of Alpha the norms, roles and status are 'negotiated' and no two groups will display the same dynamics. Potentially this could make the group rather unstable. Nonetheless most Alpha groups, despite a fairly high drop-out rate, do last for the duration. Stability remains, I would argue, largely because of the clear structure of the programme rather than explicit goals. While the weekly repetition of meal–video–discussion can be tiring for some, it does allow a certain predictability and assurance and this quickly helps the establishment of norms and fairly structured behaviour. The Alpha group, particularly through interaction over meals and discussion, usually achieves a high level of cohesion relatively quickly, especially if there are several church members present who knew each other previously. Many of these individuals would have internalized the aims of Alpha even before the course commences.

Formally speaking, it is the discussion groups of Alpha that have the clearest aims and it is this part of the course which is most cogently spelt out by the programme's organizers. It is interesting that Nicky Gumbel in his brief overview of the importance of small Alpha groups limits his account almost entirely to the broader aim of the course – in other words, the organizational goals of HTB. Gumbel maintains that the Alpha group has six main aims, of which the first is to establish a discussion group. The importance of the discussion group is to talk about aspects of the faith and this is only achieved in manageable numbers (Gumbel 1994, pp. 90–96).

A second aim is to 'model Bible study'. Questions arising from the talk of any particular week are dealt with first then, ideally, the Bible is opened for further discussion. The objective is to bring all group members into the discussion, so that everyone feels that they are participating. A third aim is 'To learn to pray together' (there are problematic aspects of collective prayer which will be discussed below). The fourth aim is 'To develop lasting relationships within the body of Christ'. The small groups engender friendship and it is hoped that this forges a sense of brother/sisterhood should conversion occur. Fifthly, 'To learn to minister to one another', including prayer for someone or 'ministry' in the form of the laying on of hands. Finally, the aim of the group is to produce new leaders for Alpha courses. Hence, the discussion group is a training ground for would-be leaders.

In their account of group goals, Cartwright and Zander (1960) argue that all goals are probably best regarded as some composite of individual objectives. It is obvious that whatever goals can be attributed to the group must reside in the members of the group. Moreover, it seems clear that groups whose members all agree upon a single goal to the exclusion of all others, both individual and collective, are extremely rare. In the typical group, there exists at least one goal which is acceptable to a majority of the group and which can properly be identified as the group goal. Group members who accept this goal are motivated to enact activities that are expected to aid in the achievement of this goal. Even those members who are not enthusiastic about the goal may nevertheless work toward it for a variety of individual or subgroup reasons.

This is an important insight. People are involved in the Alpha course for various reasons beyond the official ones stipulated by its 'supply-side'. It is invariably the case when there are, in theory, two broad and separate constituencies in the group, namely, the local church and its 'guests' – the 'consumers'. Individuals belonging to the latter have various motivations which means that those on the programme may have different aims from those stipulated in the course material. Nonetheless, there is a general acceptance by course leaders and guests that the principal core aim is to investigate the Christian faith. They will be expected to ask questions and participate in discussion. Individuals might, however, have different interpretations of what this means and how to achieve it. The Alpha course does not stipulate clearly what is involved although on the first night a leader might typically announce to the assembled that:

> This is an opportunity to discuss the Christian faith, but at the end of the course you will have to make up your own mind.

Many guests, at the onset, are left trying to understand it all. Typical responses in interviews I conducted were:

> I thought it would be run by a load of Bible-study fanatics, but it wasn't really like that.

> I essentially wanted to find out more because I simply did not know anything.

All small group members have some identifiable position, status and role. When one identifies a person's position in the group, one is at the same time identifying one's own relative standing with respect to other dimensions such as power, influence and leadership. All these variables have an impact on group dynamics and may determine the extent to which collective and individual goals are realized.

Alpha discussion groups will rarely involve more than twelve persons, although one group I attended had as many as seventeen members (they stayed together for the entire evening – eating buffet meals, watching videos, and constituting one large discussion group). Such groups may be part of a larger contingent taking part in the programme at any given time, yet rarely is this substantial.

This small size plays against the development of a clear hierarchical structure and differentiation will be simple. The democratic ethos of Alpha is part and parcel of the mutual exploration of the Christian faith which might argue against internal divisions of the course by status. However, an implicit basic division does exist. The roles of course leaders and guests constitute a form of subordination by the latter who are 'students' and the former 'teachers' and even, in this religious setting, seem to display elements of 'master' and 'novice' – the dispensing of knowledge of the divine by those who possess it to those who do not. Imparting the word of God, the undeniable truth, and a certain indefinable esoteric quality, enhances this status. In this respect the group leader gains the prestige akin to that of the Free Church pastor or preacher as the communicator of The Word to the assembled. Those with higher status as group leaders will obviously endure the course. Those more dominant and confident individuals in the contingent of guests are also the most likely to see out the duration since their self-assertiveness may allow them status recognition within the group and undermine the status of Alpha group leaders

What of roles within the Alpha group? According to structuralist theorizing each position in the group structure has an associated role which consists of the behaviour expected of the occupant of that position. Some theorists have taken this concept of role further and have differentiated between an 'expected role', a 'perceived role' and an 'enacted role' (Thibaut and Kelley 1959). The perceived role is the set of behaviours that the occupant of the position believes s/he should enact and may or may not correspond to the expected role. The enacted role is the set of behavioural patterns an occupant actually carries out. Again the perceived role may be different from the enacted role if the occupant fails to do some things that he believes s/he should do or if s/he does some things that he believes he should not do as the occupant of that position. To the extent that there are differences among these various aspects of role, the probability of conflict and group dysfunction is increased.

On the Alpha course the 'expected role' is fairly clear regarding the leadership although far less so in respect of the guests. At first the guests have little notion of either their role or that of the leadership. There are many guide-lines in the official literature on how the leadership should conduct itself, but far less is stipulated on the role of guests and how they should act because their motivation is different and some may even be participating under sufferance. Perhaps the closest Holy Trinity, Brompton, comes to the estimated role of the guest is in these written statements:

> We do not expect people to respond to the gospel after the first week. We recognise that people need time to think, watch, listen and talk through their questions and difficulties. Each person is beginning at a different stage.
>
> (Gumbel 1994, p. 20)

> We do not expect anyone to take a blind 'leap of faith'. Rather, we hope they will take a step of faith based on reasonable grounds.
>
> (Gumbel 1994, p. 21)

To watch, to listen, to be involved in discussion with appropriate and temperate behaviour is about all that is expected of the Alpha guest, while the term 'guest' suggests an invitation to a fairly formal occasion where respect for one's hosts is fairly implicit.

The 'perceived role' during an Alpha course means that the actor's role may contradict that expected by guests and leadership, especially the former. As one Alpha guest I interviewed put it:

> I did not know quite what was expected of me. Everyone was highly
> spiritual – a bit off-putting at first. I became more comfortable the longer
> I was there.

The 'enacted role' is the behaviour actually carried out through a role. In
Alpha there is plenty of evidence of how this can have negative consequences
in terms of the course's aim. One course leader stated:

> The ethos of Alpha is supposed to be softly-softly. Those in the church are
> expected to listen, encourage and discuss. However, we had one over-
> enthusiastic guest who was already in the church. He gave his very long
> testimony in the discussion group after only two weeks. After this two
> people shut up and said nothing for the next few weeks and one left. It
> was counter-productive and we had to have words with him. Also, the
> larger the group, the less the quiet people do not want to speak out.

Given the vague goals of Alpha, little can be said about the formal structure
of the programme, however most groups have informal structures and there is
plenty of scope for these to develop within the framework of Alpha.
Subgroups may emerge even among the small contingent of those on an
Alpha course. They may be formed of two or three individuals with the same
orientation, for example, displaying an outspoken hostility to what they are
being taught. Such subgroups might develop their own goals which could
prove dysfunctional. This is how the Alpha group leader put it to me:

> In the first two or three weeks guests come with a predictable level of
> hostility. They are armed with difficult questions. This is where the
> 'searching issues' like suffering will be mooted. They will be full of
> objections. They may develop a kind of clique. However, from the fourth
> week onwards they will be more concerned with experiential matters. This
> is true of the educated and uneducated. They are interested in issues such
> as 'what does it mean to find God?' or 'what does it mean to have a
> relationship with God?'. They are interested in subjects like healing and
> whether God heals. Initially they might be more concerned with the
> historical evidence of the Bible. These questions are not a barrier to them.
> Although, they only feel a need to object, they are interested in what it
> really means to be a Christian.

Motivation

Because of some of the inherent weaknesses of the structuralist sociological
approaches in throwing light upon group dynamics and processes, other
perspectives have emphasized the significance and repercussions of interaction between group members and the meanings that are generated by that
process. In the 1950s, Lewin explained that the essential dynamic of a
collection of individuals which make up a group are the interactions and,
above all, the interdependency of individuals on one another (Lewin 1951,
pp. 146–7). This approach was later developed by other prominent students
of group behaviour. One of the key arguments for Lewin was that interaction

or communication on a fairly frequent basis is *the* essence of group behaviour. This includes verbal interaction, physical interaction, and emotional interaction.

For sociologists of this school, the structuralist approach seemed to ignore the obvious nature of small groups, that is, the human motivation behind belonging to a group. This emphasis has, in fact, interested a number of rival non-structuralist approaches to group dynamics and processes. One approach, broadly psychoanalytic in orientation, was first formulated by Schutz (1955) who referred to the most important element of group dynamics as FIRO (Fundamental Interpersonal Relations Orientation). This theory attempts to explain interpersonal behaviour in terms of orientation towards other group members. It holds that every person orientates themselves towards others in certain characteristic patterns which can be explained in terms of three interpersonal needs and motivation: inclusion, control, and affection. These concepts might plausibly provide some insights into Alpha group processes.

'Inclusion' refers to the need for togetherness, to associate with others. The requirement manifests itself through behaviours designed to attract the attention and interest of others. The person who has a strong need for inclusion will reveal this through strivings for prominence, recognition, prestige and so on. Hence it is arguable that in an Alpha course some leaders or guests might wish to participate because it gratifies certain personal needs that have little to do with the stipulated goals of the course. Guests might seek to prove their intellectual prowess in winning an argument, or simply enjoy the feeling of being appreciated for being there. Group leaders might seek to gain prominence in the church by their apparent aim of 'serving the Lord'.

'Control' refers to the decision-making process between people. The need for control derives from the need to dominate others, to have power and authority over them, behind which might be the motivation to fulfil the need to be controlled. The person with a high need to control frequently displays expressions of rebellion and refusal to be controlled; while the person with a high need to be controlled is compliant and submissive to others. Those who wish to be controlled may be submissive and readily accept all they are taught on an Alpha course. In contrast, there may be certain individuals attracted by the need not to be controlled and deliberately set out to be rebellious in a setting that offers argument and even confrontation. Typically, one rather outspoken guest I interviewed brashly admitted that:

> I wanted to show that I was not having that stuff pushed down my throat. I have always been an atheist and I knew that I could prove that lot wrong. They do not know it all like they think they do.

Finally, 'affection' refers to close personal and emotional feelings between two individuals. The person with the strong need for affection will be friendly, make overtures to others, and generally attempt to establish close emotional ties with fellow group members. At the other extreme, the low-need person will avoid close interpersonal relations. The interaction patterns of any two given individuals may be either compatible or incompatible. If they are compatible, then the interaction is likely to be easy and productive; if they are incompatible, it may be difficult and unproductive.

Affection is a broad subject in group dynamics. Alpha organizers most cogently refer to it in terms of 'building relationships'. Relationships bring cohesion, the basis of not just an introductory course into Christianity but of church life. Building relationships is one of the prime functions of Alpha and is most evident in the meal and the Holy Spirit weekend which are orchestrated to enhance a sense of belonging.

Another general concept introduced by Schutz's theory is related to compatibility. Compatible groups will be more efficient than incompatible groups since relationships and interaction are more readily formed. Compatibility is reflected in the initial formation of groups, in the degree to which they are likely to continue to function and their levels of productivity. In the case of Alpha there is, however, contrary evidence. Some guests have complained, for example, of being put into groups with people of different ages, while others have preferred this. One older woman interviewed explained that:

> My church put categories of people together by age. This did not work. I for one like to hear what young people have to say. It was the older people who dropped off first. Why? Many of them had been searching for something all their lives. Because Alpha gave no quick answer, they soon became disillusioned.

Another theory which looks at individual motivation behind the dynamics of small groups is that of so-called 'exchange theory' which was first developed by Thibaut and Kelley (1959). The underlying assumption here is that individuals will seek to maximize 'rewards' and minimize 'costs'. The concept of 'rewards' refers to that which the individual finds pleasurable, enjoyable, gratifying, or otherwise satisfying. 'Costs' refer to anything that inhibits the performance of a course of behaviour. The existence of the group is based solely upon the participation and satisfaction of the individuals which compose it. Therefore the analysis of group processes must be in terms of the adjustments that individuals make in attempting to solve the problems of interdependency by way of benefits and costs. Put another way, individuals will attempt to maximize the reward of interacting with others in the group situation, and minimize the cost. In essence, the greater the inhibition that the person must overcome in order to perform a given behaviour sequence, the more costly the enactment of that behaviour. When two persons interact, each one typically enjoys some part of the interaction, but finds other parts less enjoyable or even unpleasant.

The dynamics of cost and benefits is a useful framework to apply to Alpha and important in allowing an understanding of the 'consumer' part of the programme. In short, it might be suggested that guests are seeking certain rewards, most obviously exploring the Christian faith or, alternatively, being reconciled to the possibility that it has nothing to offer. For the converted the reward might be spiritual insights or development. Other rewards already considered above might include prominence in the group, recognition, being valued, and personal prestige. We have also noted that Alpha offers the material and psychological benefits of company and companionship, therapy, and free meals.

If Alpha guests discover there are too many costs they might become disenchanted and even leave. Nicky Gumbel appreciates that there are certain things that the guest might find difficult. These aspects of the programme, I would suggest, might be awkward because they take the guest beyond merely 'exploring Christianity' and into activities not necessarily anticipated. For instance, according to Gumbel discussion groups ideally become Bible study groups, although only if it is felt that those involved are ready for it. Sometimes people may be encouraged to read a verse in public, while it is recognized that 'reading aloud can be a harrowing experience for some and they must be able to decline easily' (Gumbel 1994, p. 94).

We have seen that a stated aim of the Alpha discussion group is 'To learn to pray together'. In later weeks a guest may be encouraged to pray aloud, for example, 'Will you ask God to give us wisdom to understand this passage?' Gumbel recognizes that this is potentially off-putting and one reason why people may leave the course early. It is not just a matter of reading aloud but reading scripture in front of other people (Gumbel 1994, p. 94). Other costs might include being expected to join in discussions to a greater extent than anticipated, having to put up with argumentative and hostile characters in the group, and perhaps the more obvious variable of boredom. We have also noticed the cost of endurance and tiredness over a long evening and over the duration of the course. These are the stipulated 'disadvantages' of Alpha.

Rewards and costs may also be determined by characteristics that individuals possess such as values, skills, and needs. These exogenous factors are related to variables external to interpersonal relationships. Individual characteristics may depend on interpersonal relationships and events that participants have experienced during their lifetime, which are then carried on into the new group context and which may have negative consequences. For example, the ex-student who disliked certain aspects of university life may see little virtue in the format of Alpha. As one guest put it to me:

> I found it quite hard at the beginning – probably because I am shy rather than because of the actual course itself. However, the discussion groups afterwards felt a bit like a college tutorial to start with.

As far as Alpha is concerned, an individual involved in a spiritual search may be put off the Alpha programme by past experiences. One interviewee stated:

> I lost my wife some eight months ago. I would like to know more about the faith, but I am going to need a fair amount of convincing.

By contrast, endogenous factors are those which are inherent in the relationship itself; the reward or cost depends not only on the actions of the individual but also on the behaviour of other people within this group. With Alpha, the actions of leaders and fellow guests can contribute to the costs and rewards of participating.

All these factors related to rewards and costs are important in deciding whether to remain in the group or leave it. In short, group membership depends on the impact of costs and rewards. Analysis of any particular group must take into account more than just the stated aims of the group. Indeed, the group itself may be the object of the need (reward) of the individual or it could simply be the means for satisfying some need that lies outside of the group (Thaibut 1950). Certainly, individuals might join Alpha because of specific social and pastoral needs. The suspicion of some course leaders was that Alpha had become a pastoral tool for helping people with emotional and psychological problems and the following interviewee seemed to support this assertion:

> Sometimes I just need someone to talk to. People are friendly at Alpha and that is why I continue to go although the course itself does not really interest me.

The Environment

Physical Environment

In considering group dynamics, most of the theoretical approaches over-viewed so far have acknowledged the importance of environmental factors. Groups do not function in isolation. They are embedded in a complex environmental setting that exerts a strong influence on almost every aspect of the group process. Because of its complexity, this setting should be regarded as a mixture of several environments rather than a single one.

The small group must exist in a physical setting. The buildings, rooms, chairs and table arrangements, communication channels and the like, vary for different groups, and such factors influence their functioning in several important ways. It is a common observation that individuals tend to appropriate space and assume proprietary rights within most situations where several people come together over a period of time. For instance, when seats are not assigned in the classroom, each student typically selects a particular desk day after day. Over a period of time this becomes the student's 'property' and 'space'. Group 'territory' is also important and is perhaps typified by street corner gangs (Whyte 1943). Territory is a way of asserting the dominance of one group or individuals over another group or individuals and is expressed in terms of culturally defined 'personal space'.

Alpha courses are held in the 'territory' of the 'supply-side'. While the setting of someone's home might appear to be 'neutral', the hospitality involved does, through exchange, bring with it a certain moral obligation to conform and even accept what is being taught. If the church building provides the territory, guests more obviously find themselves in the setting of the course organizers, including proscribed seating arrangements for the evening's activities. The local community hall, where I attended one Alpha course, was subject to the arrangement of the course leaders, although compared to the church site it could be regarded as more neutral.

Relatively little research has been devoted to spatial arrangements in collective situations and interaction, but there is good evidence that they assert significant influences on the perception of status, the patterns of participation, leadership activities, and the affective reactions of group members. It is not surprising, then, that there are consistent position preferences in group situations – the choices that people make with regard to where they position themselves in the group are consistent with what is known about the effects of spatial arrangement on interaction processes.

When people are free to choose their position in a group, their choice usually reflects the cultural importance of various locations. Persons who perceive themselves to have a relatively high status in the group frequently select positions that are in accordance with this perception, for instance, they will tend to select the chair at the head of a table (Strodbeck and Hook 1961). People also choose different arrangements around a table depending on the activity. For example, Sommer (1969) asked research subjects to choose from a number of alternative seating arrangements around a table according to four different activities. The general preferences were:

Casual conversing: face-to-face
Cooperation: side-by-side
Coaching: opposite ends of table
Competing: face-to-face or opposite ends of table.

Debate continues as to whether these preferences for seating arrangements are due to cultural expectations concerning the appropriate spatial relationships in a given setting or to the feelings that various arrangements engender in the individual under certain conditions. Sommer's subjects in his questionnaire studies explained their choices in terms of task efficiency. That is, they indicated that casual conversation is facilitated by both physical proximity and eye contact; hence they chose arrangements that would maximize these factors. It is always possible, however, that explanations of this sort are rationalizations rather than true causes of the observed phenomenon.

Evidence suggests that preferences may be stimulated by the feelings aroused by particular seating arrangements (Myers 1969). It is not difficult to see that certain arrangements may produce negative feelings, while position-status relationships should make some positions positively rewarding and others negatively rewarding. The most plausible explanation of spatial preferences, therefore, is in terms of the reinforcement associated with various spatial positions.

In communication around a table there are different patterns to be observed. Steinzor (1950) discovered that comments tend to flow with people sitting opposite each other while Hearne (1957) found that, with minimum direction from a designated leader, members of a face-to-face discussion group direct more comments to persons sitting opposite them than to those on either side. However, Hearne purported that in groups with a strong directive leader, the opposite occurred – that is, more comments were directed to neighbours than to those sitting opposite. Since these studies were conducted further research has looked at many permutations including the quality and length of conversation according to seating arrangements and spatial distance. As mentioned earlier, one of the courses I attended was composed of 17 members. This large number undermined the co-ordination and control of an already fairly weak and undirected leadership. During the discussion people would tend to converse with those sitting opposite them in the horseshoe shape arrangement, just as much as they would direct comments to the leadership.

Since the leader is usually of high status in the group, it is not remarkable that there is also a relationship between spatial arrangements and leadership. Moreover, the spatial position which a person occupies in the group will have important consequences for whoever is emerging as informal leader or dominant personality and the amount of influence that person exerts on group processes. Seating arrangements themselves may produce leaders, such as being placed at the head of the table.

Alpha develops different seating arrangements according to the evening's activities. Eating arrangements may vary but generally some six to eight guests usually sit around an oblong table. However, I have noticed no stringent ordering within these contexts beyond the tendency for church leaders and helpers to sit with guests, perhaps with a 3:1 ratio of guests and leaders. Some of the guests however may be in the church themselves. True guests are rarely left to eat and talk outside the company of those in the church, or seldom left alone to converse amongst themselves. This may help to restrict contrary or hostile attitudes towards the faith, particularly the issue for discussion on any particular evening, and hinders the possible development of subgroups.

'Worship time' precedes the main event of the video presentation and comes after a brief talk by a church leader who is also likely to give out one or two notices. It is he (sometimes she) who structures the events of the evening and is the most articulate communicator within the Alpha group. It is probably this leader who will determine seating arrangements. In several groups I attended chairs were arranged in rows or in a semi-circle. Church leaders and helpers would sit next to guests with open Bibles, following the scriptures indicated in the video. The video presentation proceeds rather like an informal lecture.

television

GXGXGXGXGXGXGXGXGXG   G = guest

GXGXGXGXGXGXGXGXGX   X = church member

The group discussion follows. Alpha literature suggests that seating is arranged for comfort and where everyone can see everyone else, hence a circle of a dozen or so chairs is usually preferred (Gumbel 1994, p. 91).

(circle)

Not infrequently some groups stay in the same seating arrangement for the discussion group as for the video presentation. Here a different set of dynamics may be observable. The larger the group the greater the competition to be heard, with the more confident individuals tending to monopolize the discussion. Group leaders are thus obliged to ask the less confident to contribute.

television

(horseshoe shape)

Personal Environment

Further environments, other than the physical, are less obvious but nevertheless significant in respect to group processes. The personal characteristics that members individually bring to the group can be considered as one aspect of the environmental setting, since they may be an important determinant of the group's operational characteristics and exert a powerful influence upon its dynamics. Once the members have assembled and begun interaction, a whole set of interpersonal relationships become established. This 'personal environment' exerts a strong influence on the group.

A person's manner of behaving, their typical reaction to others, and their skills and abilities determine, to a major extent, the reaction of others to that person as a group member. In other words, the personal characteristics of each group member serve as stimuli for all other members, and those of other members serve as stimuli for each individual.

Individual characteristics influence group processes in two broad ways. Firstly, the characteristics of each member determine to some extent what their own behaviour in the group will be and how others will react to them. For example, a person who has a special knowledge of the task may be expected to use this knowledge to help the group achieve its goals and to enact behaviours designed to give control over others.

A second way in which individual characteristics influence group behaviour is a consequence of the particular combination of those characteristics. It is not a question of whether the individual has specialized knowledge of the task, but whether it is more or less knowledge than others in the group possess. In my experience, Alpha course leaders will single out members of the group known to be well-educated. Taking them aside after a meeting they might recommend reading that they believed was 'too deep' for others in the group. After a talk about creation, where I had made one or two considered comments, I was approached by the course leader and recommended to read C.S. Lewis's *Mere Christianity*.

Other variables to consider in terms of person attributes include biographical attributes, personal abilities, personality and social sensitivity.

Personal abilities result from certain background characteristics including factors such as age and gender. Age can determine the kinds of friendships and relationships that develop. Observational studies have shown that the number of social contacts and amount of social activities increase with age, which is assumed to be a consequence of increased opportunity as well as the enhanced development of communication skills. The older person often becomes more sensitive to others, more popular, and more highly esteemed by associates than younger persons. In addition, there are two other considerations. Firstly, levels of conformity are believed to increase with age, although the evidence is mixed. Secondly, with reference to leadership, assumptions are made about older people's life experiences.

The gender of the individual group member is another obvious determinant of behaviour in groups. Men and women behave differently in groups and such behaviour is usually assumed to be due to role differences imposed upon them by the culture in which they live. Numerous studies reveal that males are more aggressive and self-assertive. They are also likely to display more roughness of manner, language, and sentiments than women. Evidence suggests that males in groups tend to be more 'quarrelsome' (Ort 1950). In contrast, women are more conforming and less aggressive in group situations (Tuddenham et al. 1958).

Age and gender as behavioural attributes are frequently observable in the dynamics of Alpha groups. The confidence and sociability of certain age groups, especially middle-aged people is evident. Frequently, the young and the elderly contribute far less to discussions. Men are also generally more self-assertive. As one interviewee put it:

> I did not say a word, although I had all the questions to ask. I left it all up to my husband. I was too embarrassed to say anything. And I was the only girl in the group, that was one of the reasons why I did not enjoy it very much.

Personal attributes also include levels of intelligence and education, and occupational status. The latter refers to the evaluation of an individual's social position which translates into the rank accorded it by group members – the prestige of the position. Studies have shown that the high-status person selects a culturally valued spatial position in the group and has greater influence on the group than lower status members (Cartwright and Zander 1960). However, evidence is mixed as to whether high status implies a greater level of conformity to the group and whether the greater the level of intelligence and education the lower the level of conformity to the group. Status differences exert a powerful influence upon the pattern and content of communications in the group. In general, more communications are directed towards the high-status group member, and the content of such messages tends to be more positive than those directed downwards in the status hierarchy (Schutz 1955).

Within the Alpha discussion group intelligence and education can be important. Interview or questionnaire responses included these statements:

> Then there were these people who had scientific knowledge and argued scientifically. Most of it was over my head, so that was another reason why I kept quiet.

Bryan, a professional actor, stated:

> The discussion groups are interesting. They put people together of a different social mix. This can have interesting results. How shall I put it? I don't want to sound condescending here. I was more educated that some of the people in the group. It was a small group with only six people. One or two uneducated people had to make an effort to understand what was going on. I would make astute comments and ask deep questions. No one

else did and this made me a little unpopular. A lot of the questions I asked were beyond them. For example. I said 'don't you think that the Bible is a bit uninspiring at times?'. Let's face it some of it is boring. They didn't know what to say and the group leader would steer away from the topic. Then one lady kept on about 'her miracle'. Clearly, it was not a miracle but you couldn't tell her so. You couldn't tell her otherwise.

Another interviewee stated:

Then there was this educated disruptive person. He kept saying things like 'That's the biggest load of crap that I have ever heard'. However, he did have the effect of even getting the silent ones to speak. He had tried every religion and was desperate for some truth. Such people tend to railroad the argument. This put others off.

The disruptive individual is a major concern for some Alpha leaders. One minister explained to me:

Cementing relationships are a primary function of the discussion groups but they can be off-putting to some people. The small groups make Alpha tick and people stay the course. Undoubtedly, some people will want to dominate proceedings, while others will say nothing. This is where a good leader is necessary.

'Personality' refers to a distinct behavioural attribute. The problem is that personality is exceedingly complex and is rarely perceived as a meaningful concept in group situations. What, for example, does it mean to be 'a strong personality'? Certain core characteristics have been identified, including interpersonal orientation in response to others in interactionist situations. For example, some people display liking and warmth in interactionist contexts, and others the opposite. Another factor could be the significance of the authoritarian personality. There is a tendency for Alpha group leaders, usually men, to be selected according to their age and they are perceived by church authorities as more spiritually mature. There can also be strong characters among the guests. This can have a negative affect. As one guest put it:

Having a strong influential person in a group who is an atheist and is still not convinced at the end of the course, can deter others from asking questions.

'Social sensitivity' refers to the degree to which the individual perceives and responds to the needs, emotions and preferences of others. This can have positive or negative effects on the group, including so-called 'ascendant tendencies' – the degree to which individuals wish to be prominent in a group situation; the extent to which they assert themselves and how much they wish to dominate others. The attribute of 'dependability' is demonstrated by the individual's belief in the personal integrity and ability of others in the group. A person who is self-reliant and responsible for his actions probably will be viewed as a desirable member and will contribute to the effectiveness of the group. Quite the opposite might be the case if the member is a more demure personality.

One interviewee, Jackie, admitted that in the discussion groups some people (she noted mostly women) were reluctant to speak out:

> We knew that they did not agree with such and such a point. We would have to say 'speak up'. This tended to mean that people agreed with practically everything that was said.

Finally, 'emotional stability' is an important component of personality and refers to a class of characteristics that are related to the emotional or mental well-being of the individual. It is reflected positively by such characteristics as adjustment and emotional control, and negatively by defensiveness, depressive tendencies, and neuroticism. It is difficult to apply this in any systematic way to Alpha beyond sporadic observations and anecdotal evidence, as some people may be reluctant to talk about their past life, personal experiences, or close relationships.

Social Environment

The social composition of the group can be important in terms of group cohesiveness and the performance of the group in achieving its goals. It can have considerable significance with reference to resistance to leaving the group, morale, motivation, and coordination of efforts by group members.

Numerous studies have discovered that members of highly cohesive groups are more energetic in group activities; they are less likely to be absent from meetings, and they are happy when the group succeeds in its goals and in maintaining itself. Personal attraction, level of organization, and acceptance of group norms are important variables here. Members of high-cohesive groups communicate with each other, so it is suggested, to a greater extent than members of low-cohesive groups (Lott and Lott 1961).

Most studies seem to show that members of groups that are compatible with respect to needs and personality characteristics are able to function more smoothly and achieve goals. Conversely, incompatible groups experience anxiety and general dissatisfaction with the group which, of course, impacts its functioning. Members conform more in mixed-sex groups than in same-sex groups (Reitan and Shaw 1964). Groups whose members are heterogeneous with respect to personality profiles perform more effectively than those whose members are homogeneous (Hoffman 1959). As we have seen with Alpha, there are differences in levels of satisfaction with same characteristic groups.

Researchers have also found other significant factors related to social considerations. Firstly, higher-cohesive groups exert greater influence over their members than low-cohesive groups (Wyer 1966). Secondly, members of high-cohesive groups are generally better satisfied (Exline 1957). Thirdly, compatible groups are more effective in achieving group goals (Shaw 1959), and more likely to display higher levels of satisfaction (Fry 1965).

The amount of involvement that group members might be prepared to undertake can be polarized. With reference to groups with a high level of discussion, there is at one end of the spectrum what Hinchelwood (1987) calls the 'monologuist'. In the more open meeting, an individual can be quite dramatic and take little notice of other people and what they have to say. These dominant personalities, who seek the attention of the group, can be disruptive. Other members will often feel embarrassed and find it difficult or wish not to respond. They will tend to disassociate themselves from the group. We have already noted the possible disruption such individuals cause within Alpha groups.

Alternatively there is what Hinchelwood calls 'the silent member'. As the term suggests this one has nothing or little to say. The member appears to listen endlessly, although it is not listening in the ordinary sense. Just like the monologuist who becomes identified with the meeting itself, the silent member is protecting a similar feeling of omnipotent mastery. Identification with the group may only come when a subject touches them personally. In the words of Hinchelwood, 'When something happens in the meeting he is there only if "it's me that is happening"' (1987, p. 85). Many Alpha groups have their 'silent members'. They are not just those who are reluctant to 'speak up' but those, usually within the faith, who remain silent as a result of confidence or even a certain smugness with their belief system.

There are a number of variables associated with conformity and deviance. A higher-status member may deviate from group norms without being sanctioned if his deviancy contributes to goal attainment (Menzies 1979). Conformity in the group increases with the increasing size of the majority up to some maximum size and remains constant thereafter (Gerard et al. 1968). Deviation from group norms usually elicits sanctioning behaviour by other group members. Continued or habitual deviation may lead to rejection from the group (Homans 1975). The high-power group member is frequently the target of more deferential, approval-seeking behaviour than lower group members and exerts more influence upon the group (Lippitt et al. 1952).

This kind of approach to the wider social environment supplements or contradicts the naive approach of the early structuralist sociological work on group structures. It is a reminder that informal power relations or affective relations do exist in small groups and they might have dysfunctional aspects. Indeed, it is possible that groups function to the benefit of powerful individuals, where social status is more important than group status and where 'cliques' could develop to the detriment of the group. It is difficult, however, to apply all these observations of power and levels of conformity to Alpha and clearly there needs to be more research into these areas. Some tentative observations can be made.

In discussions after the Alpha video presentation people usually behave with a certain amount of decorum. Sometimes, since most present are already converted to the faith, everybody agrees about everything with an embarrassing uniformity – there is no dissension in the ranks. Occasionally, there are long periods of silence with just the occasional nodding in agreement. But there can be more awkward episodes with guests being extremely argumentative and even aggressive:

Example of discussion
Course leader: 'Well, who wishes to begin tonight's discussion?'
Guest no. 1: 'Not me, it is always me.'
Course leader: 'Perhaps somebody else?'
Guest no. 2: 'Don't look at me.'
Guest no. 1: 'Nobody else has much to say and when they do it's not very open-minded, they believe this stuff and will never change their minds.'
Course leader: 'Then this is someone else's opportunity.'
Guest no. 1: 'What's the point? You're only going to come up with what's written down on your piece of paper and try to convince us that you are right. Then practically everybody else will nod in agreement.'

Leadership

The leadership role is one of the most, if not *the* most important role associated with positions in the group structure. There are five definitions of group leadership to be found in most of the relevant literature (Fiedler 1967):

1   A leader may be defined as a person who is the focus of group behaviour, the centre of attention of the group. This may mean that an individual might come to the fore who is not the officially designated leader.
2   Leadership is defined in terms of group goals. Thus, the leader is the person who is able to lead the group towards its goals.
3   The leader is the person so named by members of the group.
4   The leader will have demonstrable influence of a strong personality within the group, perhaps changing the dynamics of the group.
5   Leadership is defined in terms of leadership behaviour. Certain types of behaviour are indicative of leadership, for example, the person who can exert positive influence over group members.

Although the correlations between individual traits and leadership measures are not conclusive, there is nevertheless enough consistency to permit some generalizations. The leadership of the group, to a greater extent than other members, exemplifies traits related to ability, sociability and motivation. Asch (1952) observes that the average group leader exceeds the average group member in such abilities as intelligence, scholarship, knowledge how to get things done, insights into situations, verbal facility, and adaptability. The leader also generally exceeds the group member in regard to sociability factors such as dependability in exercising responsibilities, activity and social participation, cooperativeness, and popularity. Motivational characteristics are indicated by the findings that leaders exceed other group members with respect to initiative and persistence. This may be so with Alpha groups and some may be dogmatic with a doctrinaire opinion on just about every subject.

Leadership is also bound up with issues of power within the group. The power possessed by an individual not only affects the reactions of others in the group to that individual, but also the powerful person's own behaviour. Compared with other members, the powerful member is more highly attractive to the group, perceives that he has greater influence upon it, and is better satisfied with that position. The behaviour of the powerful group member and the reactions of others to it inevitably influence the functioning of the group. Power can be said to rest on various criteria, here considered with reference to Alpha, suggesting that the basis of leadership is quite weak beyond dispensing religious 'truths' and possible personal charisma largely because of the voluntary basis of the guests' subscription:

Criteria of Power	Significance in Alpha
1 *Attraction power* – based on identification or a liking relationship, in short, 'charisma'.	Variable. Charisma partly based on 'religious criteria' – a spiritual knowledge.
2 *Reward power* – the ability to mediate rewards for others.	Not specific, but may include platitudes, for example congratulating guest for asking innovating questions: 'I had not thought of that'.
3 *Coercive power* – based on the ability to mediate sanctions.	Not specific.
4 *Legitimate power* – based on the belief that one person has the right to prescribe behaviour of another.	Largely non-existent.
5 *Expert power* – based on the less powerful person's belief that the powerful person has greater resources in a given area.	'Religious' knowledge of revealed 'truths'.

Styles of leadership vary in the group context. Lewin et al. (1967) believe that such styles can largely be divided into 'autocratic', 'democratic', and 'laissez faire'. The first style determines all policy in the group and dictates techniques and actions. The leader's attitude is impersonal and aloof but not openly hostile. By contrast, the 'democratic' leader allows the group to determine matters of policy, the general steps to the goal are allowed to be sketched and alternative procedures suggested when appropriate. Finally, the 'laissez faire' leader is essentially a non-participant in group activities. The group is given complete freedom to make its own decisions.

Alpha has a generally 'democratic' approach to leadership. Leaders are encouraged to be democratic and ask the group questions such as 'What do you feel?' and 'What do you think?' (Gumbel 1994, p. 91). The Alpha organizers put a great deal of stress on the leadership of the group. Nonetheless, in the case of the discussion group, one problem is the over-dominant leader who does all the talking instead of giving those on the course the freedom to speak and put forward their point of view (Gumbel 1994, p. 91).

Group leaders are expounding the 'truth' – the 'truth' of the gospel message is the baseline, the implicit assumption, but it is not to be put forward dogmatically. Gumbel states:

> Even if someone says something that is not correct, a good leader will respond with a phase like 'How interesting', or 'I have never heard that before', or 'It might mean that ...', and will then bring in the rest of the group to try to reach the right conclusion. (p. 91)

This attitude does not mean that the discussion group is entirely unstructured. Interestingly, it is the leader of the group who is encouraged by Gumbel to ask the group questions and to have even 'work(ed) out the questions in advance' (Gumbel 1994, p. 93). The importance of strong leadership is also recognized by Gumbel who suggests that one person doing all the talking among the guests is off-putting to others and is a sign of bad leadership (p. 1).

The importance of a strong leader is acnowledged by course convenors in local churches. Janet, a course helper, had this to say:

> The discussion groups were useful. People are very anecdotal. There needs to be a strong leader. People are likely to go off the point or change the subject and want to talk about their own problems.

Some guests played tribute to strong leadership or were aware of the dangers:

> The leaders were very 'ordinary' and unshockable. So I could ask 'all the big ones'. I suppose that this would not necessarily be the case in all churches.

> Alpha could be seen as fundamentalist or dogmatic if led by some people – the danger of promoting one sort of Christianity.

> One problem with the course was that there was no direct contact with the leader, the guy (Gumbel) who lectured on the video.

Finding people with the right leadership quality was sometimes a problem for churches and it was the minister who had to take responsibility among a myriad of other commitments.

Morale

Stogdill (1959) defines group 'morale' as the degree of freedom from restraint in working towards the goal of the group: the capacity of a group to maintain a belief in itself according to some common belief. For Stogdill, morale is lowest in an unstructured group and highest in a structured group in which members know the limits to acceptable behaviour. In addition, morale is more stable when there is an objective, measuring output such as goods from a factory or an annual profit. When the end result is something as intangible as a change in an individual's personality, the group's beliefs will clearly be susceptible to volatile changes. But what are the influences which impact this system of beliefs?

Menzies (1979) argues quite simply that, unless the members of a group know what it is they are supposed to be doing, there is little chance of their doing it effectively and getting adequate satisfaction in doing so. Lack of definition is likely to lead to personal confusion for the members of the group and to inter-personal and inter-group conflict. Members may begin to lose sight of their roles and look for others which they feel enhance their own sense of adequacy and value. In the words of Hinchelwood:

> There is merely a gap, an emptiness at the core of things. In such a gap it
> is a matter of everyone for himself.
>
> (Hinchelwood 1987, p. 54)

The individual has various methods for surviving these conditions. There may be an attempt to create subgroups. Secondly, people may disengage and, if not leaving altogether, they blunt their own distress with distance.

For Hinchelwood, morale has two basic ingredients: firstly, a belief in the integrity of the group. This is harmed if important members leave. The group may also be divided by internal divisions which are very fragmenting. Subgroups may work against each other. Secondly, the effectiveness of the group, closely related to integrity, denotes beliefs about the group's ability to do what it sets out to do. The group has to constantly clarify the scale of the task to be obtained so that people do not become demoralized. For groups suffering low morale, it is difficult to find a way out of a demoralization spiral (Hinchelwood 1987, pp. 130–31).

It is vital that Alpha groups sustain morale. The vague goals of the programme, plus the often diverse membership in terms of social and church background, can weaken morale. Leaders must constantly reaffirm aims and emphasize positive aspects of the programme, for example, publish 'forthcoming attractions' such as the weekend away. When people leave the group, especially if they are dominant personalities, there is the need to repair the damage and reaffirm morale.

Learning

Implicit in the studies on group judgement and group problem solving is the conviction that interaction contributes something to the group product that is more than the mere combination of individual products. Group members somehow exert an influence on their fellow members which leads to behaviour that would not occur when members are alone. This kind of dynamic is obviously most important in an educational setting and influences the learning environment. Individuals learn faster in groups than on their own, if suitably motivated and where morale is high (Mann 1959).

For Alpha learning must be through group discussion, not argument. Gumbel states:

> On the whole, people will not be convinced if they get involved in an argument, especially if it is in front of others in the group. They tend to dig in their heels, which makes it harder for them to give up their position later if they wish to do so. It is easier to win an argument than lose a person.
>
> (Gumbel 1994, p. 75)

Group Pressure

Finally, perhaps the most obvious element of group dynamics is group pressure. The term 'intragroup relationships' refers to the relations among the members of the group. This dynamic includes variables such as the kind of pressure exerted, the composition of the group, how successful the group has been in achieving past goals, the degree to which the person identifies with the group and so on. All these variables have been shown to be related to the level of conformity (Kelley 1952). It is clear that conformity to group norms is influenced by a variety of factors, most of all that conformity is generally rewarded by the group, deviancy is punished, or at least not rewarded.

Group pressure is also bound up with issues of power. The various conceptions of social power have in common the view that power involves at minimum the ability of one person to control or influence another person in some way (Lewin 1951). The reactions of group members to another member are determined in part by the power attributed to that person. Asch (1952) has shown that individuals are dominated more by group pressures than their own judgements. He demonstrated that a person on his own could not stand up against the group opinion perhaps when it contradicted his own senses, even when the judgement was something as objective as the length of a line. Festinger (1950) emphasized that the influence of the group is much greater still when the matter is one of belief rather than objective judgements. Evidence suggests that the mere presence of others increases the motivation level of individuals. Certain dominant individuals can increase this group pressure (Torrance 1954). Conforming to such pressures are not deterministic, and we have noted that few exposed to pressure to conform will actually do so (Zajonc and Sales 1966).

Alpha is supposed to provide an opportunity to 'explore', to ask questions in a non-pressurized environment. Invariably it will be open, depending on the composition of the groups, to many of the dynamics explored above. While there may be few overt pressures to conform, invariably group consensus, high status individuals, and the location of the meeting all impact in enhancing the power of the message. Alternatively, high status and charismatic non-churched guests can impact in a contrary way on the message that Alpha leaders are trying to put across.

Summary

What might we conclude of the group dynamics of Alpha? Clearly, traits are discernible in group relations, although groups do vary considerably. This is despite the course being a standardized product with a recognized way of doing things and an appreciation of the dynamics evident in the group situation. Firstly, the small group is acknowleged by those who put the programme together as important and at the heart of the Alpha programme. However, there are predictable and unpredictable outcomes, partly because of the application of Alpha in very different local environments. Consequential dynamics might be set in place that were unintended and not even anticipated by course leaders. Secondly, throughout the duration of the course, roles, rules, status and authority structures are not fixed but open to negotiation. Thirdly, it is not only such group structures that are negotiated but a system of 'rewards' and 'costs' which are constantly being transformed over a lengthy period of time. Fourthly, there is the significance of informal process influenced by people's previous experiences of small groups, expectations, and wider social roles. Fifthly, there is the importance of various aspects of leadership. These are not all the significant variables and more could have been considered in this respect. Nonetheless, many of those overviewed add to an appreciation of what Alpha is all about 'on the ground'.

Chapter 8

Searching Issues

Questions and Responses

Enquiring 'seekers' or Alpha 'guests' invariably have questions concerning the Christian faith. This is what the course expects and its organization is partly based around the assumption that the 'just looking' for the answers to life will have profound issues to raise. Those already in the faith also have their questions, even doubts. Some would seem to be enduring questions, others are more contemporary and relate to issues prompted by social and cultural changes.

Alpha selects certain topics to be discussed which, in turn, generate numerous questions. Some are bound to be asked by guests, others are suggested by Alpha leaders as a matter of course. Raising questions and talking through issues, then, is a vital part of 'exploring Christianity'. While the discussion group is the most obvious and important forum for issues to be explored and contested, opportunities for questions present themselves more informally throughout each Alpha evening.

HTB is well prepared to answer a range of questions and has clearly conducted its homework regarding those issues likely to come up during an Alpha course and puts them under the rubric of the 'most frequently raised objections' about Christianity. To help course leaders deal with these principal issues the brief publication *Searching Issues Manual* looks at the seven objections most frequently advanced. They seem to be presented in order in the manual according to their significance for guests and the frequency with which they are raised:

1 Why does God allow suffering?
2 What about other religions?
3 Is there anything wrong with sex before marriage?
4 How does the New Age movement relate to Christianity?
5 What is the Christian attitude to homosexuality?
6 Is there a conflict between science and Christianity?
7 Is the Trinity unbiblical, unbelievable and irrelevant?

The manual, in a very simple style, outlines the basic recommended responses to these questions, along with the relevant biblical text. They are easy to follow by the course organizers and guests. While not used on the Alpha course itself, the manual constitutes important supplementary material.

Nicky Gumbel's significant book *Searching Issues* goes into far greater depth and contains chapters on each of the above topics. Published in 1994, it was considered core reading from a very early stage. Some of these questions are also considered in Gumbel's book *Challenging Lifestyle* under such headings as 'How to Avoid Sexual Sin', or 'How to Discern False Prophets'. *Searching Issues*, however, is more concerned with the way that these topics are approached in terms of objections to the Christian faith in the context of the Alpha programme.

This chapter will discuss firstly how these questions are dealt with by *Searching Issues* along with some of the more common questions raised by guests. It is an important theme. Alpha is about exploration. What issues are brought up by seekers tells us something about the consumers' demands – the life concerns and requirements of potential converts – as well as the need for answers to enduring 'ultimate questions'. Secondly, the way in which they are dealt with in the Alpha literature throws light on the dogma (perhaps of a fundamentalist nature) extolled by its founders and relatedly, if they are advanced in a standard way, whether this leads to a further McDonaldization of the programme on a global scale.

The first topic raised by *Searching Issues* is suffering. The volume recognizes that issues concerned with suffering are 'overwhelmingly the most common objections to the Christian faith' (Gumbel 2000, p. 7). A second major issue, sex before marriage, is usually raised later in the course (Gumbel 2000, p. 8). The other issues are likely to be brought up less regularly, but are occasionally raised. This includes a recognition of the growth of the New Age and, interestingly, Gumbel acknowledges that people require a specific Christian view and response to it – indicating perhaps that a majority of guests are already church-goers. As far as homosexuality is concerned, the experience of Alpha is that some guests are gay or have friends who are and that in the church and wider society it is a topic which will not easily go away.

Another perennial theme is based on the question whether science and Christianity are in conflict. While this would seem to be an issue of faith – one that is enhanced in the secular and pluralist society – I will argue below that it is not so contentious as it once was. Among the more straightforward theological issues is that of the Trinity which, according to Gumbel, is 'often an issue for those who have been involved in the cults, as well as those with perhaps a more philosophical disposition' (Gumbel 2000, p. 8). This is the last topic raised in *Searching Issues*. Gumbel realizes that these major theological questions can only be dealt with briefly in the context of Alpha. I must state the same of my overview here since we are concerned with the attitude of Alpha itself towards a limited number of subjects and the views of guests, rather than stringently coming to grips with a range of important and often very deep and controversial issues.

At the back of the volume *Searching Issues* is a number of 'devised' questions that can be 'used by individuals or by small groups meeting together'. For example, under the broad topic of 'Why does God allow suffering?' the following more specific questions might be offered:

- What issues are raised for you by suffering?
- Nicky suggests that most suffering is caused by human sin of one sort or another. How are we to account for the remainder? (Gumbel 2000, p. 14)
- What experience have you had of God using suffering for your good?

While Alpha guests will undoubtedly have their own questions regarding issues like suffering, the course, through standardized and widely-read literature such as *Searching Issues*, not only provides the legitimate answers but presents the relevant questions.

My findings in the pilot study of what interests guests and the kinds of issues which they raise proved not that different from those found by HTB. Disparities may result from the precise question which I asked on the questionnaire: 'Which one aspect of Christianity would you most like an Alpha course to discuss?' – slightly different from that of the pilot study and different from HTB's 'objections' approach.

Some of the questions are perennial in that they have concerned believers and non-believers for centuries, including the issues of other religions, the Trinity, and suffering. Since the Enlightenment, Christianity has had to deal with issues of science and faith, typified by the theory of evolution and where the evidence would seem to contradict matters of faith. Those questions

Table 8.1 Primary objections to the Christian faith

Subject	%	No. of Respondents
Suffering	43.7	366
Other religions	15.5	130
Trinity	6.9	58
Science and religion	6.8	57
Gays	6.1	51
Sex before marriage	4.5	38
Evolution	3.7	31
Other theological issues	3.6	30
New Age movement	2.1	18
Contradiction between Old and New Testaments	1.8	15
Sin	1.7	14
Miscellaneous	3.3	28
Total	100	836

pertinent to more contemporary developments include the emergence of the permissive society, the widening acceptance of sex before marriage and the matter of gay sex.

Suffering

Top of the list of 'objections' and issues to be discussed is the problem of suffering, a perennial subject troubling those inside and outside the faith and probably the greatest stumbling block for many people over the centuries. There have of course been impressive apologetic works including C.S. Lewis's *The Problem of Pain*. Despite such literature 'the problem of pain' remains. Suffering seems to be irreconcilable with the character of a loving God. This was clear in some of the responses of interviewees:

> I wanted to know about suffering. People on the course gave me answers like God wanted to give us a choice so we can do things wrong. My niece was killed in an accident, so this has helped me cope with things.
>
> Even as a Christian I have not all the satisfactory answers as to why there is so much suffering in the world. So, I would like to know more.
>
> I found it interesting and enjoyable. The mix of Christian teaching and group discussion helped me to deal with a fundamental issue, suffering, which had previously been a major reason for not believing in Jesus.
>
> Suffering is the big issue for me. That's why I can't believe. There is simply too much suffering in the world.
>
> The issue of suffering is the most frequently raised objection to the Christian faith.
>
> (Gumbel 2000, p. 5)

The randomness and severity of suffering, Gumbel argues, seems particularly unfair. Natural disasters, war, environmental catastrophes, and accidents appear to arbitrarily take the lives of hundreds and thousands. Sickness, bereavement, handicaps, broken and unhappy relationships, poverty, persecution, injustices of many sorts, loneliness and depression – the causes of human misery and pain are endless. Gumbel's response as to why there is so much suffering is scarcely innovating and constitutes rehashed commentaries of biblical interpretation and philosophy resting on the following arguments:

- Human freedom – freedom means breaking God's laws and breaking God's laws means suffering. God loves the human race so he gave us the freedom of choice. Choosing sin means pain and suffering. This argument is rather clumsily put across in *Searching Issues* and if its logic is followed then pain and suffering results because God loves us.

God is good, hence suffering is good. There is a kind of rather curious logic here.

- God works through suffering – God uses suffering for our own good and he may deal with it in such a way as to bring us to Christ and Christian maturity. He also uses suffering to bring about his purposes which are in themselves good by definition.
- God more than compensates for our suffering – God blesses us, even in the midst of suffering. Here, the story of Job has its erstwhile function. Then there is the promise of heaven in the hereafter: 'God has indeed all eternity to make it up to us'.
- God is involved in our suffering – God is not an impassive observer. In Christ he was subject to all human torments and sufferings.

In my experience, largely as a result of sitting through Alpha courses, suffering remains the area most unsatisfactorily addressed by the literature and course leaders. In the debates following several video presentations the issue of suffering was regularly introduced. The tactic of course leaders was largely to explain it away as a result of a fallen world, man's inhumanity to man, and the indiscernible purpose of God. Another strategy was to play down its significance by playing up the wonders of creation or the promise of Christian salvation. These were not always satisfactory answers for some guests. One individual, at the end of a rather heated evening discussion that I witnessed, concluded that:

> It's all suffering. I read history and that's based on suffering. I listen to the news and that's more suffering. Members of my family are suffering. Then you tell me about the crucifixion – more suffering.

Other Religions and the New Age

One of the principal strategies taken by Gumbel in dealing with the major objections to Christianity is to play down their extent and significance, as we shall see, for example, in the way that he deals with homosexuality. As far as other religions are concerned it is worth quoting Gumbel at length:

> The impression is often given that Christianity is dying out in the United Kingdom. It is said that we live in a pluralist society in which other religions are gradually taking over. Actually, this impression of a multi-faith Britain is misleading. Only 2.5 per cent of the population are adherents of other faiths. Some 10 per cent go to Christian Churches.
> (Gumbel 2000, p. 25).

Moreover, Gumbel points out, Christianity is 'by far' the largest religion in the world.

In dealing with 'other religions' Alpha is fairly uncompromising. Jesus is the only way to God. His is the only name that can save. Here the special qualities of Christ and Christianity are stressed. Jesus as God, messiah, as the subject of worship are deemed to be qualities not found in other religions. Moreover, the resurrection lies at the heart of the Christian faith and it is only possible to have a relationship with Jesus. In the words of Gumbel: 'We cannot know Buddha or Muhammad' (Gumbel 2000, p. 28).

There are some concessions, however, towards other religions, although they tend to display a rather condescending and patronizing tone. Gumbel does not regard 'other religions' as necessarily misguided or demonic, but they are nonetheless clearly mistaken. Old evangelical arguments are trotted out at this point – especially the one which insists that 'parts of the truth' can be found in other religions. These rival religions concern themselves with creation, matters of right and wrong, and a searching for eternal truths, but on their own they are not sufficient. Thus other religions are intrinsically inadequate and are not equally true or lead to God (Gumbel 2000, p. 30).

What about those who have never heard of Jesus? Is their fate to be heaven or hell and judgement? As with a number of issues, Gumbel falls back on a certain scriptural ambiguity where the Bible is perceived as 'a practical book, not a philosophical one. It cannot answer hypothetical questions directly'. God will judge and he will be just. No one will be saved by their religion. There then follows what I think is a curious exposition. Jesus died for the godly who lived before him and those who lived after him but had never heard of him (Gumbel 2000, pp. 32–3). I am no theologian but see no justification for such a statement that would seem to contradict assertions made earlier in the chapter.

Then there are the platitudes in which *Searching Issues* seems to extol. There is the expressed conviction of the need to be humble and sensitive to the beliefs of others. We are told that there is no room for arrogance. Other faiths are not to be attacked, but treated with respect. The chapter finishes with a significant quote from a book by Alpha sympathizer Michael Green (*Evangelism Through the Local Church*):

> Far from closing our options, pluralism allows us to proclaim an undiluted gospel in the public square and in the supermarket of faiths, allowing others the same right. Let the truth prevail and let the craven silence be banished.
>
> (Green 1990, p. 5)

My observation was that guests on the Alpha course were interested in how Christianity compared with other religions. What did they actually believe and practise? For example, what did Islam and Sikhism stand for and what were the similarities and differences when compared to Christianity? These were questions not always comprehensively answered by Alpha course leaders and scarcely addressed in the literature. An inherent weakness of the programme is that there is little by way of a comparative analysis. In short, what is Christianity being compared to? While it might be unreasonable to expect that Alpha course leaders should have the necessary knowledge, the

Alpha programme short-circuits the issue by its uncompromising stand. Its dogma is at the expense of an informative and educational dimension.

That the New Age should have a chapter of it own in *Searching Issues* is significant, since it could simply have been included under the rubric 'other religion'. Although the subject of the New Age is not dealt with in the subsequent chapter of the volume, I prefer to focus on the treatment by *Searching Issues* since it would, to my mind, logically follow on. It is an oddly titled chapter: 'How does the New Age movement relate to Christianity?'.

Although he does not use the precise term 'post-modern' in his discussion of the New Age, Gumbel eludes to the possibility that 'The Enlightenment worldview and framework is collapsing around us' (Gumbel 2000, p. 53). The New Age, he informs us, is the product of a changing world. We are told, in simplistic terms, something of what the movement comprises. Its emergence is against the background of a reversal of secularization, an age of religious resurgence and pluralism, a rejection of rationalism (Gumbel 2000, p. 54). Quoting one of the charismatic movement's more academic sources, Graham Cray, Principal of Ridley Hall Theological College, Cambridge, Gumbel insists that we live in a 'pick-and-mix culture' and the New Age is an attempt to construct a new worldview.

There is more involved in Alpha's treatment of the New Age. While recognizing that it has some origins in Eastern mysticism, occultist practices and beliefs in reincarnation of other world faiths (although this is not clearly stipulated), the movement is labelled as demonic despite its concern for health, peace, ecology and spiritual enlightenment. Here, a familiar biblical quote is inserted: 'After all as St Paul reminds us "Satan himself masquerades as an angel of light"' (2 Corinthians 11:14). Then, according to Gumbel, there are all the practices to be found in the New Age which are condemned by the Bible: astrology, horoscopes, clairvoyance, spiritualism, spiritual guides and tarot.

The significance of the New Age is regarded by Gumbel (in contrast to the World Religions in Western societies) as 'enormous'. The New Age *is* a true rival. Examples are given of its magnitude; for example, that 25 per cent of Americans dabble in it. Mainline bookshops all have large New Age sections, a growing number of companies endorse the movement's techniques, doctors recommend forms of alternative medicine associated with the New Age, while TV programmes like the Crystal Maze have a New Age flavour (Gumbel 2000, p. 57). Its influence, according to Gumbel, is everywhere. This is not a new contention since the subject has proved to be something of an obsession with evangelical Christians – a development that I have discussed at length elsewhere (Hunt 1998). By contrast, in the survey only 2 per cent of respondents raised New Age as their primary issue of concern.

The tendency of evangelicals is to see the New Age as a self-centred movement which carries the ultimate blasphemy: the worship of the self and the search for self happiness, satisfaction and success. It has no concept of sin. Similarities between the New Age and contemporary Christianity are played down. In earlier publications I have explored the similarities between the New Age and the charismatic movement. They include a preoccupation with healing, human and spiritual potential, the stress on the immanence and manipulation of spiritual powers, a theological dualism, and the emphasis on the individual's 'experience'. The need to disassociate with any similarities and sustain a boundary maintenance, leads evangelical Christians to apply deviant labels and to demonize the rival New Age movement (Hunt 1998).

Like other Christian writers, there is an inclination in Gumbel's Alpha literature to lump all alleged sinful activities of the New Age together without discrimination and this is clear when he states that:

> (the New Age movement believes that) Guidance comes from within, and many feel led to advocate abortion, homosexuality and promiscuity.

The moral and Christian decline of society becomes intertwined with the emergence of a rival religious movement. Like 'other religions', followers of the New Age are depicted as sincere people seeking spiritual truths. They are, of course, grossly mistaken and find themselves in Satan's backyard.

The New Age, Gumbel tells us, fails to realize who Jesus was and merely reduces him to some 'ascended master'. It fails to realize that salvation is not through man but God and (this is stressed) 'the New Age does not get near the truth about God the Holy Spirit' (Gumbel 2000, pp. 64–5). It searches for a spiritual power, but there is no greater power than the Holy Spirit. Thus, in the spiritual marketplace, Christianity wins out. On the other hand there is a recognition that the New Age has filled a gap and that the church should take notice:

> ... those of us who have been in the church need to repent of our rigidity, rationalism and failure to make the church relevant to the culture in which we live.
>
> (Gumbel 2000, p. 57)

The matter of other religions is also tackled in Gumbel's book *Challenging Lifestyle* (2001). The chapter entitled 'How to Discern False Prophets' deals less than charitably with what is frequently known as forms of quasi-Christianity: those expressions of religion which have some familiar aspects of Christianity but are outside the remit of historical Christianity. The chapter begins by looking at examples of 'doomsday' cults including the disastrous events at Waco with the Branch Davidians and the events at Jonestown in 1978. The chapter makes a brief reference to Mormons (the fastest growing church in the world), Jehovah's Witnesses and Christian Scientists. Their beliefs are not expounded and there is little differentiation made between them either in terms of their beliefs and practices or where they depart from mainline Christianity.

While 'other religions' in all their manifestations is something of a preoccupation in supporting Alpha literature, questionnaire responses, interviews, and discussion groups in Alpha courses also tend to reflect the subject as a major concern for the guests. 'Other religions' was the second most mentioned issue at over 15 per cent. Rarely was the subject raised by Alpha group leaders and where it was it was usually in passing. In most cases they were summarily dismissed. For example, Islam was often portrayed by course leaders as a brutal, fanatical religion, where people are stoned to death for breaking social and religious taboos and regulations.

Sexuality

As far as the evidence regarding guests who attend Alpha at HTB is concerned, the main reason why people delay in becoming Christians is the matter of sex before marriage. For Gumbel, the Christian point of view 'can be seen more as a moral objection than an intellectual one' (Gumbel 2000, p. 8). Clearly, the modern Christian church is fighting a rearguard action in respect of a profound change in public attitudes. Gumbel acknowledges that a sexual revolution has taken place, that sex saturates the media and, as he puts it, 'Sex has become the idol of our times'. By way of argument, the sexual revolution is tied to another 'alarming revolution', according to Gumbel: the decline of marriage and the family as a social institution. It follows that there is a relationship between the two.

There are some quite extraordinary generalized comments to be found in *Searching Issues* including the following statements:

> Many people find themselves trapped in promiscuity which destroys their self esteem, exposes them to sexually transmitted disease and often ruins their ability to form a lasting relationship.
>
> (Gumbel 2000, p. 38)

> Pre-marital sex increases the chances of extra-marital sex.
>
> (Gumbel 2000, p. 43)

Alternatives to pre-marital sex are considered by Gumbel including masturbation ('a small sin') of which he says:

> It is not a good idea, but should not be taken too seriously unless it becomes excessive.
>
> (Gumbel 2000, p. 49)

In his arguments on sexuality, however, Gumbel largely extols a standard Christian teaching: that the one-partner (heterosexual) relationship is for life and for the best since 'God does not want us to get hurt' (Gumbel 2000, p. 42).

My research suggests that matters related to sexual morals, such as sex before marriage and homosexuality, appear to be less contentious issues than the findings of HTB might suggest, although they were more likely to be raised by the young members of Alpha groups. Nonetheless, 4.5 per cent considered the issue of sex before marriage as their major concern related to Christian teaching and over 6 per cent similarly registered the controversy of gay sexuality. My view is that the scarce concern with the subject of sex reflects the fact that the great bulk of subscribers to Alpha were convinced Christians and had already made up their minds on these issues. However, a fair few displayed strong views with the matter of gay sex being the most difficult subject for Christians to deal with. I will not discuss Alpha's attitude to it here since gay sexuality forms the subject of Chapter 13 where the question is raised concerning its apparent homophobic stance.

Science and Religion

It is a sign of secularity that, where there appears to be conflict and contradiction between faith and science, Christianity has continued to concede ground to science (apart from the Bible belt in the USA). It is interesting that *Seaching Issues*, a book which is key material for the largest evangelizing initiative in the world today, should all but scoff at the so-called 'Monkey Trial' of 1925 where J.T. Scopes was prosecuted for violating state law by teaching the theory of evolution in high-school (Gumbel 2000, p. 85). Such attitudes, we are told, bring Christianity into disrepute.

Various subjects are advanced in the broad issues of science versus faith and this was evident in the research findings – subjects such as miracles and evolution. Gumbel's approach is not to suggest that science and faith are incompatible. God is rational and has created a natural world of order. Scientists are therefore exploring what God has 'rationally' made (Gumbel 2000, p. 85). In an interesting argument Gumbel suggests that Christian belief allows experimentation and exploration of the natural world, whereas 'This would not have been the case under belief systems which regarded forms of matter as gods' (Gumbel 2000, p. 86). This is obviously a comment implicitly directed at those world religions which include notions of animism. Neither, in Gumbel's view, do science and scripture contradict; indeed, they complement each other. Nonetheless, the God who creates the rational world is also responsible for miracles.

As far as evolution is concerned, Gumbel perceives much of the theory of evolution to be just that: 'still only theory'. He distinguishes between what he calls 'micro' and 'macro' theories of evolution. Micro-evolution does not conflict with the Bible and is the means for variation and development of the species *within* the species. Macro-evolution by contrast, evolution *from* one species to another, such as apes to humans, for Gumbel is still unproven and remains so much theory. In this context, the Genesis account of creation is briefly explored: 'there are many different interpretations of Genesis held by sincere Christians', from that of a literal six-day creation, to gradual evolution over a vast time span, the endorsement of the Big Bang theory, to Genesis 1 as a poetic form (Gumbel 2000, p. 90):

> In the light of the uncertainty and differences of opinion among genuine
> Christians, I think it is unwise to be too dogmatic about the issue. (p. 92)

This is an illuminating statement because it neatly side-steps age-old
controversy and indicates the fact that it is on the subject of science that
perhaps Christianity has conceded most ground to secularity. Gumbel insists
that various attitudes are deemed acceptable by Christians today. While not
wishing to upset the literalists, the concession to scientific evidence is made.
There are plenty of quotes from the scientists, the theologians and apologists
in *Searching Issues*, to justify numerous positions. It is interesting, however,
that while concessions have been made to science, they have not been offered
in respect of sexuality. In fact, as we shall see, scientific arguments are used to
booster moral imperatives when it comes to the subject of homosexuality.

Issues of science versus faith did interest respondents and the discussion
groups that I was involved with. 'Science and religion' was mentioned by
nearly 7 per cent of respondents as being of primary concern, with a further 4
per cent specifically focusing on the topic of evolution. It was not a topic that
the Alpha groups, in my experience at least, spent much time discussing nor
sufficiently dealing with in any great detail.

Theology

Theological issues were mentioned by Christian and non-Christian guests
alike. The Trinity was the major issue for Christians, although non-believers
were more prepared to raise the issue of the divinity of Christ. The Trinity is
fairly extensively explored by Gumbel in *Searching Issues*. He falls back on
the familiar argument that although the term 'Trinity' fails to appear in the
Bible this is not to suggest that it is unscriptural (Gumbel 2000, p. 100).
Gumbel's publication briefly explores what the Trinity is, the biblical verses
that support it, and a historical account of its creedal acceptance. In dealing
with the nature of God, argues Gumbel, the Trinity remains a mystery,
stretching the boundaries of our understanding and the limitation of human
language in explaining it. There are the familiar analogies presented: three
stumps in one wicket, the shamrock leaf and the Union Jack flag. Yet,
interestingly, the chapter concludes with the analogy of psychotherapy.
Patients need a reference point in their treatment. They have to discover and
accept who they are, where they have come from and where they are going. In
spiritual terms this means the role of God the Father in where they come
from, a role model of God the Son in knowing where they are going, and a
facilitator or counsellor to help the patient get there (God the Holy Spirit).

In addition to the Trinity, two other theological issues were most likely to
concern Alpha guests. One was the apparent contradiction between Old and
New Testaments, at just under 2 per cent. This included issues of Grace versus
the Law, the observance of the Sabbath, and divine justice. Issues of sin were

primarily important for 1.7 per cent of respondents. In the discussion groups I joined, the topics most singled out for discussion were the definition of sin, the origin of sin as related to creation and human nature, sin and culture, and outmoded concepts of sin. Non-believing guests had particular problems with the term itself as meaning 'wrong doing'. One described it as 'Victorian sounding', to which the course leader argued that 'As a Christian, the more one uses the term, the more acceptable it becomes'. In such a way, the 'seeker' is acclimatized to what might be referred to as 'Christian-speak'. Other topics that were theologically related included whether personal life events are a result of God's intervention, and the matter of free will or predestination. Some issues were denomination specific. For example, respondents who were Roman Catholic raised issues such as prayer through Mary or the saints.

Finally, a wide category of miscellaneous subjects was advanced by Alpha guests. Many were linked to moral questions such as the just war or abortion. Others were related to the history of the Christian church – especially as a conservative force in upholding unjust socio-political orders, and the implications of major doctrinal divisions within Christianity.

Summary

'Searching Issues' is an important and intriguing topic. It provides a measure of many things, perhaps most of all the thinking and needs of the religious 'seeker' or church members (since many Alpha guests are already in the church). At the same time it tells us about secularity and cultural trajectories. The issues raised inform us about wider cultural and moral concerns and how they have impinged upon the church. They are, moreover, topics which say something about the church's relationship with wider society, as well as its boundaries with rival faiths and new expressions of religiosity. Other issues, mostly theological or related to suffering remain perennial.

Chapter 9

The Supply-side of Alpha

Supply-side Christianity

In Chapter 2 we explored the notion of a 'supply-side' religiosity. While it is a theme under-developed in post-modernist writings, it is more clearly articulated by North American rational-choice theorists. For those such as Stark and Iannaccone (1994) religion is now increasingly 'marketed' and likewise 'consumed'. Their argument is that while the individual exercises considerable volition and makes rational choices in subscribing to a particular religion, the growth of a supply-side religiosity can be identified whereby traditional religious structures, as well as new innovating religions, adapt to the needs of religious 'consumers' in the 'spiritual marketplace'. In responding to the requirements of the religious seeker, religious movements and organizations may attempt to forge attractive packages which take into account consumer demands – even imitating and improving upon rival brands, perhaps borrowing and adapting beliefs and practices for their own ends.

The unique commodities offered by the religious 'producers' are the spiritual, emotional, psychological, and practical benefits demanded by religious consumers. The supply-side of a spiritual marketplace, however, can mean significantly more than providing for customer 'needs' and there may be numerous other dynamics to be observed. One is the possibility that the supply-side of religion may seek to create a demand through advertising and strategies taken with the aim of ultimately creating a 'monopoly'. Hence, rather like business corporates, religious suppliers can generate or endeavour to create a demand, even where it does not exist, and convince consumers of their needs in the spiritual marketplace (Finke and Iannaccone 1993).

In the uncompromising environment of religious pluralism and the competition for a limited 'market', mainline Christian churches are now obliged to see themselves as units in a market, competing for the time, loyalty and finances of their own clientele. In this situation, so the rational-choice theorists speculate, churches largely behave as secular, commercial units operating in a spiritual marketplace: with an eye to mass appeal, advertising, displaying a sensitivity to competition, commodity attraction, 'profit' innovation, and so on.

Does this kind of perspective lend to an understanding of Alpha, particularly its supply-side and inherent organizational dynamics? Arguably, in charismatic circles such a market approach is particularly important because of the emphasis on winning converts, church-growth, and the long-awaited expectation of an imminent revival. Clearly Alpha has proved a powerful, if over-hyped, product in the spiritual marketplace and potentially is the means by which many of these goals might be realized. It has the capacity both to deal with a consumer demand and to create a demand through its advertising techniques. This chapter therefore considers the implications of a distinct form of supply-side Christianity via the Alpha programme, through the relevant recently developed sociological frameworks.

Alpha, as we have seen, is a fairly standard product advanced by its well-organized and directed supply-side. Although it was put together by one church, Holy Trinity, Brompton, in terms of content and structure it reflects a specific theological and cultural milieu. This enculturated package has subsequently penetrated other churches throughout the UK for over a decade. In recent years the programme has been exported in its original form on an international scale and to very different cultural contexts ranging from that of the USA, to the ex-Communist nations of Eastern Europe, to a variety of Third World countries. This apparent top-down dissemination of a standardized commodity obviously makes HTB a very powerful producer in the charismatic-evangelical world. In broad terms HTB could be seen as much a business organization as a centre of Christian outreach and a leading contemporary charismatic church. It thus constitutes the supply-side of a distinct religious product.

Here we consider the implications for contemporary Christianity of the standardized and widely distributed product of the Alpha programme through the concepts of 'globalization' and 'McDonaldization'. Applying them to Alpha is a useful enterprise since the programme provides a testing ground for core sociological typologies and theories with reference to contemporary religion. While the concepts prove to be useful exploratory tools, as we shall note, they do not always apply stringently to the Alpha product. It is clear, moreover, that there are limitations in their application to religiosity and, at a broad level, we might speculate that the notion of a spiritual marketplace is perhaps best comprehended as a metaphor rather than primarily understood in terms of literal and macro-economic structures, although a number of these are certainly observable. Perhaps above all, the significance of Alpha lays in its near-monopoly in evangelical circles. No other equivalent course comes anywhere close to achieving such a high profile. This is of particular significance given its global reach. Hence, it is legitimate to discuss Alpha's market impact in terms of globalization and its vastness of scale.

'Globalization' has become something of a buzz word in recent years – and not just in sociological circles since the term now enjoys widespread common usage. This is perhaps understandable given the profound changes which have taken place internationally and their significance by way of economics, culture and, as far as we are concerned here, the sphere of religion in general.

However, as a core concept in sociological thinking there remains some debate about its definition and its principal ramifications.

While acknowledging the complexities, it is increasingly obvious that a discussion of religion in any particular society or indeed any political–geographical region of the world, including the industrialized nations of North America and Europe, will only be valid with reference to the globalized context. In recent times, even the most distant reaches of the world have become more easily accessible through economic networks and rapid advances in technology and communication. Thus, it is necessary to look beyond the boundaries of any given society for the full impact of what may be understood as an extension of the changes brought about by modernization and its economic dimensions. Now there is a global interconnectedness of what McLuhan (1996) has referred to as the 'global village', which implies that the world is now a smaller place and that national, political and cultural boundaries are breaking down. Multinational corporations, international financial markets, transnational communications systems (such as satellite TV) and transnational political organizations (including the United Nations and the European Community) all function outside the jurisdiction of individual nation-states, yet have a significant influence on them.

The dynamics of globalization, as Roland Robertson (1992) notes, are far from new: they have been impacting for several centuries and there has been no straightforward line of development. However, many aspects of globalization are increasingly marked by their scale and intensity (Bonnett 1994). Religion is a case in point. Although for centuries the major religions such as Islam and Christianity have had an influence which transcends national boundaries, globalizing forces bring numerous other consequences. Robertson (1993) maintains that while religion may, at first glance, appear to be peripheral to globalization it is, in fact, at the heart of it. Recent history suggests that what he refers to as 'national societies' are related to different cultures and traditions as their economic and power structures become interdependent at a global level. This is true of religious culture and tradition as much as any other social dimension.

The global spread of Western religion is by no means novel. Missionaries have taken their variations of Christianity across the world for centuries. Since the nineteenth century many North American sects, including Jehovah's Witnesses, Christadelphianism, Mormonism, Christian Science, and indeed Pentecostalism, have made their way from 'God's backyard' to all parts of the world. The process continues into the twenty-first century. What is unique about the current wave of movements, however, is the extent to which they carry an Americanized cultural package – much exemplified by the so-called 'Health and Wealth gospel' with its emphasis on a get-rich-quick philosophy (Hunt 2000).[1]

While Alpha is a UK-based, not a North American, package there is the discernible impact of the teachings and practices of the Vineyard movement that had already enjoyed a global influence through the planting of its own churches and via the Toronto Blessing in the mid-1990s. To this is added, as we have already explored, the unique dimensions of an enculturated form of Pentecostalism: middle-class and therapeutic in orientation with a distinct theology and praxis. It is this package that has permeated many regions of the world and different cultural contexts in what might be refered to as the 'mass marketing of God' (Smark 1978).

McDonaldization – an Overview

For George Ritzer (1996), McDonaldization denotes global patterns of consumption and consumerism and is a process of rationalization exemplified by the American fast-food company McDonalds. It represents standardization and a near market monopoly, and dispels the myth that a free global economy brings endless variation and upholds consumer choice through competition. What McDonalds produces is the same all the world over, the same items and the same image, yet what McDonalds implies is not limited to the food industry. Education, work, health care, travel, leisure, dieting, politics and increasingly other aspects of social life are subject to the same processes.

It may be difficult, given its nature, to believe that religion can be reduced to the dynamics of McDonaldization. However, the churches as bureaucratic structures, alongside their need to communicate with the secular world and the dynamics of the evangelizing enterprise, are forced into certain constraints. Over the years there has been a tendency to bureaucratize and 'package' Christian lifestyle and image, to simplify dimensions of faith, and to standardize aspects of church life and experience as almost items of consumption. This has been particularly true of the evangelical wing of the church. Certainly much is exemplified by many North American ministries with their mass-produced publications and visual technologies.

To understand the significance of such processes for contemporary religion we have to range further. One of the most comprehensive ways of understanding McDonaldization is to see it as a natural outcome and extension of Max Weber's model of a bureaucracy. Indeed, McDonalds takes the Weber ideal model of bureaucracy to its furthest conclusion: McDonalds is a bureaucracy writ large – as applied to the business enterprise. Potentially, an exploration of this theme provides useful insights into the processes associated with the supply-side of Alpha and its implications for the local church context.

When Weber developed his classic model at the beginning of the twentieth century he suggested that, whatever its function or purpose, a bureaucracy displays certain characteristics: clearly defined goals and methods, strict rules and regulations to be applied in particular situations, a division of labour, specific roles and professional conduct, specialized training where necessary, and where work is performed without emotional attachment to either work associate or client. All these variables are part of an over-arching rationalism. In taking bureaucracy to its conclusions, McDonaldization displays its own identifying characteristics and all are related to the relentless drive for the maximization of profit. These characteristics are 'calculability', 'predictability', 'control' and 'efficiency'. A study of these central elements will help us understand to what extent Alpha is a form of evangelical McDonalds. It will permit us to conclude, however, that the programme displays only some dimensions of these essential characteristics.

Alpha – an Evangelical McDonaldization?

At first glance it would appear that a standardized Alpha package has been deliberately and systematically exported across the world by its instigators from one church in the UK, namely HTB. Perhaps then, it is not too unreasonable to describe it, as I have before, as a form of 'evangelical McDonaldization' (Hunt 2000). Certainly there is much to suggest that Alpha has at least developed this potential. There is a kind of ideal model of the course both in terms of its content and strategy. Given its scale the implications are considerable, not least in terms of how the message is put across, the image of Christianity portrayed, and the theological content which is advanced. With the growth of Alpha it is clear that the programme is moving towards large-scale adoption, even a near monopoly. While there are similar courses to be found, such as Emmaus, none is anywhere near the scale and market penetration of Alpha.

As we saw in the opening chapter, Alpha in several respects epitomizes the church-growth imperative of many charismatic congregations and their increasing tendency towards mass-marketing and commercial mobilization. One clear implication of this tendency is the conscious creation of a 'brand', including a brand name and distinct image. This image was first to be observed on the Alpha posters. A group of Christians from the advertising industry gave their free time to design the distinctive Alpha posters. One of them was Francis Goodwin, managing director of Maiden Outdoor, which operates its own poster sites. Goodwin claimed:

> We wanted people to feel that an Alpha course is a perfectly normal thing to do ... We needed to establish the Alpha name in the world outside the church community and to link its logo with the name, thus helping create a brand image. We chose posters to give the campaign an impact at street level and to communicate with a large audience.[2]

The tendency of Alpha to display aspects of McDonaldization can be observed beyond a mere standardized image and is evident in aspects of 'calculability', 'predictability', 'control' and 'efficiency'.

Calculability is two-sided. First, the ability to quantify every aspect of a process makes efficiency more attainable. Waste can be eliminated, energy saved and economy of scale utilized. Secondly, quantity is promoted as a beneficial commodity. For McDonalds 'quantity tends to become surrogate for quality' (Ritzer 1996, p. 60). The chain previously had the policy of advertising on large signs the numbers (in billions) of hamburgers it has sold. The implication is that such huge numbers must represent a quality product, although it may be argued that quantity is at the expense of quality.

In terms of calculability, like the advertizing of McDonalds, HTB is very keen on boasting of the number of Alpha courses running worldwide, the number of churches involved and the number of people who have passed through the programme. Its global application suggests quality and effectiveness, and thus thousands of satisfied customers. However, as we have seen (Chapter 1) there is a tendency to over-exaggerate figures and round them upwards. The reality behind Alpha's image is not always so impressive. As noted in the previous chapter, in those churches surveyed the course was often on a small-scale and many were infrequently run or even given up altogether.

'Predictability' is also an aid to efficiency in the McDonaldization process. If the customer knows with certainty what he or she is purchasing then less time is spent in choosing at the counter. It is the same all over the world – the same image and the same product. What results is a fairly standard package. In fact, it is probably the case that most people have already decided what they are going to buy before they enter a McDonalds restaurant. Predictability is also less threatening to the consumer. If one knows everything about a situation and there are no surprises, then peace of mind is enhanced. This also applies to staff whose tasks may be mundane but are not threatening because of unpredictability. Predictability similarly enhances efficiency in the manufacturing process as supplies are easily quantified and suppliers are known to produce a standard item.

It is difficult to suggest that Alpha works precisely in this way. Alpha is a one-off experience for most people, unless they choose to repeat the course. Sometimes people do come back a second or even third time. It appears to have a psychological security for those who have come to be known as 'Alphaholics' – they are attracted by the course's human company, personal attention, and pastoral care. For most guests, however, there is little idea of what to expect and this may lead to ultimate disappointment. Alpha is, in theory at least, a learning process for those who have little or no knowledge of the Christian faith. Efficiency is not important in this context because the aim is different: to educate through the means of a simple, standardized programme.

The characteristic of 'control' is considered by Ritzer (1996):

> ... for organizations to gain control over people gradually and progressively through the development and deployment of increasingly effective technologies. (p. 101)

Control reduces the behaviour of those involved in a process, be they producers or consumers, to a series of machine-like actions. Then, says

Ritzer, once people behave like machines they can be replaced by machines. The process is all too evident in the commercial world where bank clerks are replaced by automated telling machines, shop assistants are reduced to being one part of a conveyor belt passing over a scanner, and the restaurant chef becomes a timer set to take prepared fries from the fat after a predetermined cooking time.

Specialization is also a key aspect of McDonalds' control dimension. One person cooks hamburgers, another creates milkshakes, another dresses the buns, and so on. Control does not have to be only by machine, the technology prescribes pre-written protocols to which the operative must adhere for full effectiveness.

The advantages of such strict control for business firms are that variation is reduced to a minimum, costs are kept down and efficiency and rationality increased. There is a minus side however. Max Weber understood the process of rationalization as being inevitable and resulting in the increasing constriction of humanity in an 'iron cage of rationality' which was systemized and dehumanized. Ritzer's conclusion is similar, and he brings a pessimistic prophecy of ever-increasing captivity to McDonaldization in that workers are reduced to dehumanized individuals going about their daily business like robots, pre-programmed, controlled and unable to break free – a veritable brave new McWorld.

Influential in the development of McDonalds was Ray Kroc who offered the original McDonald brothers a partnership before buying them out. McDonalds was followed everywhere with the most exacting fidelity. Kroc's obsession with detail became legendary. He dictated that McDonalds' burgers must be exactly 3.875 inches across, weigh 1.6 ounces and contain precisely 19 per cent fat. He even specified after much experimentation, how much wax should be on the wax paper that separated one hamburger patty from another. Such obsessiveness made McDonalds a success but created a culture that was against innovation. When a team of his executives suggested the idea of miniature outlets called MiniMacs Kroc was outraged because they implied modifications.

In industry and commerce control is exerted over the machine and technology and also the pre-written instructions to which the operative must adhere. In terms of Alpha, this would suggest that those who subscribe to the course in local churches should cleave to the recommendations of HTB. This is why HTB runs two-day conferences instructing those churches who wish to subscribe and will send instructors to visit congregations on request. In this way HTB penetrates local parishes and churches and subsequently attempts a standard practice. HTB is keen that everyone gets it right. How to conduct Alpha at the grass-root level is something that it has given much attention to. For that reason there is plenty of literature and 'plastic' media material generated to support local churches and to enforce the recommended way.

The video is the most obvious means by which local church environments are penetrated. There are aids for church leaders and course administrators, such as the video *How to Run the Alpha Course, Telling Others: The Alpha Initiative*, or the 15-minute promotion pack *Introductory Video* which includes material from Alpha courses and conferences held at HTB. These, and such tapes as *Alpha Worship* which has a '16-track recording of hymns and songs suitable for use on Alpha', undoubtedly further enhance the tendency towards control. The video is very much a standard product and in this way the cultural environment of HTB is taken into the context of the local church. The man on the screen replaces the real-life person in the church.[3] In the two-day conferences the principles and practicalities of the course are made clear in a 'Model Alpha Session'. Nicky Gumbel is frequently quoted as saying 'Running Alpha without attending a conference is like driving a car without taking lessons'. Elsewhere he states that 'As in baking a cake, the best way to run Alpha is to follow the set recipe' (Gumbel 2001a, p. 22).

So far we have only skirted around 'efficiency' in relation to the process of McDonaldization although it is intrinsically linked to control, calculability and predictability. Efficiency is the selection of the best method to achieve a given end after all the options have been considered and the goals of an organization have been clearly identified. Hence, efficiency might be the way of applying notions of McDonaldization to Alpha. The programme is, as we have seen, a result of years of evolution and perfecting a design for a practical and constructive programme of evangelism. Its evolution and drive for efficiency has meant that it has retained a certain simplicity in its style and content. Commenting on the logic behind Alpha, Damian Thompson, a freelance writer specializing in religious affairs, has remarked that its ingenuity lies in its simplicity and ability to reach people 'where they are':

> British Christianity has stumbled across the big idea that has eluded it for most of its feeble Decade of Evangelism. It is not so much a big idea, as a small one brilliantly executed. Its popularity owes little to mission strategies or the thaumaturgical extravagances of the Toronto Blessing. Its milieu is mundane and domestic.[4]

Standardization may not, however, necessarily enhance efficiency or cost effectiveness when it applies to the Alpha programme. Alpha organizers do not operate like a business enterprise in being concerned as to whether Alpha is particularly cost-effective. Here the McDonald analogy breaks down because the essential aim of Alpha is very different. Organizing and running courses can be expensive in terms of finance, human resources and church involvement. There may be few guests and no conversions. Results or profits are difficult to quantify and qualify by way of the number of souls won and spiritual paths embarked upon. Those who endorse Alpha would undoubtedly argue that costing cannot be put on conversion or spiritual journeying.

From another point of view, the great strength of Alpha may also be said to be its major weakness. Its ingenuity lies in its simplicty. Alpha brings a quick 'service'. There is the minimum use of resources (church hall and video, plus booklets and other Alpha paraphernalia) and a fairly short stay in its site of consumption (three hours per week over ten weeks, although obviously the aim is to bring people permanently into the church). The menu is very limited: there is no choice of what is discussed in the programme. But there are drawbacks. The McDonalds burger is simple and basic, but is hardly a culinary delight. It might likewise be argued that Alpha lacks the theological richness which would come with a longer, more detailed course.

For Ritzer, McDonaldization means that 'quantity tends to become surrogate for quality'. In the Alpha parallel there are important implications. Does the theological content of Alpha mean that quantity is at the expense of quality? Being 'relevant to modern man' and putting the gospel message across in a simple way may leave little scope to explore personal spiritual experiences, church history, and the wide-ranging nature of the faith in different historical and theological contexts. This partly explains why it does not raise contentious issues which have long plagued Christendom such as infant baptism, the nature of communion, or the ordination of women. Perhaps more importantly Alpha may still leave people 'hungry', especially since there is nothing stringently organized post-Alpha. It could be regarded, then, as a kind of spiritual drive-through. However, this rapid 'service' is supplemented by the uncharacteristic feature of McDonaldization in attempting to come to know the customer (guest) as 'a real person' and to create a sense of group association and identification, not to mention emotional attachment.[5]

There are other problems observable in Alpha's simplicity. I found that simplicity could equal inflexibility. Inflexibility in group discussions meant that useful exchanges were often cut short because the course leaders were either forced back to the standard booklet on themes to be covered or limited by the time restraints of the evening's discussion period. Moreover, a few individuals I interviewed, both clergy and lay, argued that Alpha tends to present a 'quick fix theology', that it was pastorally weak, not always practical in dealing with real human problems such as marital breakdown and bereavement and cannot be expected to do so in such a short space of time and minimal contact with guests. According to one interviewee:

> the world is revealed in a 30 minute package ... Alpha is marketed to provide an answer to everything but it isn't. It is not the be all and end all even for those of us who readily endorse it.

Alpha is, in theory at least, efficient because it is a standardized product, yet it is also an ongoing project. As we have noted, those who put the programme together are prepared to accept recommendations. In an interview I was told by Nicky Gumbel that the course organizers at HTB constantly take feedback from churches on how to improve the product. It is not then, the 'finished product'. We may expect that in the future Alpha will be modified according to consumer demand and the advice of local churches. In this respect, Alpha organizers, rather like Japanese car manufacturers, take notice of not only the requirements of customers but the recommendations made for efficiency by those on the shopfloor.

Alpha on the Ground

While the McDonalds burger may be a fairly standardized product, Alpha has considerable variation when applied 'on the ground'. Localized contexts, theological preferences, church tradition and culture are not always taken into account by those who advance Alpha since it is assumed that the package of basic Christianity is a common denominator to all. HTB does not envisage a great deal of difficulty in applying the programme to the local environment. It is however aware and concerned about unwarranted improvization and customization. For such reasons the programme is accompanied by a copyright statement. Through the statement HTB maintains that it has always been happy to allow those running a course the flexibility to adapt it where deemed necessary to cater for particular local needs. However, HTB claims that there have often been misunderstandings and that the 'loss of integrity in some courses has given rise to considerable confusion'. Perhaps of most concern are the deliberate changes in the content of the course made at a local level. HTB insists that it has no problem with the programme being shortened but the question remains as to when it is so shortened that it ceases to be an Alpha course. At the same time, constricting the course does not apply to certain aspects of it. By way of illustration we may note that course leaders are implicitly instructed not to leave out the section on the Holy Spirit (its main charismatic element):

> **Alpha Copyright Statement** (paragraph v, part b)
>
> The Alpha course may be shortened or lengthened by varying the length of the talks. Not all the material need be used; additional material may be used. This is subject to the proviso that such alterations do not change the essential character of the course. Alpha is designed to be a series of fifteen talks, over a period of time, including a weekend or day spent away together, and teaching on the various topics contained in the book Questions of Life. This teaching should neither be departed from nor qualitatively altered in an Alpha course for the reason in paragraph (iv) above (i.e. *causing confusion and uncertainty as to what the Alpha course really is*) (emphasis is that of HTB).

Local traditions and denominational structures constitute the cultural sites upon which not only Alpha impinges but they, in turn, impinge on the course as a universal product. While clearly more research needs to be conducted into how it adapts to local environments elsewhere in the world, my survey has indicated a fair degree of variety on the ground (or what might be referred to as 'localization' even in the context of the UK).

The pilot survey indicated that there were considerable localized variations in the application of the Alpha programme because of practical needs and theological and traditional differences. The national study has substantiated this. Some churches shorten or occasionally lengthen the course for a variety of reasons. Perhaps more importantly it has to be recognized that tradition and doctrinal preferences are not discarded overnight and to some extent they impinge upon the structure, content and the working philosophy of Alpha.

One of the problems associated with Alpha is that while it seeks to be as universal and popular as McDonalds (it is interesting that McDonalds uses different adverts to attract different groups), it has, unintentionally perhaps, reached a niche market despite attempts to attract groups rarely touched by evangelism such as the young and prison inmates. Most bureaucracies and organizations, business oriented or otherwise, will display certain cultural attributes. So it is with Alpha.

As already suggested, one complaint is that the general culture of Alpha is too middle-class. An Anglican minister, in a disappointed tone, explained to me in an interview how a woman had left the course after only one week because the group was predominantly middle-class and educated, and consequently she 'felt left out and intimidated'.[6] Another clergyman had problems with the Nicky Gumbel video presentations and was thinking of starting his own customized course complaining that:

> He (Gumbel) is an old Etonian. He is middle-class talking to middle-class people. Because of this Alpha is a bit intellectually demanding for some.

Neither were guests always endeared to Gumbel and the cultural milieu that he represented as these interview extracts suggest:

> Gumbel was the problem. He was being over-hyped. In the video it looks at if flowers are growing out of him. Then his wife will suddenly appear with a huge beaming smile and the lighting on the picture will go soft. This is really all unnecessarily contrived.

By contrast, adaptability and flexibility were accepted by many of the clergy interviewed as advantages of Alpha. For instance, a Baptist minister instructed his course leaders to run the programme within the framework of Baptist traditions and to further the cause not only of his denomination, but of Protestantism generally. A course taught at a Salvation Army citadel ran a more streamlined version in order to be more attractive to the public. This omitted five topics including the three on the Holy Spirit (for theological reasons) which were replaced by the single topic 'What about the Holy Spirit?'.

In determining the degree to which a standard Alpha product is applied on the ground, beyond denominational doctrines and culture, the important determining factor is often the course leaders. They are the gatekeepers of Alpha – often highly motivated, elite church volunteers 'on the ground' dominating events. Some faithfully follow HTB's instructions, others do not. All this adds to the richness and diversity of Alpha as an evangelizing programme.

Summary

This chapter has considered the question whether Alpha can be seen as a form of evangelical McDonaldization. To conclude, I would like to say more about the strive for efficiency inherent in McDonaldization and as applied to Alpha. We have observed that efficiency, as perceived to be enhanced by a standardized package, is not always to be found at a local level. Efficiency, as we have suggested, is about the best possible means of achieving a desired end. Alpha's strive for efficiency can be undermined in fairly obvious ways. In terms of a highly structured course, designated routes to maximize efficiency quickly become institutionalized and counter-productive. The enthusiasm of those who administer the course runs dry and the hard work involved means burn-out. The result could be that the course may become rather routinized with the enthusiasm and spark being dampened.

On the ground, at the local church level, Alpha does not always live up to the glossy image of its slick advertising. There is frequently the human element to be observed. It is not that any of the courses I attended turned out to be a failure, although on occasions they did look amateurish. For the most part, they were generally well-organized and executed by dedicated clergy and lay people. At the same time, like any other aspect of life, Alpha could become ritualized and lose its momentum. As I discovered in some instances, there were often long periods between Alpha courses. Those who had run the course for some time not uncommonly admitted to being exhausted, overworked, and rarely helped by others in the church, which led to a certain disenchantment. This routinization is also enhanced by rationality. Max Weber understood the process of rationalization as being inevitable and resulting in the increasing constriction of humanity in an 'iron cage of rationality' which was systemized and dehumanized. The implication of this for Alpha is that a rationalized and standardized product reduces the course workers to minute parts of the great machinery of HTB – where potentially people become unemotional cogs. This would all seem to work against the end of Alpha, that is, to enhance the spirituality of all those involved.

The proof of Alpha's efficiency, much like that of McDonalds, is in the eating. In terms of the monopoly tendencies of the latter we might note that all but 4 per cent of American consumers will visit a McDonalds at least once a year. Around 32 per cent of all French fries and nearly one-fifth of all eating in a public place is undertaken at McDonalds. Hence, it is not surprising that the *Economist* magazine has used the cost of a Big Mac in various world cities as more or less a serious basis for an index comparing the relative value of currencies.

Can such comparisons be made with Alpha? Possibly so, if we are referring to its near monopolization. In terms of percentages, more people within the churches visit Alpha than any comparable programme, while the religious seeker is far more likely to attend Alpha than any other programme that the churches have cared to put on. In that sense Alpha is undoubtedly a success. The implications, however, are yet to be fully explored.

Notes

1 See the impressive account of the exportation of North American fundamentalism in Brouwer et al. (1996) *Exporting the American Gospel*, New York: Routledge.
2 Quoted in an article by Dominic Kennedy, *The Times*, 9 September 1998. Previously, the design of contemporary Christian posters had put the advertising team behind Alpha into more than a little hot water. It was they who had designed the much-derided Christmas 1996 poster for the Churches Advertising Network which proclaimed 'Bad Hair Day? You're a virgin, you've just given birth and now three kings have shown up'. Alpha posters have generated no such controversy.
3 One of my fears is that I will one day be made redundant by a video of myself lecturing to an audience of undergraduates.
4 Damien Thompson, *The Times*, 2 February 1998.
5 In one group I belonged to I was not allowed to leave for home unless I had been hugged by at least six church members! Hardly the treatment one would expect at the local McDonalds.
6 At one church I surveyed Gumbel's upper middle-class accent was frequently the source of great amusement. There was a fair amount of fun and frivolity in mimicking his accent as the video progressed. On one occasion a rather radical member of the group described HTB scathingly, on the evidence of the video, as 'a middle-class glee club'.

Chapter 10

Who Joins Alpha?

Most of my research into Alpha over a period of five years has been primarily concerned with understanding and accounting for the 'consumer side' of the course in the churches. This is also a principal interest and focus for Holy Trinity, Brompton, although undoubtedly for different reasons. Among the key questions that I have centred on regarding Alpha in the churches are the following: What do guests expect to get out of the programme and, indeed, what do they get out of it? Does Alpha satisfy a range of spiritual, emotional, psychological or less specified needs? Are they satisfied or disappointed? These questions have been partially addressed in earlier chapters and they will be more stringently approached in the next and following chapters.

There are certain needs that the guests displayed which we have already considered above. One set of requirements may be linked to the attraction of joining the Alpha group (perhaps any group) and may have repercussions for the group dynamics of the programme. This is observable in terms of fulfilling a need for 'belonging' at a very broad but meaningful level, of winning appraisal, or perhaps to 'prove' one's powers of argument or persuasion. At the same time, there may be a desire to answer important and relevant questions – the 'searching issues' that are an integral part of 'exploring' the faith and possibly an expression of the wish, especially for the already committed, to know more of the dimensions of faith or concerns central to a spiritual maturity.

In this chapter we will explore the social background of Alpha guests and consider whether certain characteristics seem evident. If so, we might ask if there are any implications for the programme as an evangelizing initiative. In short, does it have limitations, especially in fulfilling the needs of the customers or guests? Later we shall explore the significance of the church and religious background (if any) of those who subscribe to the course. At this point we are concerned with the basic question related to the consumer side of Alpha: what *kind* of people join the course? There is obviously a relationship between these two questions since the matter of which kind of people join Alpha is undoubtedly linked to the range of needs catered for by Alpha as the supply-side of the religious marketplace.

Social Background

Is there something distinctive about the social background of Alpha guests? If so, are there particular types of people that Alpha tends to attract and what are the implications? Conversely, are there categories of people which the course is unlikely to reach or simply does not appeal to – for example, certain age groups, ethnic communities and, as already implied, social classes? The pilot study that I conducted in 1999 found that if generalizations could be made it is that the backgrounds of those who joined Alpha courses in the churches studied were in many respects close to that of the average church-goer and member as revealed in the findings of *Christian England*, probably the most comprehensive study of churches in the UK of late (Brierley 1992). While those attending Alpha appear to cut right across the board in terms of social background, some social groups are evidently over-represented. The findings of the survey with its sample of 837 respondents did not differ considerably from the pilot study. The social categories are discussed here along with a consideration of the likely reasons why there are over-representations and what the possible repercussions might be.

Occupation

A substantial majority of Alpha guests in the greater number of the churches in the survey might be described as lower middle-class: those with lower professional, clerical and administrative jobs – representing a wide spectrum of white-collar occupations. By contrast, skilled manual workers and semi- or unskilled workers were under-represented. This general lower middle-class profile of Alpha guests, as judged by occupation, was reinforced by educational profile with a high number achieving professional qualifications, a degree award, or with diploma or certificate in some occupational specialism or another. The survey also found that about one-third of those attending Alpha courses were not in paid employment; of these one-half were retired and a further one-third were housewives. There were no significant differences between those working and those not working in terms of other social variables such as occupational background, father's occupation, education and rates of social mobility.

The middle-class background (if this is a suitable term to describe those from a range of white-collar occupations) of Alpha guests should not surprise

Table 10.1   Alpha guests: social background
by occupation – all churches (%)

Upper professional	8.6
Lower professional	24.1
Clerical/Administrative	53.7
Skilled manual	9.5
Semi- or unskilled manual	4.1
	100

us unduly given that a good number of church members attend the average Alpha course and that charismatic-oriented churches have congregations that are known to be predominantly of this background (although as we have seen, the sample includes a few non-charismatic churches as well). It also true that in terms of broad occupational criteria a good two-thirds of the general population in the UK could be described as middle class, even if Alpha appeals more directly to the lower professional, clerical and administrative groupings. One important implication of this is that such a middle-class contingent may also be self-perpetuating in that Alpha largely works through network contacts – proving the principle that like really does attract like.

There is however more to consider regarding the over-representation of the middle classes on Alpha courses, that is simply that a higher proportion of such people attend church and are more likely to be involved in the pursuit of all things spiritual. Here, there is nothing particularly new in what the survey reveals. With the development of empirical research into the nature of religion from the mid-twentieth century in Western societies, one of the primary concerns of sociologists of religion has been with class and aspects of belief and institutional belonging. In a series of investigations it was found that the lower classes were noticeably absent from the mainline churches and also that the affluent and the poor express their religious beliefs in different ways. For example, lower-class people are more likely than middle-class individuals to pray in private, to believe uncritically in the doctrines of their faith, and to claim intense religious experiences which they rarely make public. By contrast, the middle class, at least in the USA, appeared to display a greater religious commitment and institutional belonging such as church attendance, seek a sense of community and fellowship with like-minded believers, and discuss aspects of faith.[1]

We have already noted (Chapter 3) that it is middle-class people who are attracted to the charismatic churches for a variety of reasons including dealing with negative aspects of professional life, as well as taking advantage of the battery of healing and therapeutic techniques on offer. More broadly, there are the cultural trappings that are evident in the whole Alpha 'package', the video, literature, discussion groups and so on. Since many so-called guests are already in the church, it should not be astonishing to find them as middle-class people subscribing to the middle-class enculturated course which Alpha appears to be.

The attraction of the middle classes to organized religion is by no means limited to the traditional churches or the charismatic movement. There are numerous studies over the last few decades that have found that the New Religious Movements including the Unification Church, Scientology and some that are based on one variety or another of Eastern mysticism have also proved to be particularly appealing to the more affluent although they do tend to display a rather younger profile. Initially, the charismatic movement was, from one perspective, merely another 'new religion' emerging at the same time and appealing to not dissimilar social constituencies.[2] More recently, the New Age movement, or certain strands of it, have also been discovered to offer an attraction to the more affluent and educated sections of the population.[3]

A whole variety of explanations have been provided for the appeal of the new religions to the middle classes including the charismatic movement.[4] Some of the explanations given may be relevant to our discussion. They include experimentation and alternative lifestyles that challenge prevailing mainstream values,[5] the answer to the moral ambiguity generated by contemporary culture,[6] and the decline of community and a sense of belonging lacking in wider society.[7] Many of these social and psychological problems, so the sociological literature has suggested, could be overcome by expressions of religion that offer an emotional and ecstatic spiritual experience in movements which combine all the attributes of a surrogate family with a strong system of beliefs. In short, providing a sense of belonging with a clear and stringent set of doctrines.

Many of these explanations of the attraction of the new religions to the middle classes were rooted in observations of the social changes taking place in the 1960s and 70s. They may not have the same appeal at the beginning of the twenty-first century. However, one theme which did come out of empirical works in those decades may now have more credence. Pre-dating theories of post-modernity, some studies focused on the new religions and the search for identity. Earlier commentators attempted to establish a link between the new religions and such a search that is precipitated by the contemporary world dominated by bureaucratic structures and fragmented social roles. The new religions are said to address this need by promoting a holistic concept of self-identity especially through therapeutic movements and mystical cults.[8]

Applying some of these explanations of the rise of new religions to the relationship between Alpha in the mainline churches and the attraction of the middle classes is an arduous enterprise. Perhaps the most promising explanation is the matter of identity and its link with therapeutic techniques and experiential experiences. This is not to rule out the attractions of providing a sense of belonging, a strong moral system, or an alternative lifestyle (although these variables may be bound up with the matter of identity). This would bring Alpha close to what Stark and Bainbridge (1985) designate 'client cults' – organized and structured cults which offer services to their followers including healing, spiritualism, and techniques of 'personal adjustments' in dealing with the needs and aspirations of the membership. This is frequently achieved by signing up to a course that prepares and educates followers to deal with their personal requirements. Many such cults offer the ability to control and change one's social identity and self, consolidating all of the individual's fragmented social identities into a single, central, religiously-defined self which is strengthened by the strict control of the more authoritarian and, in the case of those that are of Christian sectarian form, fundamentalist church type groups.[9]

Alpha may approximate *some* of these needs found among contemporary client cults. It does not insist on 'conversion' but looks forward to the conversion experience as an ideal, as the climax of spiritual searching. Its tendency towards fundamentalism along with its therapeutic techniques evident in the Holy Spirit weekend may plausibly point towards the construction of a new 'Christian' identity well-geared to the contemporary age – one which provides a strong belief system, a sense of community and belonging, but does not insist on a strict 'fundamentalist' lifestyle. In short, it achieves a balance between belief and commitment, and advocates an easy-going 'comfortable' form of Christianity.

While these factors may explain why a charismatic-style Christianity is popular with the middle classes, they do not fully explain why people join Alpha – a programme which constitutes merely a possible *means* by which people may adhere to such an enculturated expression of faith. For the most part, the genuine guest who joins Alpha (that is, those not already in the church) will have little understanding of what the programme entails. Interviews with those who join Alpha rarely highlighted these considerations and failed to prove such sociological speculations. The variables such as 'the search for identity' are difficult to quantify. They were also conspicuously missing in questionnaire responses.

What are we left with? I would suggest that a key explanation as to why the middle classes predominantly subscribe to Alpha is more to do with the cultural emphasis on educational and intellectual pursuit. In short, the format and cultural trimmings of the course itself. Fairly formal lectures (albeit by video presentation and discussion groups) are very reminiscent of the way the art subjects are taught in higher education, that is, lectures and seminars. Casual conversation over the Alpha meal-time adds to this appeal. This is all part of the middle-class Alpha package.

Although the emphasis on the middle-class cultural trimmings of Alpha and its obvious attractions to a middle-class constituency is an integral part of the sociological analysis, it does face the danger of making vast deductive generalizations about churches and guests. The churches surveyed were located in very different geographical and demographic areas. Some were urban, others suburban or rural. Others had a greater representation of professional people or manual workers on their courses – roughly in line with the general profile of the churches running them. At the same time other factors such as gender and age cut across class considerations, while 14 per cent of those taking Alpha in the survey had no educational qualifications at all. Thus, while the Alpha course does appeal to the middle classes, it is far from limited to them.

The research findings of both the pilot and national study showed that a fairly high percentage of those attending Alpha courses were not in paid employment, which may mean that Alpha is more attractive to those who have more free time and less work and family obligations than others. They

Table 10.2 Alpha guests: social background by education (%)

Professional qualification	11.8
Degree	18.2
Certificate/Diploma	32.1
'A' Levels	12.8
GCSE	9.6
None	13.6
Misc./Unclassified	1.7
	100

might include retired people, as well as those who are freer to organize their time, conceivably housewives and students.

One of the principal reasons why people dropped out of an Alpha course was because of work or family commitments. These results meant either that some guests were suffering fatigue (hence attending a course became a 'cost' which outweighed any 'reward'), or that a number of people attended irregularly. Of those not working, the largest category are the retired, in fact well over one-third of those not in employment. The next largest categories are housewives, students, unemployed, and disabled respectively (see Table 10.3). The unemployed are another group who presumably have time on their hands and can organize their lives more freely. The same may well be true of guests who do not have family commitments, in particular, those who are single or have grown-up children (see Table 10.4).

The matter of available time for the spiritual voyage offered by Alpha should not be under-estimated. Many studies of the processes of conversion and joining of religious groups and organizations have underlined the importance of the time and opportunities involved in interaction with members and involvement with group activities (Loftland and Stark 1965). During what amounts to socialization into the movement, recruits learn to redefine their social world to that of a new 'religious' setting.

The model of conversion developed by Bromley and Shupe (1979) in their work on New Religious Movements shows that conversion is frequently a

Table 10.3 Alpha guests not in occupational work (%)

Retired	38.1
Student	22.7
Housewife	21.9
Unemployed	11.1
Disabled	5.4
	100

Table 10.4 Alpha guests by marital status (%)

Married	57.8
Single	26.7
Widowed	8.9
Divorced/Separated	6.9
	100

'structured event' arising from relationships with members. Constant interaction is more likely to provide the experience of role models in the group. Another example is provided by the study of Snow and Machelek (1984) which shows that the greater the level of 'commitment' the greater possibility of conversion by the acceptance of a 'master theology' and the submergence into a subculture through a large number of collective experiences and activities. These are complex and detailed studies which cannot be given full justice here, but we shall return to such accounts of commitment and conversion in the next chapter. What can be recognized at this point however, is the *opportunity* for certain people to be involved in Alpha.

Age

HTB's analysis of the profile of over 400 guests undertaking one of its own courses found the average age to be 27, with the 18–35 age group being the most prevalent. Alpha's organizers are fairly convinced that it works best with this age category. Further research by the largest independent Christian Research organization estimated that around 2,000 people under the age of 35 – more than 75 per cent of those taking part – had completed an Alpha course at the church in 2001. While this might seem to be convincing evidence of Alpha's attraction to this particular age group, I would suggest the research merely underlines the unique social profile of HTB rather than a universal tendency. In short, the average church has an older church profile than that of HTB. Nonetheless, the attraction for the young would seem to be quite strong. In 2002, Christian Research indicated that 22,000 people under the age of 34 attended Alpha courses in the autumn of 2001.[10]

My initial sample in the pilot study in 2000 found that there was a wide spread of age categories of those taking Alpha, ranging from 16–85 years. Similar data was produced by the national survey. Beyond that, Alpha appeared particularly popular among those between the ages of 30–40 years, a somewhat older age category than that advanced by HTB. The under-thirties and over-seventies were conspicuously under-represented. As far as the young were concerned, the relative absence of under-thirties, especially the under-twenties, is not good news if Alpha is seeking to win over a new generation of church-goers. Indeed, I found in the survey that most attempts to establish Youth Alpha were unsuccessful (this programme will be discussed in Chapter 12). The lack of interest by younger age groups in Alpha is perhaps surprising, given its accompanying cultural package.

At the other end of the age spectrum, the relative absence of the elderly is probably easy to explain and could feasibly be accounted for by physical incapacity especially in the light of the sheer endurance of an Alpha course for some older people. Indeed, as we have already seen (Chapter 4) it was the more elderly respondents who were likely to see this as the main disadvantage of Alpha. Its contemporary form of presentation, in fact the entire cultural package, could be alienating to older people just as it is more attractive to the young. Several course leaders that I spoke to expressed the view that the course did not work for older people; they might sign up but soon dropped out.

Some older people that I interviewed appeared to struggle with this cultural dimension. Helen, a woman in her early seventies, stated:

> Yes. Alpha is orientated to the young. This meant a period of adaptation for me.

Albert, of the same age group also had a difficulty with the course:

> I was not at first endeared to Alpha because it was too slick and obviously aimed at a younger generation.

It was also clear that the older generation of people already in the church often disliked and even objected to Alpha on theological grounds, namely its charismatic element.

Of the people who could be described as middle-aged, those between 40 and 60, the sample of Alpha course guests indicated a higher proportion of individuals not in the faith but who might be depicted as part of that small constituency of 'earnest seekers' or others who were returning to church life after several years of absence. Alpha may be a way back for those wishing to return to the fold in mid-life, perhaps after they have settled down into secure patterns of work and social life, particularly after their children have left home.

In some respects the attraction to distinct social groupings endorses extant academic findings regarding degrees of religiosity through the life course. As far as the latter is concerned there is probably a great deal to concur with Richter and Francis' findings of when and why people leave the churches. A large component of church-leavers, they discovered, are those who give up in their teenage years or early twenties because of other distractions and family responsibilities (Richter and Francis 1998). There is evidence, to be discussed in the next chapter, that some Alpha guests are discovering church life anew via what the course has to offer. Finally, although the age categories I have utilized are somewhat arbitrary, it is the 30–40 group to which Alpha appeals to the greatest extent. It may be that the general cultural milieu of Alpha is

Table 10.5 Alpha guests by age categories (%)

−20	6.4
21–30	7.8
31–40	35.1
41–50	20.0
51–60	17.5
61–70	11.4
70+	2.5
	100

attractive mostly to this age group, while in all possibility there are a greater number of first time 'seekers' to be found among them.

Gender

It is perhaps in the area of gender where Alpha is found to most approximate broad church attendance figures. *Christian England* presents evidence that a greater percentage of church-goers are female (58 per cent in England, 62 per cent in Wales, 63 per cent in Scotland). Women are clearly over-represented on Alpha courses, simply reflecting the fact that they are generally over-represented in the churches. Thus, they are plausibly involved in Alpha for the same reason they go to church on a regular basis. The question is, essentially, why is church attendance higher among women than men?

The link between female over-representation in the churches is not one which has frequently been discussed. Among the more detailed analyses is that of Tony Walter (1990) who argues that the higher rate of church-going for females can be attributed to a search for solutions to a number of negative social and psychological experiences. In short, feelings of guilt, anxiety, and dependency are all concerns that need to be psychologically addressed. Solutions and compensators might also be sought for such deprivations as poverty, low status and lack of opportunities of which a number might be linked to the limitations of female social roles and child-raising in particular.

Table 10.6 Alpha guests by gender (%)

Male	37.5
Female	62.5
	100

Is Alpha providing positive functions for women in some way, perhaps by fulfilling a social and psychological need and, in the long term, encouraging integration into church life? Are these the essential 'rewards' for women? Much remains speculative. Certainly there was little to cull from interviews or questionnaire responses to suggest that Alpha is significant in this way. Nevertheless, while such variables are notoriously difficult to identify, they should not entirely be ruled out.

The greater participation of women in the Christian churches may be part of a wider picture of involvement in religion generally. Women are also over-represented in the majority of New Religious Movements. Many of these new religions appear to provide women with liberating roles, pathways to self-identity transformation and image construction, and provide an alternative source of authority and power through distinct beliefs, rituals and symbols (Cook 2000). The new religions are also attractive in the way that they deal with gender issues. In particular, they venerate female attributes and offer a greater sense of status, liberating women from the constraints of gender roles and sexuality (Palmer 1994).

By way of its theology and culture, it is difficult to argue that Alpha meets many of these requisites. In various respects the course extols quite a conservative attitude to women. Although women are encouraged to be course leaders and, in fact, are heavily involved in Alpha in a practical sense by undertaking the cooking, administration and organization generally, it does tend to advance views of traditional gender roles, especially within marriage, and would seem to reinforce traditions within the church.

While Alpha might attempt to be attractive to 'modern man' its appeal to women is not always obvious. Why this appears to be the case was a question that I put to some interviewees, both clergy and Alpha guests. One interviewee, Brenda, noted the greater number of women on the Alpha course that she had attended. I asked her why she thought that so many women were attracted. She suggested that women were over-represented in the church generally and the reasons why may be the same as to why they join Alpha. She explained:

> Women are more sociable, they like to join clubs and things. There is undoubtedly a greater camaraderie. There was good friendship at the Alpha I attended and this has continued since. You know how it is. Women like to talk. We had a fair few on Alpha courses who had just moved into the area. They liked talking to older women. I think that they were looking for some sort of mother figure. I enjoy talking to younger people too.

Janet, another Alpha guest, focused on a fairly simple explanation for Alpha's attraction to women:

> Why is Alpha more attractive to women? They simply know more about its existence. Women generally have a larger network of friends and contacts than men. They are more likely to talk about it and pass on their experiences. It is all about networks really.

Ethnicity

Finally, as far as ethnicity is concerned, the sample of churches surveyed were unrepresentative of the population as a whole in that their congregations were largely white. At the same time, it is my observation that very few black churches (which are usually of the Pentecostal persuasion) have endorsed Alpha, although they may increasingly be doing so (Church no. 2, a Pentecostal congregation, had a strong non-white background, athough a higher percentage of those who were white joined Alpha courses at the church). The resultant findings were not otherwise at odds with predominantly white churches.

Church Background

It was evident from early in my research that many Alpha guests were already attending a church or had a church background at one level or another – most attended on a fairly frequent basis. The pilot study suggested that this was an indication of Alpha's weakness in that it was failing in its primary aim of reaching the unconverted and unchurched.

On such evidence, I earlier argued that Alpha could best be understood as a movement of revival. Here, there is nothing particularly new. One famous sociological study has shown that the large-scale evangelizing campaigns, typified by those of Billy Graham, had long served this function, that is, that most attendees were already converted (Lang and Lang 1960). Attending such rallies reinvigorated the faithful and functioned more as 'status confirmation rituals' (such as 'altar calls'). In short, they provided a sense of belonging, identity and revival for those already in the faith, or brought back into the fold those who had gone astray.

I concluded after the pilot study that this rejuvenation is what Alpha has achieved, largely through a charismatic form of Christianity. It is clear then, that as a vehicle for revival, Alpha is extending charismatic Christianity to the churches, including those previously untouched by the Renewal movement. According to interviews and questionnaires, it is apparently the charismatic

Table 10.7 Alpha guests by ethnicity (%)

White	86.2
Black	6.2
Asian	2.2
Other	5.2
	100

element which provides a deeper expression of the faith. Charismatic Christianity therefore continues, for good or for bad, to carry on the same function that it has for over four decades in spiritually revitalizing those already in the churches. This has been by far its major achievement, indeed one of its principal aims. Although I still share this view, I have modified it somewhat since most churches will put at least some of their members through an Alpha course as a 'dry run'. In other words, they will try it out with those in the church before going public. This trend may have distorted some of the statistics generated, in that church-goers are over-represented, nonetheless the general findings point to the same conclusion: many Alpha guests are already in the church or, at the very least, have something of a church background.

In this overview of the church background of guests we need to go further. Alpha may assume at least some knowledge and a level of experience of church life. In this respect it could prove attractive because it may be pitched at a suitable level for individuals who might be seeking to return to the church after a period of absence. In the questionnaires respondents were asked: 'Have you ever belonged to a previous church?' Typical responses included:

> As a child I went to a Baptist church every week but faded away.

> Born a Roman Catholic, and that was it really.

> I was a choirboy when young. That was my only reason for going to church.

> As a child I was sent to a Catholic Church. Nothing much happened after that.

One interviewee detailed his experience in this way:

> Yes, I was a regular church-goer during my teens and was confirmed. I used to be in the church choir. I was a lot younger then, although I always believed in God. However, church-going became a chore when I was made to go as a teenager and conversely it was also a refuge from an over-possessive parent. Once I was married and had children my husband and I would still go to church but mostly on special occasions or a duty thing because we hadn't been for a while. Once I decided I wanted to go on Alpha I spoke to my parish priest and tried going to my local church but unfortunately it held too many unhappy memories. We then tried the church we were married in but people seemed more distant. We now regularly go to St James' where we took the Alpha course and feel we belong there although it is some miles from our home.

Many of this category of people, on the evidence of the questionnaires, appeared to be considering returning to the faith (and church) after a fairly long period of absence. Numerous reasons were presented for having giving up. However, the profile was of a cluster of individuals seeking to explore or reconsider their faith in later life (see Table 10.8).

Table 10.8 Church background at time of taking Alpha course (%)

Already in church which is running course	57.8
On fringes of church which is running course	13.6
Agnostics with some experience of church life	16.3
No church experience, non-believers	8.0
Belonging to other churches	4.3
	100

Table 10.9 Unchurched guests' previous church experience at time of taking Alpha course (%)

None	69.1
Attended church as child only	18.5
Left as teenager	12.7
	100

Summary

The general picture which emerges in terms of those who join Alpha is that a fairly high percentage of people come from relatively broad social origins regarding occupation and to a lesser extent educational background. If anything, manual occupational groups were under-represented. Ethnic groups are also thin on the ground, while men are also less evident. The young and the old are less likely to be found on Alpha courses. The amount of free time, by way of allowing a greater commitment, is also important for at least some subscribers to Alpha.

In terms of church background there are some overlapping circles according to people's commitment to the faith (and probably their knowledge of it) and their experience of church life. Those at the core are largely already dedicated to Christianity but wish to develop spiritually or to experience a 'refresher course'. In addition, there are a number of prodigal sons (and daughters) returning or considering returning to the faith, probably at a later stage of life. Next are those outside of the faith. What Alpha brings to all of the above categories is a distinct form of Christianity that is essentially charismatic in orientation. Beyond these sets of people are a miscellaneous group of individuals who have a variety of non-religious reasons for being involved. These are themes which will be discussed in more detail in the next chapter.

Notes

1 For an example of one of the earliest post-war studies see Demerath (1965). We should, however, be wary of US studies as applicable to the UK given the cultural differences, not least in respect of religiosity.
2 Barker (1984), Downton (1979) and Ellwood (1979).
3 Heelas (1996).
4 Barker (1992) and Wallis (1984).
5 Bellah (1976) and Wuthnow (1976).
6 Anthony and Robbins (1982).
7 Gordon (1964), Marx and Ellison (1975).
8 Westley (1978).
9 Bird (1978) and Dreitzel (1981).
10 *Alpha News*, March–June 2002, p. 1.

Chapter 11

Is Alpha Working?

Measuring Success

The issue of who joins Alpha in terms of their range of spiritual, emotional and psychological needs is related to the much broader concern of whether Alpha is working or not working. This central question is not easy to answer because it ultimately depends on what is meant by 'working'. At the same time, there has to be an acknowledgement that Alpha's principal aims are rather vague and their fulfilment virtually unquantifiable. Despite these difficulties there are several possible dimensions that can be explored and by which we can discuss the success or otherwise of the programme. The first is whether the programme is a suitable introduction to the Christian faith or adequately serves as a refresher course for the already convinced. Secondly, whether it is reaching the unconverted – in other words, is Alpha winning new converts and bringing about the future possibility of the reversal of church attendance decline?

The discussion of Alpha in this book is largely informed by a national survey of courses run by 31 churches, and supplemented by research into Youth Alpha, Student Alpha and Prison Alpha. The level of success in these latter settings will be considered in the next chapter. Our consideration here is Alpha's impact in the churches – the programme's primary focus and concern.

Perhaps we need not spend too much time on the first theme: is Alpha a suitable introduction to Christianity? Not all those within the churches would identify Alpha as the ideal starter package or even suitable for spiritual edification. We have noted already that Alpha has its critics. This should not surprise us greatly given that Christians of different traditions are unlikely to agree on all fronts as to what constitutes 'basic Christianity'. While there are discernible core historical Christian doctrines such as the Trinity, the Atonement and the divinity of Christ, what else may be included in an introductory package is entirely subjective. For the Alpha organizers it is the charismatic element that is obviously to the fore: the charismata, healing, spiritual warfare, and so on. Some would disapprove of this. There is also, as we have seen above, the debate as to what level Alpha should be pitched, raising the dilemma as to what degree of knowledge and understanding of the faith should be assumed of those guests who attend. In that sense Alpha is a bit 'hit and miss' in attempting to appeal to those inside and outside the churches. Simultaneously, we have noticed the middle-class enculturation of

Alpha's self-styled 'introduction to Christianity' which may be alienating to some.

First Impressions

Admittedly, given the number of courses running and the number of people who have taken Alpha, it must be doing something right. Yet the question here still needs to be addressed: has Alpha turned out to be what the guests expected it to be? In short, is there a mismatch between the customers' requirements and the supply-side offers? These are important questions given that most of those dropping out of Alpha courses do so within the first few weeks.

Questionnaire respondents in the national survey were asked 'What were your first impressions of Alpha?'. Just under 30 per cent saw merits in Alpha's format with the attraction of meal–video–discussion and small groups being particularly welcomed. The next largest category, just under 20 per cent, were struck by the friendliness of the meeting – perhaps indicating the attraction of Christian hospitality rather than the format or content of the course. Thirdly, just over 13 per cent respondents indicated a 'mixed reply' – highlighting both positive and negative aspects of the course, many of which were the basis of other response categories such as 'friendly but boring'. Comments regarding the video constituted the fourth and fifth highest categories. Here there were both positive and negative attitudes. The emphasis on the video is perhaps understandable given its visual nature and central position in the Alpha programme. Next came Alpha's simplicity. Among the detailed comments by the guests was the uncomplicated way that the message was put across and the effective means by which the teaching of 'the basics' was achieved.

Those who found Alpha primarily 'boring' in the early stages registered at under 6 per cent. The video or 'Gumbel' were most commonly flagged up by those responding in this way. Others found the discussion dull largely because it was too structured in the hands of course leaders. In short, it did not allow sufficient exploration. Under 4 per cent provided an unqualified positive acceptance: a *very* positive appraisal. This was a surprisingly low figure, indicating that Alpha has some way to go before it is perfected. Such responses were more likely to come from course leaders or new converts.

In relating their initial impressions, respondents sometimes put their views across in more detail. One interviewee, John, stated:

> My wife talked me in to going along but I was quite pleased to do so since I always ask all the difficult questions. She told me what it would all entail and that there would be no commitment expected. I was fairly open-minded and felt that it would give me the opportunity to raise questions about the faith. My only fear was that Gumbel would be like Billy Graham, OTT, over-dramatic, over-doing it. He did a bit, although he was not as bad as feared. Yet, Gumbel did get under my skin. He's a bit over-enthusiastic.

Table 11.1   First impressions of Alpha (%)

Good format	29.9
Friendly	18.1
Mixed replies	13.2
Liked video	12.9
Disliked video	7.0
Simple to understand	5.9
Boring	5.7
Very positive appraisal	3.9
Miscellaneous	2.1
Not stated	1.3
	100

My first impression was pretty much as I expected – all these people keen to convert you and over-doing it with the feel good factor and the Bible.

Not what I expected at all. But then again, its been a long time since I've been to church. Perhaps I should not have expected too much.

Questionnaires and interviews indicated Alpha's tendency to solicit a response, either positively or negatively, at a fairly early stage. Among the more positive responses of guests in the first few weeks were the following:

I had the first chance in my life to ask some questions I'd always wondered about.

It was very friendly and I did not feel left out even from the early stages.

From the beginning it was all very, very interesting, informative, supportive, it made me want to know more.

This was the first time that I felt that I could discuss freely my doubts, fears, etc and still have a good laugh.

It was all quite easy to understand even if you had no previous grasp of Christianity.

It does work for many people. Although I do not agree with all the presentations of the course. It's amazing how people listen to Nicky Gumbel for so long.

There were also more negative initial responses:

Everyone was highly spiritual – a bit off putting at first. I became more comfortable the longer I was there.

At first it was a bit boring. Then, as we started to read scriptures and had discussions, it got better. In time the course really challenged my preconceptions.

> Most of the participants didn't need to be there. The great majority were
> in the church and all were politically correct. I found that a bit daunting
> until I had acclimatized myself.

While the matter as to the adequacy of Alpha as an introduction to
Christianity is only briefly discussed here, I shall return to the question in the
conclusion of this volume and raise a few more pertinent issues.

Coming to Know of Alpha

A second way of marking the success of Alpha is in terms of its outreach – the
number of people who know of Alpha and recognize it as a Christian course.
This perhaps allows the opportunity of gauging the actual or potential
'consumer side' of the spiritual marketplace. As we saw in the Introduction,
the organizers of the programme believe that the course is identified by a
relatively high percentage of people both inside and outside of the church (12
per cent of those asked). In that respect, the poster and advertising campaign
with its familiar Alpha logo would seem to be fairly easily recognizable,
suggesting that advertising campaigns do work. However, there is contrary
evidence. In the nationwide survey I asked how those in the Alpha course
came to know of the programme. Many on the course were already in the
church and most initially became aware of it through the church they
attended rather than through the various forms of advertising.

Since the greater number of guests came to know of Alpha through their
church, this confirmed the fact that the majority were in the faith already and
that the courses were organized by the church that they regularly attended (in
rare instances people subscribed to courses run in other churches, generally
because their own church did not partake of Alpha). In total, over 66 per cent
of the 837 respondents came to know of Alpha in this way. There were some
variations between churches with 30 per cent of guests in one church finding

Table 11.2 How did you get to know of alpha? (%)

	Pilot Study 1999	Main Study 2002
Through my church	69	66
Friends	15	20
Media	13	5
Poster	2	5
Leaflet	1	1
Miscellaneous	1	2
	100	100

out about Alpha by this means, with nearly 90 per cent at the other extreme. Despite this variation half to-three quarters of guests subscribed to the course directly through their churches.

The second most common way of coming to know of Alpha was through a friend or close associate at just less than 20 per cent. The evidence suggests however that many of these respondents were already churched and heard of Alpha through friends in their congregation. The media (either advertising or media reports) and posters were the third and fourth most common way, both at around 5 per cent. Leafleting of homes was responsible for less than 2 per cent of people joining a course. There were variations between churches regarding all these ways of joining a course. At one church nearly 20 per cent of guests were attracted by posters, while at one-third of churches no one was attracted in this way. Despite variations, it is clear from these findings that the aim of the Alpha initiative to move away from social networks to direct advertising has largely failed.

Perceived Advantages of Alpha

Questions in the main survey also attempted to measure the success of Alpha in terms of the programme's perceived advantages and disadvantages.

Good for spiritual development Many interviewees praised Alpha for enhancing their faith. In fact the largest category of respondents, over one-quarter, thought that this was its principal advantage. The great majority of these respondents were already in the churches. The course appeared to bring a deeper level of spirituality especially through the weekly topics on how to read the Bible and those related to the Holy Spirit.

Allows a discussion of the faith The second largest category of respondents, again around one-quarter, believed that the primary advantage of Alpha was

Table 11.3 Perceived advantages of Alpha (%)

Good for spiritual development	27.8
Allows a discussion of the faith	25.7
Non-threatening environment	15.4
Simple to understand	12.1
Provides knowledge of the faith	7.9
No advantages	5.0
Back to basics	2.1
Miscellaneous	2.9
Not stated	1.1
	100

the chance to discuss the faith – a viewpoint expressed by those inside and outside of the church. Respondents welcomed the opportunity to raise issues, although some, through the questionnaires and interviews, complained that there was insufficient time or that the discussion was too structured by course leaders.

Non-threatening environment   While a small number expected the Alpha environment to be intimidating, several respondents commented especially on the programme's user-friendly philosophy and the generally welcoming attitude of the churches involved. Many were endeared to the opportunity to meet people from all walks of life participating in a non-confrontational discussion.

Simple to understand   While some respondents found themselves out of depth on the programme (often causing them to drop out in the first few weeks), the great majority had little trouble understanding what was put in front of them. Scarcely any complained they were being indoctrinated or intimidated into accepting an alien system of beliefs.

Provides knowledge of the faith   Both churched and unchurched guests welcomed the opportunity to broadly discover the faith (which of course included the opportunity for discussion). This is Alpha's raison d'être and, indeed, what the great majority of guests required. Many respondents spoke in terms of 'Alpha making Christianity relevant to daily life' or 'for me, Alpha means getting back to basics'.

   Few were keen to stress the virtue of the whole Alpha format as a constructive, contemporary and relevant package: meal–video–discussion, socializing in general, and a pressure-free friendly environment.

No advantages   A small minority of respondents saw few or no virtues in Alpha. A number in this category dropped out during the course, some continued under sufferance, others still continued but in a more vociferous and confrontational way.

Back to basics   Those who stressed terms such as 'it was good to get back to basics' did so for two broad reasons. Firstly, they welcomed the opportunity to be refreshed in terms of basic doctrine such as 'Why did Jesus die?'. Secondly, others tended to see 'back to basics' as the way Alpha negated liberal teachings that had crept into the churches, including a denial of the virgin birth of Christ.

Alpha's Failings

Supplementing the perceived advantages of Alpha was the straightforward question 'What do you think the major disadvantage of Alpha is?'. There proved to be a diverse set of answers, so many that they had to be placed under more generalized headings (see Table 11.4).

Too long/tiring Complaints that the Alpha programme proved to be too long and boring was most frequently directed from the younger and older age categories, as well as those who felt that they had 'heard it all before'. The latter contingent were frequently drawn from those who claimed that they were obliged to attend by family or friends or asked to do so by their churches. Nearly 12 per cent found the course 'tiring', especially after a hard day's work or family responsibilities. This was not just a response from younger age groups but older people too, many of whom often struggled to attend every week and concentrate for three hours or more at a time. One respondent put it this way:

> It is too tiring. You cannot expect people to have a long day at work or looking after the kids and then turn out for what amounts to a long slog week after week.

Too simplistic As we have already noticed, Alpha faces the problem of finding the correct level in which to 'pitch' itself. For some the level is too difficult, for others too simplistic. Needless to say, the latter were those already in the church, although noticeably there were those outside who thought that it might have been more intellectually demanding. Its over-simplistic approached tied in with issues of boredom. Another frequent complaint was that the rigid structure of the programme prevented the discussion of issues raised in previous weeks.

Video Over 10 per cent of respondents pinpointed the video as the greatest disadvantage with Alpha. It was perhaps the major reason why people regarded the course as boring. Others found it too long or objected to Gumbel's talk and demure, sometimes that his humour wore a little thin. A

Table 11.4 Perceived disadvantages of Alpha (%)

Too long/tiring	43.8
Too simplistic	14.2
Video	11.3
Culture	9.6
Theological component	6.1
No disadvantages	5.6
Boring	5.0
Miscellaneous	2.3
Not stated	1.3
	100

number of respondents would have liked other speakers or other means of 'getting the message across'. In this respect, Alpha's standardization was counter-productive.

Culture   Over 10 per cent of the respondents claimed that Alpha was too middle-class in orientation. Many pointed out that this was most evident in the video. The more discerning saw the cultural bias in the charismatic teachings and practices. A few respondents suggested that there should be different Alpha 'packages'. This would be in respect of the denomination of the church putting on the programme and background of those attending.

Theological component   The most common grievance about the theological component of Alpha was that it promoted only one view of Christianity, one which was charismatic, fundamentalist, and limited in what was discussed. Some respondents felt pressurized into accepting a particular type of Christianity with a number complaining of the over-emphasis on the Holy Spirit. A few respondents from the churches found its attitude too liberal. This was the case with a small handful of Protestants objecting to Alpha's acceptance of Roman Catholicism.

No disadvantages   An uncritical acceptance was most likely to be expressed by those who derived a great deal from the course. Those who had gained 'rewards' at very little 'cost', namely who had been converted, felt sufficiently aided in their spiritual development, or had returned to church life. An uncritical laudation also came from course leaders. While the 'cost' of organization and effort was often considerable, the 'reward' frequently came from the intrinsic satisfaction of running the course and seeing others benefit from it.

Boring   We have already noticed in 'first impressions' that some respondents found Alpha boring and tedious. Others thought that the evening and the entire course just went on too long. A few found the discussions uninspiring. The more educated and those longer in the faith had a particular difficulty here. In regard to boredom, a small number mentioned the discussion groups, in particular, that other guests dominated the proceedings.

Miscellaneous   Under this heading were those who disliked the meals – especially eating in public, and those who took a personal dislike to the course leaders or questioned their ability to lead. Others complained that they were getting little out of the course in general or that after Alpha 'there was nowhere to go'. Some wanted a little more controversy, perhaps with guests from different denominational backgrounds.

These categories of positive and negative responses appeared to cut across all types of churches and the various denominations. If anything, it was the charismatically oriented churches which were more likely to return positive responses related to 'spiritual development' and a 'non-threatening environment'. Those with no/or little charismatic orientation were more likely to speak, by way of a positive response, in terms of 'knowledge', 'simple to understand' or 'enjoyed the discussion'. The latter were also more inclined to have found little advantage in Alpha.

The question on the questionnaire, 'Any other comments you would like to make about Alpha?' allowed respondents to put over their own unsolicited views (see Table 11.5).

The 'any other comments' category attracted little further discussion other than an elaboration of earlier stated 'advantages' and 'disadvantages'. The highest response at over 25 per cent was that those asked would recommend Alpha to others. Given that the majority taking Alpha were already in the church, many would seem to do just that, at least within limited church circles and, to a lesser extent, this was the case with unchurched friends, relatives and work associates.

Why Join Alpha?

The question as to whether Alpha is working necessarily relates to whether or not it satisfies the requirements of the guests. We have already considered the perceived advantages and disadvantages, but on this 'consumer side' we need to know why people were motivated to join Alpha in the first place and whether their needs were satisfied.

The quantitative methods of questionnaires and interviews yielded a good deal of evidence as to why people joined. Those who were administered questionnaires were asked the direct and simple question: 'Why did you join Alpha?'. There were a number of smaller categories of responses which, nevertheless, amounted to a sizeable proportion of answers that did not

Table 11.5 Any other comments? (%)

Would recommend to others	26.2
No further comments	22.5
Has serious limitations	13.8
Insufficiently deals with issues	9.2
Good tool for evangelism	8.4
Too middle-class in culture	5.2
Excellent course	5.2
Problem with theology	2.9
Boring	1.39
Miscellaneous	5.1
	100

directly appear to relate to a clear pursuit of knowledge about the Christian faith or a spiritual journeying. These reasons for joining have not changed since the time of the first Alpha 'National Initiative'.

Running the course   A small group of people attending an Alpha course did so for no other reason than that they were involved in running the course for their church. Sometimes this could bring an imbalance to the composition of Alpha groups. In a number of the smaller churches surveyed half those participating were group leaders.

Advised by church leaders   A similarly sized group claimed that their primary reason for joining Alpha was that they had been advised to do so by their church leaders or had initially taken the course when it was first introduced as a 'dry run' before going public or, as one interviewee put it, 'I guess that I was following the party line'.

Wanted to join 'something'/hospitality/company   A larger constituency comprised those who had attended Alpha because they were looking for something to join and admitted that they could have signed up for practically anything. Included here were a handful of individuals who apparently were pragmatically taking advantage of an Alpha course in order to embrace its hospitality or for company. From this group were drawn the so-called 'Alphaholics' – people who would repeatedly sign up for the course. Hospitality and a free meal was not without an appeal. Here 'rewards' may just about outweigh the 'costs':

> I never say no to a free meal. The disadvantage is being obliged to watch through a dull video.

Greg is a pensioner and already in the church. I asked him why, since he had been a Christian for ten years, he had joined an introductory course in Christianity. He stated that he was encouraged to do so by his church on the grounds that he could learn a great deal from it. However, he was mostly

Table 11.6   When did you join Alpha? (%)

1996	2.6
1997	7.5
1998	10.9
1999	18.5
2000	36.9
2001	18.3
2002	4.9
	100

Table 11.7   Why did you join Alpha? (%)

Refresher course/Spiritual development	51.1
Spiritual searching	14.4
Invited/Persuaded by friends/family	13.9
Wanted to join 'something'/hospitality/company	11.8
Running the course	5.0
Advised by church leaders	3.8
	100

attracted by the prospect of socializing with church members and of meeting people from other churches. 'It was', he explained, 'like a little party every week. Something to look forward to'.

Invited/Persuaded by friends/family   The third largest category of people, some 14 per cent, attending Alpha courses were those who insisted that they primarily did so because they were invited or persuaded by others – friends, relatives or work associates had brought them along. Many in this category admitted that they felt obliged to attend and had no real interest or commitment. Indeed, a number stated that they would have probably dropped out if they had not felt morally beholden to see it through as a result of loyalty to someone they knew:

> I was invited by my wife. She more or less insisted I came.

Spiritual searching   The second largest category had commenced an Alpha course because they either knew of somebody connected with a church or had, on the fairly rare occasion, responded to the advertising campaign of the national initiative. It was this group of people, along with other categories discussed below, who seemed to have joined for what might be interpreted as a genuine motivation to know more about Christianity. Among them were around 5 per cent of respondents who were outside of the faith, had little previous knowledge of Christianity, and largely appeared to be on an earnest spiritual journey. More will be said of this group below.

Refresher course/Spiritual development   The main reason for people joining Alpha, at just over 50 per cent, were those previously convinced of their Christian faith and who were using it as a refresher course. Alpha thus promised a kind of personal spiritual renewal, sometimes after a period of backsliding, scepticism, or disillusionment. Typical responses were as follows:

> You forget a lot over time you know. Or you think you know some of the basics of the faith but take for granted what they mean.

> Just what the doctor ordered to consolidate my Christian faith.

Alpha brings an opportunity to hear experiences and doubts of all age groups and to help each other progress in the faith.

Most of the participants didn't need to be there. They were already Christians and church members. I found that a bit daunting.

I regarded Alpha as part of my spiritual journeying. I am already a Christian but I need to go further in my faith.

'Not for me': Why People Leave Alpha

Beside the question as to why people join Alpha, we may ask why people opt to leave. It may be one thing getting people to an Alpha course, it is another keeping them there. The drop-out rate, estimated by HTB at about 30 per cent, is obviously high. My research took some account of those who left. The situation in one church I surveyed was not untypical. In 1999, it ran two courses: 24 guests were already in the church, 10 dropped out, one claimed a conversion experience and joined the church after taking the Alpha course, and four were never seen again. The fact that only one person was converted may be a reason for rejoicing. However, the question is why people do drop out or, for that matter, endure the course but are not convinced of the evidence and arguments. Is the message irrelevant? Is the Alpha package unattractive? Is the church environment alienating? The evidence of the pilot study, which was confirmed in the national survey, was that a good many are lost in the first few weeks.

It was hard to trace, and even harder to talk to, people who dropped out. As a matter of policy, the great majority of churches surveyed refused to pass on the names and addresses of those who left. Moreover, since churches participating in Alpha courses are instructed by HTB not to chase up those who have left, contact addresses often simply did not exist. Despite the limitations, I did manage to speak to a handful of individuals who forwarded the following reasons for deciding to leave:

Sheer endurance of the course   These people tended to have strong work or family commitments. Some older participants simply found it all 'too much'. Those already in the churches sometimes dropped out because of competing church obligations such as scout groups or organized sports.

Found the environment intimidating   Interviewees who had dropped out frequently spoke of the unfamiliarity of surroundings, problems of eating in public, or feeling obliged to be involved in discussion groups. In this respect 'the disadvantages of Alpha' reproduce themselves in the reason why people left. The 'costs' of involvement were simply too high.

The Church has not changed. It does not inspire   Although Alpha wants to 'sell' an attractive package of Christianity, 'on the ground' it does not always come across as the slick product run at HTB. Often it seems second-rate, run in draughty church halls, and reinforces the negative experiences of some. In this respect, 'first impressions' are important.

Alienated by the Holy Spirit Day   Some guests opted out at this stage, a third of the way through the programme. In many respects it is a watershed – welcoming to some, alienating to others.

Did not like the Bible readings   The early use of Bible readings for those without a Christian background can be a problem, especially if guests are expected to read chapter and verse aloud. The 'cost' of embarrassment or unfamiliarity eclipses any 'reward' of those delving into the faith.

Did not like video   As indicated above with the recorded 'first impressions of Alpha', the emphasis on a visual media presentation is valued by some but not others. After a few weeks the guests are familiar with the format and see a ten-week course as too long and gruelling.

Besides a handful of interviews, I can also relate the experience of one church in regard to Alpha guests dropping out of the course. St Mary's, on the advice of the vicar, had given up the Alpha course after having run it for three years. He felt that it was not working for several reasons when offered to guests outside of the church. Firstly, that it was not 'basic' enough. It was established with the assumption that guests already had some knowledge of the faith. However, the Alpha course leaders found that many unchurched people simply did not have even the basic understanding of Christianity. He provided the example of a young man who was enthusiastic about the course but had very little knowledge. This particular individual dropped out after a few weeks complaining that he took for granted that guests would all be at the same basic level. This proved not to be the case, some had a good understanding, others displayed practically no knowledge. Secondly, the vicar complained that guests from working-class backgrounds had been unintentionally driven off and alienated by the middle-class culture of his church and the Alpha course. Thirdly, he expressed a dislike of the video and wanted church members to give the talk each week. Unfortunately, he had experienced great difficulty in finding suitable volunteers. The vicar noted that those who had a busy working day were also likely to drop out of the course early. For these who attended in the evening, the course had become part of an exhausting endurance test.

Is Alpha Winning Converts?

Is Alpha winning converts? Is this *the* key question? It is clear that many converts are claimed by Holy Trinity, Brompton, through its own courses, while *Alpha News* heavily focuses on those who have experienced conversion and undergone changed lives. The newspaper is full of personal accounts of conversion at HTB and other churches, not just in the UK but across the world. It may well be, however, that HTB is rather atypical, possibly because it has been running Alpha for far longer than other churches and has thus experienced sufficient time to perfect its strategy and establish wide networks of individuals who constitute Alpha guests. It is also probably the case that the greater expertise of HTB and the high profile which it enjoys has led to a larger number of claimed converts than have been achieved by churches in the provinces. I would suggest that it is doubtful whether many local churches, at least in the UK, can provide examples of a significant number of conversions.

Little research has been conducted into converts won by Alpha. I know of only two in-house attempts to do so that have been subsequently reported by HTB. The first, by the Anglican diocese of St Albans in 2001, discovered that about one in six of the people who had taken an Alpha course over the previous five years decided to 'come to faith'. The survey found that of the 6,307 people who had attended Alpha, 1,010 were described as 'conversions'. Of these, 597 went on to confirmation. This seemed to mirror the findings of a similar survey in the Lichfield diocese a year earlier which revealed that 4,687 people had attended Alpha with 992 being described as 'new Christians'.[1]

Few denominations have openly claimed growth through Alpha. One, however, is the Baptist Union. An edition of *Alpha News* in 2002 reported Alpha's role in the growth in some Baptist churches (this was part of a survey carried out into Alpha in 1999 by the BU). More than half the churches running Alpha boasted that their Sunday congregations had increased. One-quarter claimed to be up by 10 per cent. Baptist churches running Alpha also apparently attracted more candidates for baptism. Some 67 per cent of all baptisms in the Baptist Union were performed in churches running Alpha, although those churches made up only 40 per cent of the total. Membership was also allegedly up in 37 per cent of Baptist churches running Alpha.

To these examples can be added the findings of research conducted by some of the churches under study. One church had run courses twice a year for five years, mostly with about 40 guests. It claimed 3 or 4 converts each time around, not always at once but as part of a longer period of spiritual journeying. In this instance, a few Alpha guests went on to be baptized and joined the church some time after attending an Alpha course.

Claiming a high level of success (far higher than any of the others surveyed) was a Pentecostal church in the survey (church no. 10). In the last run Alpha group as recorded in the survey, so the Alpha leader maintained, there were 11 conversions, 7 or 8 people were still considering committing themselves to the faith, 11 or 12 had seen out the course but said 'thanks but no thanks', while 2 or 3 did not stay for the duration of the course. A Baptist church surveyed (church no. 12), had run only two courses with 15 guests attending. A handful of them had started attending church 'quite regularly' according to the course leader, and one or two were considering commitment through baptism.

Table 11.8 shows statistics produced by yet another church not included among the 31 surveyed by the national study. The figures relating to those 'now regularly attending church' are obviously significant. While they do not in themselves suggest conversion, they may be indicative of an enhanced spiritual journeying post-Alpha for previously unchurched guests. In addition there is further evidence here of the high percentage of Alpha guests already in the church or the fringes of it.

Of the 837 respondents returning their questionnaires in the main national study, 47 claimed to have 'become a Christian as a result of taking Alpha'. Table 11.9 indicates the previous church experience of those converted, in short, the number who had previously attended church some time in the past (17 in their childhood, the remainder for a period during their adult life). These individuals were thus returning to the church later in their life.

What is Conversion?

The criteria that many churches and those interviewed seemed to use for 'conversion' were those of making a commitment to the Christian faith in terms of baptism and church attendance. 'Conversion', however, is a slippery

Table 11.8 Analysis of Alpha courses held between 1998 and 2001

Date	No. of guests	In congregation	On fringe of church	Non-church	Helpers/ Leaders	Dropped out	Total	Fringe/Non-church now attending regularly
Sept. 1998	29	21	3	5	10	2	37	3
April 1999	25	8	11	6	10	2	33	9
Sept. 1999	28	15	4	9	6	3	31	3
Sept. 2000	18	7	2	9	14	1	31	10
Sept. 2001	21	5	3	13	10	8	23	too early to tell
Youth Alpha 1999	22	17	3	2	3	–	23	0
Totals	**143**	**73**	**26**	**44**	**53**	**16**	**178**	**25**

Table 11.9 Church background of those claiming conversion

None	11
Anglican	11
Baptist	10
Pentecostal	6
Roman Catholic	2
Methodist	2
Other	5

Table 11.10   Age of those claiming conversion

−20	4
21–30	11
31–40	12
41–50	13
51–60	5
61–70	2
70+	0

Table 11.11   Gender of those claiming conversion

Male	17
Female	30

term and perhaps broader than these criteria might suggest. The typical dictionary definition describes conversion as 'bringing over to an opinion, party, faith, etc; turning of sinners to God; changing into others of different character' (*The Concise Oxford Dictionary*). Implicit in this definition, as in a more popularized account, is the conviction that conversion amounts to a kind of 'road to Damacus' experience. Alpha appears sometimes to work with this definition, other times not. The latter is clear when Nicky Gumbel writes:

> Conversion may take place in a moment but it is part of a process. Jesus used the expression "born again" for the beginning of a spiritual life, and the New Testament speaks about becoming a child of God. While the birth of a child may be one event, there is a much longer process before and afterwards. The Bible uses many other images to represent spiritual growth: some are taken from agriculture, others from the ideas of building or journeying. All these involve a process. (Gumbel 1994, p. 20)

Sociologically speaking, conversion has come to mean different things and to be accounted for in various ways. While notions of conversion as a 'process' feature strongly in the sociological literature, it is interpreted rather differently. One approach sees conversion in very broad terms and defines it as conforming to a new worldview largely as a result of external coercive forces, in other words 'brainwashing'. Sargant's (1957) work on brainwashing of American POWs during the Korean War, inspired early accounts of 'conversion'. Subsequently, a number of academic studies have examined the circumstances under which people may be persuaded to accept religious beliefs and a radically different worldview which was previously alien to them. Here the emphasis has tended to be on the proselytizing endeavours of the religious group to which the individual is exposed to and perhaps eventually elected to join. Such an approach downplays the individual as an autonomous actor searching for a spiritual truth and claims to a subjective spiritual experience.

There are substantial weaknesses with this kind of theory since it cannot explain why some exposed to pressurized circumstances 'convert', while others do not. For instance, Eileen Barker (1984) found that some people were converted to the Unification Church while others failed to be as a result of attending the church's workshops and after being exposed to contracted periods of a unique ideology. The similarities between these workshops and Alpha are striking and are noted in Chapter 7. In Alpha those 'converted' would have been subject to the same 'stimuli' by the way of exposure to teachings, culture and group dynamics. Yet, as we have noted, only a small percentage of the unchurched are won over.

A second set of theories sees conversion as a process which happens over a period of time. Some of these theories were briefly covered in the previous chapter but can be elaborated on here. The earliest work in this respect was probably that of Loftland and Stark (1965) who believed that conversion was a process involving seven requisites:

- Unresolved tensions and contradictions in the life of the convert. The emphasis here is on the individual's personality, experiences and personal problems. Important here is the significance of social class, gender, age, and level of education in framing such experiences.
- An individual will probably be predisposed to coping with their difficulties by reference to religious views of the world. Thus in all possibility they will already have a religious background.
- The individual has a tendency to resolve personal problems through the appeal of religious ideas and beliefs.
- There is the fairly predictable 'turning point'. The would-be convert comes to a crucial juncture or crisis in their life.
- There is the relevance of 'affective bonds' of networks.
- There will be the negation of relationships outside of the religious group. This is easier if the individuals attracted to the group are already socially isolated.
- Finally, the religious seeker is 'converted' and becomes a fully-fledged member of the religious community.

This kind of model suggests that there is a 'conversion type', that because of their personal disposition, life experiences, and social background, some people are predisposed towards conversion. As far as Alpha is concerned it would be necessary, according to this model, to look at the social background and life experiences through in-depth interviews, however this would be a limited task since it would only tell us something about conversion per se rather than just the experience of Alpha courses.

Importantly, those converts won over by Alpha in this survey by no means show all these above variables and if they did so, then with no great consistency. Most of my interviewees were fairly consistent with the findings of Greil and Rudy (1984) who discovered that few accounts of conversion to religious groups indicate that all such variables established by Loftland and Stark are evident. These sociologists, in an examination of case studies of conversion to ten different groups, found that only the 'formation of affective bonds' and 'intensive interaction' with group members seemed to be indispensable prerequisites for conversion. In short, social background and church background, life crisis and life 'turning points' do not constitute constant variables. The decisive variables then, to put it succinctly, are attachment and high degrees of interaction with the group. Alpha's (and post-Alpha group) function here is thus vital in claims to conversion. There is, however, more to consider.

Other sociologists of religion, such as Jim Beckford (1975) in his account of Jehovah's Witnesses, see conversion as a learning process 'skilfully accomplished by actors'. Conversion in this regard is about a progressive enlightenment to accepting a system of 'truths': it is 'achieved' and 'organized'. This comes about through systematic Bible study and interaction with members of the Watchtower organization. The similarities with Alpha are again quite striking. Unchurched guests are introduced over a fairly long period of time to a new culture, are given a systematic Bible study, and are introduced to those who have a distinct worldview and cultural orientation.

An alternative account of conversion is the 'role-theory' model. Here conversion is again identified as a kind of learning process, although the emphasis is more on the interaction with the group's members and the 'model' of a convert presented to those considering joining. The model developed by Bromley and Shupe's (1979) work on New Religious Movements notes that frequently there is no great depth of individual dedication or commitment, feeling of belonging, or intense individual religious experience, while little may be known of the movement's beliefs. Rather, conversion is a 'structured event' arising from relationships with members and roles within the group.

According to this model, one becomes a convert through five stages:

- 'Predisposing factors' such as alienation or social availability.
- 'Attraction' – levels of motivation, and experience of role models in the group.
- 'Incipient involvement' (the group's claims to compliance and greater depth of individual involvement).
- 'Active involvement' (for instance, witnessing, evangelizing, and fund-raising).
- 'Commitment' (which includes the acceptance of a 'master theology' and the submergence into a sub-culture).

This might prove to be the most useful model so far since Alpha, to a great degree, is a learning process. Some of these predisposing factors are clearly evident – social availability, levels of motivation in joining, and exposure to a distinct sub-culture. After taking Alpha some guests might like to become more involved in this subculture, perhaps by attending church or a post-Alpha course.

The problem with these sociological accounts of conversion is that they largely failed to take into account the actor's (convert's) subjective point of view and experience. Thus some such as Snow and Machelek (1984) maintain that conversion is, above all, primarily a change in self-consciousness. Here particular kinds of rhetoric frequently reflect some underlying changes in consciousness and include specific types of language and rhetoric as tools that individuals use to 'achieve' the transformation of self. The person is an active participant in the creation of a 'new self'. Rhetoric is the convert's own account of conversion and is often framed in this way, and is seen as an individual choice. This decision is said by the convert to be beneficial with an emphasis on a wonderful new way of life. Rhetorical indicators include, in Christian jargon, 'coming to Christ', 'knowing Jesus', or 'having Jesus in my life'.

I interviewed several people who came to a conversion experience through Alpha. Some were going through difficult periods in their lives, others were not. Some were on a spiritual journey, others reached conversion almost by 'default' in that they were reluctant guests at first, but then arrived at a point of conversion and commitment. A few could not claim a 'road-to-Damascus' conversion, while others did.

There is, of course, an unqualifiable element of the conversion encounter – the subjective spiritual experience of the individual. This is beyond the scope of the sociological enterprise. All that we can do here is relate some experiences as expounded by the new converts and regard them as one dimension of a broader process.

Some Accounts of Conversion

Among those I interviewed were several people who had undertaken a commitment to the Christian faith. For a few others Alpha seemed to convince them that they were on the correct track. Put another way, Alpha constituted part of the spiritual journeying and may have significantly enhanced it.

Case no. 1 Lucy signed up for Alpha in 2001 after taking the Saints Alive course – a more basic introduction to Christianity. Moving from one to the other she regarded as a 'progression'. Alpha was in line with Christianity as she was beginning to envisage it. After progressing through Alpha she decided to be confirmed in a charismatic Anglican church. She saw one of the benefits of Alpha as broadly reflecting her view of Christianity, although she enjoyed being with people from different denominations with contrasting thoughts and varying traditions.

As a student in the 1970s, Lucy had studied a degree in sociology and welcomed the opportunity to be interviewed on the subject of Alpha. Over the last few years she had come to think about life and all the familiar existential questions such as 'Why am I here?' and 'Where am I going?'. These became more important to her as her family grew up and she had more time to herself. In her own words she 'just drifted into believing'. Lucy's parents were, in her account, 'believers' but did not attend church. Nevertheless she had some experience of church life. She was married in church, where her husband was a non-practising Roman Catholic, although she occasionally attended Catholic services with him.

Lucy regarded Alpha as part of a spiritual journey where she valued learning about other people's faith and experiences and welcomed the opportunity to share ideas. Alpha was, she confided, a useful course because it compartmentalized certain areas of faith for discussion. Lucy was especially interested in the historical facts behind the gospel such as the evidence of the historical existence of Jesus. Alpha provided a good environment in which to ask questions and Lucy had especially enjoyed the weekend away. However, she found it hard to relate to the healing and ministry part, despite the fact that the teachings on the Holy Spirit deepened her faith. Lucy concluded the interview by stating that 'Yes, I was converted by Alpha although I think that I was a believer a long time before I signed up'.

Case no. 2 I spoke to Chris in a telephone interview. In his discussion of conversion he shows the ambiguity surrounding the concept:

> Alpha did not change my view about Christianity immediately. Then after a while I started going to church regularly. I wanted to be confirmed and went to confirmation classes. I was given a lot of support by the church.

Would you say that you have had a conversion experience?

> I have never thought about that, an interesting question. I am not quite sure where I am although Alpha has helped … I suppose I have really. Alpha at the very least encouraged me to read the Bible.

Let me rephrase the question. Would you say that there was a particular day when the truth suddenly dawned on you and that a greater level of spirituality came into your life?

> I don't know about that. I think that I am won over now, partly by force of argument. I would regard myself as a Christian, born-again if you like, but the birth was a long and difficult one.

Case no. 3 Ryan said this of his conversion following his experience of Alpha:

> Once Jesus and the Bible meant nothing to me. I did not know that much about the faith. I was not brought up in the church and I did not go to

Sunday school. However, I am married to a vicar's daughter and I used to have plenty of arguments with him. I did have lots of questions and that's why I joined Alpha. It all came together and I got the answers. After two weeks of being on the course I asked Jesus to come into my life and I have been baptized. My life has been turned around. It followed a difficult year for me. I had a heart attack and took months off of work. Finally I lost my job, then my house. Somewhere in the middle of it I split with my wife although we are back together now. Last week the finance company came for the Porsche. I simply said 'Take it, who needs it?'

Spiritual Journeying

Let us briefly return to the subject of spiritual journeying. So far we have considered Alpha's level of success through notions of conversion. Conversion may be seen as the final stage of a process of spiritual journeying. We may also ask, therefore, whether Alpha has helped others on a quest which may or may not lead to conversion. Questionnaire respondents were asked 'Has Alpha changed your view of Christianity?' (see Table 11.12). To be sure, this question does not of itself imply a spiritual journeying, only that views have changed for better or for worse and if for the better this might include a discernible level of spiritual development. However, respondents were also, more directly, asked what it had contributed towards their spiritual development (Table 11.13).

Those 'unsure' were more likely to be those who had only recently completed an Alpha course and had not made their minds up quite where they were going in a spiritual sense, if anywhere.

What did people 'get out of Alpha' to aid their spiritual journeying? Below, to supplement some of my own findings, are the results of a small survey conducted in one particular church not taking part in the national sample.

Table 11.12   Has Alpha changed your view of Christianity? (%)

Yes	38.2
No	58.6
Unsure	1.5
	100

Table 11.13   Has Alpha influenced your spiritual life? (%)

Yes	55.5
No	32.1
Unsure	12.4
	100

These findings were passed on to me with the permission to publish. It is concerned with weekly sessions – how many attended; the value of the meal, video and discussion; and what themes were regarded as the most useful.

Findings of questionnaire distributed by church not in survey (48 filled returns)

How many sessions did you attend?

Sessions	No. of people
10	16
9	17
8	10
7	3
6	1
4	1

Which session was the most helpful?

Session	No.
Who is the Holy Spirit?/ What does the Holy Spirit do?/ How can I be filled with the Spirit?	21
All	11
Why and how do I pray?	8
Who is Jesus?	4
Does God heal today?	4
Why and how should I read the Bible?	3
Why did Jesus die?	2
How can I resist evil?	2
What about the church?	1

How do you rate each part of the evening? (1–5) 5 high, 1 low

Food	5:33, 4:12, 3:3
Video	5:27, 4:15, 2:1
Discussion	5:25, 4:13, 3:8, 2:2

Are you interested in being part of a further study/discussion group?

Yes: 42, Not yet: 4, No: 1, No response: 1

The view of the course leader at this particular church was that many benefited from Alpha in terms of their spiritual journeying. What proved most effective were the teachings on the Holy Spirit with its strong charismatic twist and answers to the questions 'What does the Holy Spirit do?' and 'How can I be filled with the Spirit?'. 'How to Pray' was also a popular session. Here, 'spiritual journeying' is practically equated with being exposed to charismatic teachings and practices.

Summary

Is Alpha working? I began this chapter by stating that the answer depends on what is meant by 'working'. While there is a fairly high public recognition of Alpha as a Christian programme, it is not entirely clear if there is a widespread understanding of what it amounts to. Thus, preliminary enquiries by the unchurched as to what it all entails may not be substantial. More research needs to be conducted into this area. Given a relatively high profile, it is clear that the number of guests outside of the church is probably low. The greater contingent is already in the church and constitutes committed Christians, although there is a sense in which Alpha brings in those on the fringes of the church – perhaps those who attend infrequently or only on special occasions. This fact was acknowledged by many clergy and course leaders that I interviewed. These are my findings. By contrast, HTB has a more triumphantist attitude towards Alpha's success. Yet this attitude can be supplemented by the findings of a report passed on to me by HTB, *Alpha Initiative Highlights Report* (see Appendix).

Clearly Alpha has impacted UK churches and thousands worldwide on an impressive scale. It has carried its unique culture and arguably a distinct theology to different denominations and church traditions. Alpha is doing some things for some people. It seems to be rejuvenating those already in the church through charismatic teachings and culture. A greater exploration of this tendency will be discussed in the conclusion of this volume. This is the story in the churches – the mainstay of Alpha. But there is more to the story, more to Alpha's reach and impact. It has also sought to reach out to the young, students and prisoners as distinct social categories. How has Alpha fared here? This will be the subject of the next chapter.

Note

1   Lichfield diocese study, *Alpha News*, March–June 2002, p. 2.

Chapter 12

Alpha in the 'Hard Places'

Then the righteous will answer him ... 'When did we see you sick or in prison and go to visit you?'

(Matthew 25: 39)

In 1978, Douglas McBain, a leading Baptist advocate of the charismatic renewal movement, wrote in the *Renewal* magazine of the Spirit's call to the 'hard places'. His contention was that in some notable respects renewal and revival in the churches had its serious limitations. Renewal undoubtedly had appeal to the middle classes but it was clear that certain unchurched social constituencies had scarcely been touched. Evangelism, McBain argued, needed to be directed in earnest to inner-city areas and the under-privileged sections of society (McBain 1978). Those who had little hope in this world did not have much of a stake in the next either. Despite McBain's pleadings and admonishments, renewal has not impacted upon the 'hard places'. No large-scale evangelizing programme devised then or since has effectively reached these social groupings.

As we have seen, Alpha has its appeal to the same people long attracted to renewal, albeit several decades on: to the middle classes and those who can identify with its distinct cultural trappings. But what of the 'hard places'? Does Alpha work in any meaningful sense with those outside of a particular cultural context, especially those who are unchurched? Perhaps the most difficult challenge would be in applying the programme to the lowest sections of society: the poor, the unemployed, and the uneducated.

Arguably, among the 'lowest of the low', so to speak, would be prison inmates. Yet it may be to such marginalized often desperate people that Alpha could potentially appeal, as did the gospel initially and throughout the centuries: to those who are disadvantaged in this world or who have perhaps made a mess of their lives. The gospel *a la* Alpha could bring hope, meaning and solace, and even a means by way which those in prison could reconstruct their lives. The prisons, then, could provide a good measurement as to whether Alpha is working, especially since the programme, or one variety of it, is deliberately aimed at this constituency by Holy Trinity, Brompton.

In this chapter we will look at Alpha in some of the hard places. We begin by considering the impact of the course in penal institutions. The appraisal is based on my research of the programme's application in a number of prisons and focuses on interviews of people who have been responsible for running the course, as well as prisoners that have been, as it were, captive guests. This chapter is not limited however to an overview of Alpha in the prisons. It also looks at another 'hard place': evangelism among the young. In some respects this is a more difficult and complex task since the young are made up of numerous fragmented groups which cut across social class and other divides such as ethnicity and gender. However, it is possible to be reasonably focused on this age group because Alpha certainly sees the need for addressing the gospel to younger people and has developed specialized student and youth programmes. These will be considered below, after an overview of how the programme has impacted in the UK prison population.

Alpha in the Prisons

During a visit to one prison that I surveyed in the course of my research I was informed by the chaplain of the declining importance of the prison chapel in his institution. It was built at the core of prison life over 150 years ago, a time when many of the antiquated institutions now in use were built. At one time the chapel was located at the centre of the 'street' of cells in the main prison, where all the wings converged. Here the prisoners' spiritual and pastoral needs were administered to by the clergy and the chapel was literally at the centre of their lives. In a sense the cells were like the small dwellings occupied by monks in a sobriety since they also converged around the place of worship and were conducive to monastic life in that they were totally cut off from the outside world.

In this particular jail, the chapel and chaplaincy had been relocated to the end of one street, although it still provided fairly easy access for the prisoners. It was no longer the centre of prison life. In other prisons today the chaplaincy can be found in even more peripheral locations. At another prison I visited it was to be discovered tucked away in a portable cabin. Along its edge ran barbed wire. It was a plain-looking building which had nothing about its exterior to suggest its function except for a small sign above the door stating 'chaplaincy'. This peripheral site symbolized the increasingly marginalized position of the Christian faith in the prison and reflected its general social decline in the outside world. Some rather anachronistic throwbacks however remain. One is that component of the Prison Act of 1952 which specifies that those appointed as prison chaplains should be clergy of the Church of England (or the Church of Wales in Wales). Senior chaplains, then, will be Anglican. Roman Catholics and Free church representatives are also to be found and often constitute part of a 'chaplaincy team'. Legally speaking, each new prisoner should be given a visit by their allotted chaplain within 48 hours of his/her incarceration.

The Christian mission in the prisons has undoubtedly declined. In the multi-ethnic society, the religious faiths of inmates from the various ethnic groups are now catered for. Some prisons have the Islamic equivalent (Imams) to the full-time Christian chaplain and there are generally arrangements for the spiritual and pastoral needs of other prisoners of other ethnic and religious backgrounds to be met. There have been further changes too. Once Christianity was the central element of rehabilitation and an important element of control within the prisons. Now, in a world of the therapeutic and of a myriad of programmes of secular counselling, the mortification of the body and the call to repentance has far less significance and application. For evangelizing Christians, however, this is not sufficient. Ways have to be found of reaching the unsaved behind bars. This is true today as it ever was. Enter Alpha.

On paper at least Alpha would seem to be doing well in prisons across the world and enjoys the same near-ecstatic coverage as the standard Alpha courses in the churches, at least in terms of the number of courses run. In 2002, it was apparently administered in over 80 per cent (125 out of 158) of jails and correctional institutions in the UK, compared to a mere 8 courses in 1996. A total of 7,000 prisoners had been through the programme by 2000, although the HTB publication, *An Introduction to Alpha for Prisoners and Caring for Ex-Offenders* (undated), suggests that this figure is as high as 15,000. Alpha, in total, is run in prisons in 30 countries in diverse parts of the world including Australia, Poland, Zambia, and Bermuda. The ambitious aim of HTB, as put forward by the *Alpha for Prisons Training Manual*, is to '(introduce) Alpha into every prison in the world' (Gumbel 2001b, p. 10). To support and extend its reach in penal institutions of all kinds there is an Alpha in Prisons office located at HTB, including its own staff under its director, Paul Crowley.

Like other applications of Alpha elsewhere, the official literature is full of the usual brash triumphantism of its impact in the prisons:

> All over the world prisoners are becoming Christians.
>
> (Gumbel 2001b, p. 11)

> I have absolutely no doubt that Alpha has made a significant contribution to the reduction of crime in society.
>
> (Sir Peter Woodhead, HM Prisons Ombudsman)[1]

The Alpha literature presents plenty of testimonies of prisoners 'coming to Christ', including that of a convert in HMP Dartmoor:

> I became a true Christian 11 months ago after being on five Alpha courses. The first couple of times I only came to have a chat and a cup of tea. But after the fifth one something hit me. Something inside of me said, 'that's you'.
>
> (Gumbel 2001b, p. 47)

The fact that Alpha directs itself to prisons as a distinct evangelizing mission is not, of course, surprising. The call to the hard places has long been part of the Christian mission. At the same time, many prophecies in the charismatic movement over recent years have been predicting mass conversions in the prisons. This is linked to the enduring belief that God often begins revival with the lowest sections of society and, after all, the current revival may be the biggest ever – at least according to the prophecies. One prison chaplain I interviewed, who himself had administered Alpha courses, and was aware of the significance and repercussions of such prophecies, referred to the motivation of many in running Alpha as a kind of 'evangelical masturbation'. In other words, an attempt to force revival and fulfil prophecy. This is perhaps a little unfair to those who would earnestly seek to reach out to the hard places and cater for the spiritual and practical needs of prison inmates. Nevertheless, the point is taken.

The aim of Alpha in the prisons according to Nicky Gumbel is threefold: to win converts, to rehabilitate ex-offenders back into society, and to reduce re-offending. His aim is clear in *Alpha for Prisons* which regards the mission as imperative across many Western societies with their increasing crime rates and where more and more people are incarcerated each year. The publication points out that there are over 65,265 men and women in UK prisons; that the prison population increases by 71 inmates per month; and that approximately 80 per cent of young offenders leaving prison will re-offend and return to jail within two years (Gumbel 2001b, p. 10). Alpha, so its advocates suggest, can save the day by bringing a way to salvation and simultaneously reverse these figures and thus perform a public service. The programme, perhaps not surprisingly, has the full support of the UK Home Office. The question remains however: is Alpha working? Before we address this question something should be said about how the course is organized within such institutions and the sample of prisons that were researched in my survey.

Alpha is administered in one of two ways: either by a local church of a single denomination that is invited into the prison by the chaplaincy, or by ecumenical chaplaincy teams. Both means have their advantages and disadvantages. The former can give a basis of support and follow-up for any new converts whether they remain in jail or leave into the outside world. Chaplaincy teams are, on the other hand, more broad based and can act as a check on the inexperience and perhaps counter-productive over-enthusiasm of those church members coming in from outside. The view of HTB is that local churches and the chaplaincy should work hand in hand and not infrequently this is what happens. Those church members who are sympathetic to Alpha can edge themselves in and spread the wider culture and theology of the charismatic movement. In reality, the relationship is not always easy: theological differences, praxis, and problems of institutional life tend to get in the way.

Alpha runs its own annual training day for chaplains at Newbold Revel Officers Training College. In addition, most international Alpha conferences hold a seminar on Alpha in prisons which focuses on worship, talks (including a model Alpha evening), prayer ministry, and small group training. There is a weight of specialized booklets to be purchased (as well as the rest of the standard Alpha literature), including *Alpha for Prisons: A Training Manual, An Introduction to Alpha for Prisons*, and *Caring for Ex-Offenders*. *Alpha for Prisons* is the key publication and constitutes a fairly detailed manual of how to apply the programme and 'get it right' in a sensitive and difficult context.

There are various ways in which prisoners are made aware of the Alpha initiative. The first is through informal networks which, in many regards, are the mainstay of prison life. Inmates who have taken the course, particularly if they have been converted, are regarded as the best means of reaching others. The central prison notice-board and posters placed in various parts of the prison are other possible ways of informing prisoners. Then there is the 'Alpha Appetizer Event' to which prisoners and officers alike are invited. This is staged by the Alpha team proposing to run the programme, with the obvious setting for the event being the prison chapel. The prison guests are shown the video 'God Who Changes Lives' where Paul Crowley, a small-time youth offender, gives his testimony. He may even go to give the talk in person, accompanied by a team from HTB. If the Appetizer Event is organized by the local church, then one church volunteer to every six inmates is recommended in order to stimulate close contact and interest. The task of the Alpha team, besides the practical task of arranging the rudimentary catering, is to give testimonies, explain the programme and be available for a time of ministry. Each guest is ideally given a Bible and an Alpha manual as part of the 'appetizer'. On completing the course prison guests might be presented with an Alpha certificate.

Alpha could be said to break the McDonaldization mode in the prisons. However, while establishing its own 'model' for prisons, the departure from the standard course is minor. To gain a greater understanding of the modifications and HTB's distinct approach to applying Alpha in such institutions, I interviewed Rachael Robertus, the assistant of Paul Crowley.[2] She explained that the course is not especially customized but that some of the material is adapted according to specific needs. Firstly, Alpha is often 'fast-track' – sometimes reduced to two weeks with courses occasionally running back to back, although the ideal is still to run it over twelve weeks. This is because people may be in prison for only a short space of time. In other prisons it may be a longer course administered once a year. Much depends on the category of a particular prison. Although serving a meal will frequently be out of the question in the institutional setting, a social time of tea and biscuits is encouraged.

Secondly, Robertus explained that although she did not want to make generalizations, it was clear that because of their background (that is, poor, uneducated and possibly young offenders) the attention span of many prisoners would be short. For this reason Alpha leaders in prisons are encouraged to present only parts of the video, perhaps in conjunction with a talk, or to take fairly lengthy breaks between showing the essential parts. Thirdly, inmate guests are ideally separated into groups where they remain for the duration of the course in the usual Alpha fashion. However, security arrangements in the prison may not always allow this so the discussion element may be omitted. While the highlight of Alpha is the Holy Spirit day (rather than weekend), this may change considerably depending on the security category of prison.

The Alpha literature acknowledges that the programme in the prisons is, of course, dealing with a unique clientele. For this reason some interesting innovations are recommended. One is to show clips from well-known movie pictures to illustrate the theme for any particular session. It is suggested that the clip is not explained since this may weaken the impact. The theme 'Why did Jesus Die?' could, *Alpha for Prisons* tells us, include the scene from *The Mission* where Robert De Nero has a huge weight of armour cut away from the natives that he used to hunt for slaves. Alternatively, the final dramatic scene from *Indiana Jones and the Last Crusade*, or even Bruce Willis in *Armageddon* may be shown. The session 'How can I resist evil?' might include *Return of the Jedi* and 'What about the church?' could plausibly show *Mr Bean in Church* as a 'Funny example of church life' (Gumbel 2001b, p. 34).

There are a number of other recommendations. *Alpha for Prisons* suggests that for very small groups singing should be avoided and replaced by a CD of worship songs. A number of particular hymns and songs are suggested, including old favourites to stir the memory, typified by *Amazing Grace* and *When I Survey the Wondrous Cross*. New worship songs from the repertoire of the charismatic movement include *Lord I Lift Your Name on High* and *Blessed be the Name of the Lord*.

HTB also takes the mission to prison inmates beyond the Alpha programme by encouraging churches to support those who have left prison. Adverts can be found in *Alpha News* asking for churches to attend conferences organized by HTB aimed at developing those who are interested in prison ministry or the care of ex-offenders (some 14 per cent of churches involved in Alpha apparently have such a ministry up and running).[3]

Various pieces of literature inform those who wish to be involved. *Caring for Ex-Offenders. A Handbook for Churches* is HTB's manual and is foreworded by the former Archbishop of Canterbury, George Carey. It serves as a handbook to support those who have been converted by Alpha or by some other means while in jail, although it also seems to suggest that prisoners who are not converted and are about to leave prison could be adopted and gradually brought to faith and church life (ideally, of course, through the Alpha programme):

> If the church runs the *Alpha* course, it is an excellent starting point for anyone new to the faith. If someone has done the course in prison, they will feel comfortable with the set-up.
>
> (*Caring for Ex-Offenders 2001*, p. 37)

For the most part, *Caring for Ex-Offenders* is a sensitive, astute handbook which understands the realities of prison life and the complexities of rehabilitation and the issues related to settling ex-prisoners who might be young offenders, drug abusers, sex offenders, or mentally ill. It deals responsibly and intelligently with the matter of integrating non-offenders into church life, working with police and probation services, and in providing practical help in finding accommodation and employment. One recommendation when dealing with someone who has been released is that a support team should be picked on the basis of age, sex and ethnic background. The handbook recommends liaison with police and probation services. It seeks to work with other Christian groups such as the Prison Fellowship, but in doing so spreads its unique brand of Christianity.

Caring for Ex-Offenders appreciates that there may be many expressed fears and concerns about the whole issue of welcoming ex-offenders into the church, and suggests splitting them up in different house groups. The practical needs of the ex-inmates are also sought to be met, such as providing clothes, shoes, arranging housing benefits, and the gift of a Bible. However, there are slightly worrying parts of the publication. Under the issue of why people take drugs, it explains that 'Some of the factors which lead to people taking drugs are spiritual attack, and demonic influences – an important aspect when people are not responding to treatment' (Gumbel 2001b, p. 57).

An Appraisal

I conducted a number of interviews with those who could provide useful insights into Alpha as applied in penal institutions. They included prison chaplains, course leaders from local churches, and prisoners who had attended as guests. I attempted to draw a sample of those associated with different types of prisons in various parts of the country and different categories of prisons or those catering for different types of offenders: women prisoners, juvenile offenders, or those gaoled for sex crimes. The categories of prisons in the UK are as follows: A – prisons with serious offenders who present a potential grave danger to the public; B – local prisons which may relocate prisoners depending on the offence; C – low-level security prisons; and D – 'open' prisons.

While seeking a broad sample there was, however, a certain amount of 'snowballing' in that some chaplains recommended colleagues that I should speak to in other prisons if it was felt that they could provide particular insights into Alpha. I also attended a number of sessions on the course in a sex offender's prison. Most interviews were conducted by phone although two took place within the walls of a prison. Most, but by no means all, of those contacted were prepared to speak about Alpha. Of those who did, the majority preferred to be anonymous. I have not named the prisons where Alpha was researched but the type of institutions were as follows:

Prison no. 1 An average-sized classification B prison in southern England. Although listed in *Alpha News*, the course was not currently being run in this particular jail since the chaplain had some reservation about its format and theology.

Prison no. 2 A small category B local prison in the east of England which exclusively serves the county in which it is located. The prison has run a handful of courses with mixed success.

Prison no. 3 A fairly large prison (just over 600 inmates) that serves as a local C category institution, while also catering for high-security status prisoners covering a large area in the west of England. Alpha has been run in this prison alongside a number of other evangelizing initiatives.

Prison no. 4 A young offenders' institution on the southern coast of England. The chaplaincy that runs Alpha claims 'significant success'.

Prison nos. 5 and 6 These institutions are two small jails under the auspices of a single chaplaincy. One is an open prison with about 150 prisoners, the second has 220 inmates all of whom are incarcerated for sexual offences. These range from paedophiles, to pornographers, to rapists. Some two dozen are 'lifers' for violent sexual offences.

Prison no. 7 A medium-sized B category jail in the north-west of England. It claims a 'mixed success' for the Alpha programme.

Prison no. 8 A large category B prison situated in London. The course is administered by a group of local churches closely linked to HTB.

Prison no. 9 A women's open prison in south Wales. The chaplain has run Alpha but is sceptical about its achievements.

Prison no. 10 An open prison in the eastern part of England. The chaplaincy claims 'a measure of success' with Alpha.

Prison no. 11 A young offenders' institution in the west of the country. The chaplaincy here spoke very enthusiastically about the merits of Alpha.

Is Alpha working in prisons? As with the Alpha courses run in the churches, the course in the prisons needs to be examined carefully and a balanced appraisal at least attempted. As noted, the majority of, but not all, prisons run Alpha. The programme is, as a matter of courtesy, held with the co-operation of the chaplaincy. Even some of the chaplaincies which do embrace Alpha have at least a few misgivings, but many display various levels of enthusiasm. Some are very pleased about the arrival of Alpha. A number of the chaplains who I interviewed praised HTB for its endeavour, level of support, and understanding of the difficulties encountered in the institutional setting of the prison. It was pointed out that HTB, time and time again, has shown its thoughtful application: it has proved effective in delivering the necessary practical and moral support (back-up material requested is likely to arrive in the post the next day).

There were those chaplains who lauded a well-constructed course of evangelism, the cheap material, and the standard of people from local churches who ran the course. There was praise for the handling of the Holy Spirit day, including 'ministry time'. Especially with the support of those Christians who had worked in prisons in a voluntary capacity for some time, the course worked well. For many chaplains Alpha achieved what it claimed to do in teaching the basics of Christianity. One chaplain I interviewed, although critical of certain aspects of Alpha, saw the advantage of teaching simple Christian doctrine to the prison population. The prisoners enjoyed meeting people in the outside world, had no particular Christian grounding at school and had rarely attended Sunday school. Yet, these were men and women with their own needs. Alpha was, in his words, 'filling a gap'. Other chaplains had similar points to make.

Alpha, however, has its limitations in prisons and it is clear that the course faces particular difficulties despite all the hype that surrounds it in such institutions. Some of these are practical restrictions. One chaplain who had run Alpha for two years at his previous prison explained to me that while he did not have a great problem with the course he decided not to continue with it at his current post. He felt that in his experience Alpha was inappropriate for the prison context. It was not sufficiently flexible enough for this environment without radically modifying it beyond what was acceptable to HTB. He warned of the dangers of, in his words, 'what someone has called the McDonaldization of Alpha': that the package is being applied without a great deal of consideration for the prison clientele. For one thing, many inmates in his prison were on remand, which meant that they tended not to stay for any great length of time, thus the course was too long for their needs. Neither, as an over-worked chaplain, did he have the time for a course of Alpha's length, although he was beginning to look at a 'fast track' customized programme. For another chaplain it was the Holy Spirit day that created logistical problems since many prisoners went on home leave at weekends and their family and other obligations were obviously the priority.

In measuring the success of Alpha much depends on the category of the prison and the regime inside any given institution. One chaplain pointed out the practical difficulties of organizing a course for the needs of the whole range of prisoners in some jails. Those in high security cannot mix with other prisoners, while some were locked in their cells at 7 o'clock in the evening and could not attend. A number of prisoners may only eat in their cells, so the Alpha communal meal is excluded from the programme (although HTB has been known to ask for a special dispensation for inmates to eat together in the context of the course). Moreover, chaplains and prisoners have busy timetables and it is not always easy to fit Alpha into a crowded regime. Contrary to what might be expected, prison life can be busy and bristling with activities. There are 'windows' during the day to run the course in many prisons but this is still difficult for prisoners who had their 'performance target' of purposeful activities which usually means occupational work. There are always the unemployed and disaffected but they constitute a limited section of prisoners.

Time restraint is another practical problem. A course leader who had run the programme in both churches and prisons related that he had always attempted to give Alpha guests the best he could offer: the best food, the best hospitality. Prison, however, did not lend itself to this. There were only tea and biscuits provided, while the whole evening was compressed into a mere ninety minutes. Since the video took up half this time, there was little opportunity for discussion – *the* element of the Alpha course that the prisoners seemed to most enjoy. 'It all seemed so second rate', the course leader suggested.

Some chaplains tried to overcome these limitations by improvising. However, the question was then about the *degree* to which there is improvisation to the possible detriment of the integrity of the course. At one prison the Alpha team had stuck to the copyright as much as possible but there had to be modifications for important reasons. While there was ministry in the Holy Spirit day, this was often limited in its application because of the prisoners' personal or psychiatric problems. As it was put to me by one course leader:

> We play down the emotional side of things. We do not create that kind of atmosphere that gets people emotional. It is not helpful in a prison environment. People are away from their homes and friends. They are vulnerable.

A further problem that was frequently mentioned by those who run Alpha in the prisons was the programme's cultural inadequacies. In its standard form it is scarcely conducive to reaching the hard places. One chaplain put it succinctly: 'Alpha's middle-class ethos was not for the lads.' Because of this he had abandoned Alpha and customized a number of alternative evangelizing programmes. They included the shorter *Why Not?* and *Beyond Belief* programmes, both of which are based on video presentations and have different speakers, male/female, black/white, and more relevant themes for the prison setting. Even more appropriate was the video *Top Ten* which discussed each of the ten commandments in reverse order. The chaplain explained that:

> These were successful since they challenged the lads, especially *Top Ten* –
> it is what I like to call 'the original offenders course'. They do not claim to
> be fix-all like Alpha. Rather they show human frailty and mistakes and
> offer the way forward through the gospel challenge.

Then, the chaplain also explained, there was Alpha's over-emphasis on the Holy Spirit. Most people in his experience were converted on Alpha courses through the triumphantist dogma on the Holy Spirit. When tragedy happened and life went wrong they could not cope. This kind of triumphantism is inappropriate in prison where life is far from wonderful and problems cannot be easily fixed. On the subject of the Holy Spirit another chaplain pointed out that his Alpha team had to be careful how they used the Holy Spirit ministry. He had bowed to the persistent request of local churches to run an Alpha course in his prison. He was aware of the dangers of ministry exacerbating the prisoners' emotional problems:

> I asked them specifically not to do the hands on thing. But of course that was precisely what they did. I came in as three of the team were laying hands on a prisoner. He was in a terrible emotional state and this lasted for weeks. Guess who ended up picking up the pieces?

Not all the course leaders used the video presentation. One explained that while there was a mixture of people at the jail where he ran the course, they were far from the type attracted to HTB's culture as projected in the video and inmates found it difficult to associate with the very polished presentation and middle-class culture. It was put cogently by this particular leader:

> HTB may try to show videos of different races etc. in their congregation, but there is no getting away from their expensive clothes and sparkling teeth. Gumbel talks of squash clubs and university friends. We have to reinterpret the video after showing it to prisoners. We need special courses for prisoners. We also warn 'guests' beforehand of what to expect, but just to listen to basic points. It is necessary to explain that we cannot do things like elaborate meals.

The experience of some course leaders differed in many respects however. While the opening video is based on the life and conversion experience of Paul Crowley and is meant to speak from an 'insider's' point of view, some prisoners found it uninspiring. Indeed, a number I spoke to claimed that it was patronizing. At an open prison, by contrast, where middle-class prisoners who had committed 'white-collar crime' of one sort or another were catered for, Alpha was more of an attraction. On the other hand another chaplain was surprised at how well lower-class prisoners took to the video. Gumbel obviously had his own language, but the prisoners soon adapted themselves to it. He pointed out that we should not underestimate prisoners' capability in understanding that Alpha is a specific cultural package.

There were also theological objections advanced by some chaplains that I spoke to. Many were not dissimilar to those encountered in Chapter 5. There were also more specific criticisms. One was a conviction that there was a lack of theology relevant to prisoners. Another chaplain complained that Alpha does not talk about issues that have concerned the church for nearly 2000 years: poverty, sickness and, more recently, the social environment that is conducive to crime. Some of these were the experiences of the inmates. A situation of poverty and psychiatric problems were relevant to the lives of more than a few. Alpha is wide of the mark here.

Another difficulty with Alpha in the prison context was the quality of the teams that administered it. Of course, as much can be said about running the programme outside of prisons. Nevertheless, prisons obviously offer a particular challenge. There were some teams of high quality. One chaplain paid respect to the 'excellent' practice of two team leaders heading a complement of eight from several churches who came in to run the course in his jail. In another prison I was personally impressed by the maturity and warm spirituality of the team, long in the faith and having spent a fair time as volunteers in the prison environment. They understood the needs of prisoners and the specific limitations of Alpha which they actively sought to overcome.

There were dangers however with inexperienced Alpha teams administering the course. A chaplain of one large prison stated that because people in prison were vulnerable he was careful only to have those involved in Alpha whom he trusted. Certainly, there were plenty of local churches who wanted to come in and convert the inmates with some zest, not necessarily through Alpha courses, but he was wary: 'We do not want to use "wild cards", and one church is definitely banned'. For another clergyman it was the charismatic inclinations of some teams which was the main problem. A local church often came in to hold the service on Sunday. The service was, he said:

> ...frequently a bit of a circus, with inmates not quite knowing what to make of the charismatic/evangelical way of doing things. The team often had false expectations about revival in the prison and the course put prisoners' expectations too high.

Some teams were inexperienced and were unprepared for the prison context. One chaplain related:

> This church wanted to come in to do the Alpha presentation. These were local cronies of HTB. I had reservations about letting them in but I agreed to do so. On the Sunday evening the team came in ten minutes late, culturally disorientated and complaining that they had been physically searched and that this was unnecessary because they were Christians. Two were real daisies. One of these seemed particularly dazed after his ordeal and wandered around the prison courtyard in a confused manner mumbling over and over again to himself 'Thank you Jesus. Thank you Jesus'. He shouldn't have been allowed within a million miles of the place.

The key question is undoubtedly – is Alpha winning converts? There is little doubt that Alpha does have its attractions for both chaplains and inmates, perhaps inaccurately described as the 'supply-side' and 'consumers' respectively. The potential customers are obviously of a particular ilk. Often they are desperate men and women, sometimes with acute personal problems and in many cases disowned by their families. Some are in denial, others overcome by grief for what they have done. There are obviously hardened criminals too.

At prison no. 1 some 120 inmates (or one-sixth of the prison population) came to the church services. For most, claimed the chaplain, it was an opportunity to get out of the cell and little more. This was also true at a young offenders' institution where the young men were using chaplaincy activities to give a good impression as their parole dates drew closer. Some might even feign conversion. Similarly, the motivation for joining an Alpha course, as might be expected, was not for reasons of spiritual growth.

According to one course leader, prisoners were attracted for various reasons. Alpha was a recognized brand. Some prisoners were aware of it from the 'outside' and looked at it as inmates. Many obviously had time on their hands and wanted to do anything to relieve the boredom of prison life. Others, as it was put to me, 'were attracted by the cookies and coffee'. Inmates also want to have contact with the outside world, to talk to people and hear about their experiences and take the opportunity to discuss their own problems.

By contrast, some prisoners were seeking something relevant to them, something to believe in, something to make life meaningful. The leader of the Alpha course at the sex offenders' prison was convinced of its merits:

> It undoubtedly works although it is not for everyone. What is particularly useful is looking through the evidence of God and Jesus. Quite a few come along. We have run eight courses. Twenty signed up to the first and fifteen to the last. Only a couple dropped out. What they particularly enjoy is the discussion. They like to be asked their opinion because that is not something which happens all that often.

Another course leader from a local church lauded Alpha in no uncertain manner. Its appeal was across the board to all classes of prisoners, from those incarcerated for only a few months, to 'lifers'. Alpha also allowed them to try to come to terms with the crimes they had committed. A kind of momentum would often build up during the course, one of mutual support and friendship between prisoners. Through Alpha many inmates came to understand how God could forgive them for what they had done. Many however, particularly where the crime was grave, could not forgive themselves. This remained a serious block to proceeding in a spiritual journeying. Nevertheless, over half those who had taken the course continued on their way by undertaking the Bible study course that had previously been run for several years in the jail. Some prisoners had even begun their own prayer group.

Compared to what appears to be the case in the outside world, most prison guests were not typically of a church background, although a few were. At the sex offenders prison, most of those who attended had some faith and were seeking to find out more. Questionnaires were administered by the team and practically all found it useful and strengthened their spiritual commitment. Some wanted Alpha tapes after the course had finished. Others had fallen from grace and were attempting to find their way back. Most of the chaplains and course leaders interviewed could not argue that there was a big demand. Sometimes it was difficult for chaplains to bring together enough prisoners to run a course.

Then there is the problem of measuring 'success'. The claim at one young offenders' institution was that it had been successful, but no figures or examples could be given regarding changed lives or conversions. At a medium-sized prison the chaplain maintained that some prisoners were 'undoubtedly touched and changed'. A handful were converted and displayed 'fundamentally changed lives'. Some are generally moved and interested.

Others, after six weeks or so, say 'it is not for me'. Many dropped out very early in the course. The chaplain saw Alpha as a possible way of enlightening people and setting them off on a spiritual journey but it was not the only possibility. He was open-minded to the needs or spiritual 'blank page' of the prisoners, even if it was Buddhism or New Age that fulfilled such needs.

For those converted there is a particular problem of persecution and ridicule. I interviewed one prison guest, Andrew, who was a Christian convert before attending Alpha. In his own words, he 'came to the Lord while in jail'. As a fresh convert he had sat through the Alpha course. 'It's OK', he stated, 'but it does not go far enough'. He went on to explain that it taught all the basics. However, it did not convince. People may go through the course thinking that they are forgiven, but a real conversion does not often take place. It does not result in changed lives and when the course is over, they often slip back into their old ways. He also confided in me that:

> It is not easy being a Christian here. There is a lot of ridicule. When I first
> let it know that I had become a Christian I had to take a lot of stick. But if
> I did not have my faith, I would fall to pieces.

Another prisoner told me how, after he admitted conversion, a fellow inmate had come up to him, spat on the floor and said 'JC is an FC', turned his back and walked off. The problem of persecution for new and old converts in the prison environment remains acute.

My sample of prisons researched is a small one: less than 10 per cent of all those embracing Alpha. There are undoubtedly success stories. However, I was struck by the remarks of the first prison chaplain I interviewed. On asking what Alpha had done for his institution he gave a sigh, followed by a sardonic laugh. He went on to explain that:

> The Alpha literature gives the wrong impression. I would say that there
> are, how shall I put it, pockets of awakening. It is simply not big time with
> people falling over themselves to get in.

So, how many are being won over? Rachael Robertus at HTB admitted to me that there were no statistics on conversions or altered lives, but there was anecdotal evidence. It did however seem, she suggested, that Alpha was breaking the cycle of re-offending over two years. *Alpha News* also carries many stories of released prisoners returning to the straight and narrow, even if they are not converted.

The reality is that in prison Alpha is still small time. Another chaplain had run three courses and was just about to commence a fourth, the groups ranging from 4–10 guests. He could claim that six had offered themselves for confirmation, one already had a church background and expressed a faith. Another chaplain spoke realistically about conversion: Alpha is more likely to be part of life-long searching than a road to Damascus conversion.

Perhaps to conclude we can look at the experience of one prison which I think is fairly typical of many others. This particular (open) jail was one of the first to put on the course. Alpha had been run four times with different results. First time around 15 prisoners came along and all saw it through to the conclusion. It was, in the words of the church minister who led the team from outside, 'highly successful'. Second time around it was down to only 9 guests. It was 'relatively successful'. The third time it was 'an utter disaster' with no takers out of 400 prisoners – it had reached 'critical mass' despite a high turnover of prisoners. The chaplain had left it for some time before bringing in the fourth course. On this occasion it was given a big send off with HTB representatives attending and conducting the Holy Spirit day. This particular chaplain concluded that there was not a particularly high demand for Alpha in the prisons and probably, in his experience, about the same percentage of uptake in the local village which had roughly the same population as his jail.

Student Alpha

While there has been no specialized Alpha course in the same way that is evident with Youth Alpha (discussed below), students are singled out as a constituency which HTB feels has potential for converts. Alpha apparently is now run in 87 student establishments across the UK including 60 per cent of universities. As with other specialist applications of Alpha, conferences are periodically held at HTB to teach course leaders and inform the 'just looking'. For example, more than 240 people – half of them students – attended the second Alpha for Students conference at HTB in September 2001.

In studying the application of the programme in this context I first interviewed Lizi Cope, in charge of Student Alpha at HTB.[4] There were, she claimed, 150 groups involved in teaching the Alpha programme in universities and institutions of higher and further education. Her role was to develop means of teaching the course in ways that were culturally relevant to students. But these are early days, she insisted, and Student Alpha had been running for only two years. The Student Alpha office had the broad function of supporting the courses running in practical terms, offering advice, sometimes personnel, and even financial help. There were no thoughts towards developing a distinct course for students because it was perceived that the standard Alpha course largely served students well; it had a 'lecture', and provided time for argument and analysis as in the good university tradition. Thus there is no special manual for students; it is merely mainstream Alpha applied to the college and university setting. As yet, HTB did not have sufficient feedback to warrant substantial changes. Some evidence suggested that the courses were going well, others less so. Universities, Lizi explained, were all different and it was difficult to know what were the determining factors for a successful course. Among those perceived to be important were the number of Christians on campus, and whether Christian groups in universities were prepared to co-operate in running Alpha, while the more successful were deemed to be those run by students themselves.

There are three ways of running Alpha in the universities. Firstly, through Christian groups of students on campus. One chaplain was happy to leave its administering to the Christian Union since it was students running it for students. The problem here, as HTB's publicity officer Mark Elsdon-Dew explained to me, is students' commitment to exams, holidays, and people graduating and leaving their institutions. Hence, there was often a lack of continuity.[5] Secondly, via the chaplaincy with the programme being led by the chaplaincy team. Thirdly, a ministry team of a church with a reachout to students. Here students were generally invited to take the course in a local church. In its own way of doing things HTB has a fair few students who are incorporated into mainstream Alpha with 3 or 4 student groups. I had the feeling that it is the latter that HTB prefers. In more than one institution that I surveyed the student Alpha groups had been incorporated into the local churches and had come together for the weekend since it would be 'a change for them' outside of the institutional setting.

An Appraisal

In my survey of universities and colleges seven were selected through a random sample taken from a list of 57 in *Alpha News*: two in London, and one each in Wales, the west of England, the south of England, the north west of England and Scotland.

What are the advantages and disadvantages of running Alpha in the student setting? Jenny, who had twice run Alpha as chaplain of a Welsh university, believed that it was a true and trusted brand name. She was sufficiently impressed as to intend to run it at her new post at another university. Jenny admitted to 'buying into the package' because some students knew it from their pre-university days and she was confident of offering it to 'freshers' because their parents would probably be least likely to have heard of it. While she believed that the format was 'sound' there were difficulties however. She had problems with the Gumbel 'lecture' since students were undoubtedly tired of yet more 50-minute lectures. She wanted to create her own Student Alpha but was not entirely sure in which direction it would go. However, she was convinced that one component of the course would remain: the meal which offered students the attraction of free food.

At her previous university, as Jenny explained, the courses had attracted about 12–15 students, yet she expressed her disappointment that all bar one were either in the church already or on the fringe of it. The drop-out rate was, however, low. Many of these Christian students were not charismatic oriented. This created problems and in Jenny's words a fair number had objections to the charismatic teachings, while the Holy Spirit weekend proved to be 'utterly alienating to some'. While she and members of the chaplaincy team, including a Catholic nun, had no difficulty with it, many of the students were 'freaked out' by the phenomena observable during 'ministry time', and did not know what to expect next.

Other chaplains were unhappy with the charismatic teachings and at least one claimed that the talks on the Holy Spirit 'stuck out like a sore thumb' and unbalanced a course that was otherwise a generally good introduction to Christianity. One particular chaplain had problems with the way that Alpha dealt with certain topics:

> I would not touch the follow-up material like *Searching Issues*. Here, Alpha shows its illiberal attitudes. What about homosexuals? Well, they go to hell. What about believers in other religions? Well, they go to hell too. I'm a liberal fembo type of cleric and have trouble with the way some things are taught. How can I approach these subjects in simplistic ways to students?

Some chaplains I spoke to were only considering taking Alpha on board. A student chaplain at a northern university had never run the course himself and was not sure if his institution had previously run it. Although he had been in the post for only a year, he had studied Alpha, especially its theological content. He believed that it lacked a balance. There was no problem with the charismatic element but it was the only strand of Christianity represented. There was little, he complained, on social issues. Moreover, there was no flexibility to deal with the various Christian traditions. He had students from different church traditions and a variety of church backgrounds. Sometimes this proved a real problem. Alpha did not promise to help in this regard.

Some success could be claimed at the institution in which I work (although Alpha has now been discontinued). I spoke to two students who had been converted by Alpha, and others who had been brought back into the faith. More widely, most chaplains I spoke to could boast of Alpha's success. For example:

> We had one convert. He was already asking questions before he joined Alpha. He took a year off and went to work in the Third World. When he came back he changed his degree from physics to theology. He is now going to enter the Christian ministry.

But Alpha has not always proved successful in institutions of higher education. I contacted the Roman Catholic chaplain at a new university in London. Two Alpha courses had been run two years earlier. In her words, they 'flopped horribly'. Few students turned up and most left before the end of the course. There were various problems. As with many of the newer universities there were several sites which made it difficult to co-ordinate any extra-curricular activity. It was clear that she had some reservations about Alpha, and her Anglican counterpart even more so, especially in promoting 'one sort of Christianity'.

Students seemed to dislike the 'hard sell', so several chaplains complained. This was perhaps surprising given its attempt to ease people into the faith. A chaplain explained to me that other campus evangelizing initiatives had encountered the same difficulty. For example, rock concerts had been set up followed by a Christian evangelizing talk. The students took an instant dislike to this. The university also took in a high number of students from poor backgrounds, foreign students and mature students who were not attracted to the Alpha cultural package. She believed that there was a consumer side: 'students are searching for something but I do not think that it is Alpha or at least in the way that it is presented'.

I also interviewed the chaplain from one London university who had run Alpha for three years. I questioned whether it had worked and, if not, why he no longer ran it. It was, he admitted, partly successful. He explained that 60 per cent of the guests on the last occasion were already in the church and belonged to the Christian Union. Only seven were unchurched although they did see it through to the end. Posters had been put up everywhere but had only resulted in a handful attending out of thousands of students. If it was to be run again, then there would have to be some large attractive event to draw attention to it. The previous course was reduced to eight sessions with 'How to Read the Bible' omitted and only one teaching on the Holy Spirit being used on Holy Spirit day. This particular university also suffered from being spread over twenty sites, so the chaplaincy and Student Union (which had taken some time to reach a trusting working relationship) tried to draw attention to courses being run in local churches. I asked whether students were spiritually searching. The chaplain did not think so on the whole, and conjectured that:

> We live in a grossly materialistic society. Twenty years ago the problem for the evangelical enterprise was trying to bridge the gap between God and man. Now there is the cultural gap, a second bridge if you like. There is the lack of any biblical knowledge and Christian basis among students. Then, they do not know what the questions are. Alpha answers the questions but does not adequately raise them.

The chaplain and members of the Christian Union had sought to improve this by organizing meetings above a pub: 'a pre-Alpha course'. This was used for general discussion and to raise broad issues about the Christian faith, then if people were interested they were taken along to Alpha courses in local churches. The chaplain also used the Emmaus course as an evangelizing initiative but even then only parts of it. Many Christian students, he believed, changed their attitudes in the university context; some became more liberal. Neither Alpha nor Emmaus were sufficiently flexible to deal with the complexity of issues around the faith. The chaplain's wife, the vicar in a local parish, had run Alpha but it proved to be a flop. In its place she put on a course based on the Gospel of Mark. Some of those who had joined had never even heard of such a gospel. How then, the chaplain asked, could people deal with Alpha?

Finally, by way of example, I can briefly mention the experiences of two other universities. I spoke to the female chaplain in a Scottish university. She had been trying to get Alpha off the ground for several years. Although registered in *Alpha News*, it had never run. The reason was not so much the lack of students as guests, but resistance from factions within the Christian Union. She felt morally obliged to work with them. However, one particular group had theological objections and would not comply.

At a southern university the course, according to *Alpha News*, was registered but this was not actually the case. The chaplain had run it elsewhere but not at his current institution. Rather, he used Emmaus along with some very small snippets of Alpha material. His view was that 'Alpha is not theologically complete'. Anything to help people was useful, however Alpha did not have the answer for all human dilemmas. Individual students came to him with personal problems and tragedies. Waving a copy of *Alpha News* at them with all its triumphantism was not useful. The chaplain encouraged people to go to Alpha in the local churches if that was what he felt they needed – those on the fringes of the faith or those who wanted to fully immerse themselves in Christianity. However, many students have bad experiences of organized religion and, he explained:

> Students are miles away from Alpha. It simply is not where most students are at and as far as I'm concerned HTB is very pushy in sending out the glossy brochures. I get very fed up with them at times.

Youth Alpha

According to the Alpha literature, youth clubs and schools, as well as thousands of churches around the world are busily running the Youth Alpha course. Unlike Student Alpha, Youth Alpha has its own specially designed manuals aimed at two age groups: the 11–14s and 15–18s. While the syllabus is broadly the same as the main Alpha programme, it is refined for young people. Also used are the book *Questions of Life* and other distinctive training manuals which give guide-lines on how to communicate the course with its own distinctive gospel message to youngsters.

Analysing Youth Alpha is another way of exploring the broad Alpha programme and its success or otherwise. Yet there is more to the aims of research than that. Alpha Youth plausibly provides indices to the possible future of allegiance to the Christian faith. Research suggests a clear link between age and religious belief which does not augur well for the future. The evidence suggests that belief in God increases up the age scale, as does belonging to religious institutions (Gray and Moberg 1977; Gerard 1985). This is so for various European countries irrespective of other social variables such as gender and social class, and appears to be the case with most Christian denominations. Here the importance of previous religious socialization is imperative. As Peter Brierley (1992) points out, socialization into church life is an important ingredient in sustaining the young in the faith.

In recognizing the difficulties he quotes Reginald Bibby, author of *Fragmented Gods*, a major book on Canadian church life who states:

> As things stand, there will be an ongoing decline in church attendance during the 1990s. The reason is simple: people who attend as adults are primarily people who attend as children. Active churchgoers seldom come out of nowhere; they are homegrown. And the proportion of children being exposed to religious instruction outside the school day has dropped from three in four to less than one in four at present.

Brierley believes that the situation is more or less the same in the UK. We might surmise then, that evangelizing the young remains one of the major challenges of the contemporary church (Brierley 1992, pp. 30–32). However, there is good indication that the younger age cohorts will not, in time, endorse a greater religiosity in old age and this means that the long-term picture appears to be one of continued religious decline, at least in terms of mainstream Christianity. In this respect, Grace Davie (1994) notes that opinion poll data over a period of time in the UK indicates that younger generations are less religious than older ones. Moreover, she notes that not only have the young left the churches, they are, it seems, rejecting even the nominal belief that may potentially grow into a greater religiosity in old age. The findings of my national survey was that in terms of guests there is the relative absence of those under 30, especially the under 20s. This is probably why HTB felt it necessary to have a distinct and separate course for the young and for students.

Youth Alpha does not have a centralized co-ordinator as does its prison equivalent. Neither was it originally really HTB's brain-child and I got the distinct impression that HTB did not quite know what to do with it. Rather it was the invention of an Anglican curate, Chris Noble, who put it together while training for the ministry. Noble had modified the standard Alpha course that he ran with the help of the youth leader at the church. Initially, he had shown only parts of the video, and modified Gumbel's talk for a younger audience or for young people who had parents in the church, making them shorter for 15–18 year olds. He also modified other evangelizing material as part of this package. Interestingly, the part of the original Alpha that is retained is the Holy Spirit day which keeps its entire format.

The *Youth Alpha Manual* is based on Gumbel's *Question of Life* but modified by Simon Jones, a leader of an evangelically-minded church in Pinner, London. The topics covered remain the same as in the standard Alpha programme but are explored through relevant stories and anecdotes. Each topic is simplified and scattered with youth-appealing jargon such as reference to the historical evidence of Jesus that 'another guy reported' or that Jesus did 'amazing things' (John 11.43). The lure of reference to the Bible being full of 'sex scandals', and the fact that the Holy Spirit lives in a Christian means that they will not do such things as 'slagging others off' is further evidence of cultural concessions to youth. Besides these concessions, the underlying philosophy of Youth Alpha appears to be different. It seems oriented more towards evangelism and teaching the fundamentals rather than to discipleship and conversion.

Mark Elsdon-Dew at HTB admitted that his church does not really promote Youth Alpha and for this reason *Alpha News* tends to play it down. Nevertheless, seminars were held at HTB where youth leaders could exchange ideas and consider the future direction of the course. We can note that HTB does not run its own Youth Alpha groups. Cynics might suggest that this is because the church does not have young people of this age category or, more exactly, that many of them are away at boarding school. More recently, HTB has taken Youth Alpha much more seriously and it is being developed by John Brant who is overviewing the programme for the future.

It remains difficult to speculate how widely used Youth Alpha is, especially since HTB does not keep tabs on it in the same way as it does with its other Alpha programmes. Moreover, finding out about Youth Alpha was not simple. Although I had been reliably informed that the programme was being run by 50 per cent of those who subscribed to the mainstream programme, it was difficult to find a list of participating churches and equally difficult to contact leaders of the programme. Nonetheless, I was able to find four churches and a juvenile offenders' institution, as well as an ecumenical initiative who were willing to allow me to research into their Youth Alpha courses. There were limitations, however. In particular, it was difficult to sit in and participate in the same way that I could for mainstream Alpha courses and Prison Alpha.

An Appraisal

Youth Alpha in a United Reformed church   The attraction of Youth Alpha to some churches is perhaps obvious. I spoke to one elder of a United Reformed church about the predominance of elderly people in his church and the conspicuous lack of younger generations to replace them. Alpha was perceived to be a way of attracting the young. Youth Alpha, however, had failed to get off the ground in this particular church. A number of children of church members had volunteered or, in his words been 'persuaded', to attend an Alpha group. They were asked to bring friends along. Some attended but it appears that the course fizzled out before the end.

Youth Alpha in a Methodist church   A leader of Alpha Youth at a Methodist church spoke enthusiastically of its success. Twelve youngsters had been invited, all of whom were associated with the church in some way. They either had friends or relatives in the church. Apparently some were now attending church services or showing further interest by joining the church's youth group.

Youth Alpha at a juvenile offenders' institution   The associate chaplain of a young offenders' institution – attempting to rehabilitate 380 young males – spoke of 'quite a few baptisms' (about half a dozen per year). In regard to the motivation of those who attended Alpha the chaplain explained that 'many are just keen to get out' and that good behaviour (including attending Alpha) was a means of doing so. Nonetheless, a sufficient number of young men seemed interested in the faith and he was running a post-Alpha course. Some even took Alpha over and over again. Many of these 'repeaters' were already converted but Alpha seemed to reinforce their faith in the problem of the institutionalized setting and the difficulty of upholding their faith among wayward youth. On the other hand, repeated attendance also partly trained them to evangelize with other boys. Alpha in this setting was a customized course which also took material from the Navigators programme which is now used in the university setting and which focuses on discipleship, relationships with God, prayer and how to read the Bible. Simultaneously, it took into account the fact that many in this institution were educationally disadvantaged and some seriously emotionally or psychologically disturbed. At the time of communication, there were 14 boys on the Alpha course, four on the post-Alpha programme.

Youth Alpha in Anglican churches   I can briefly discuss the level of success, or lack of it, at two Anglican churches that I contacted. Both had tried Alpha on only one occasion but it failed abysmally. One did not get off the ground, while the other was abandoned after only three weeks.

An ecumenical initiative   I also enquired about a Youth Alpha initiative organized by several churches in a small town as an ecumenical initiative in a Christian café known as Noah's Ark. The young people involved would meet on a Friday evening after the café had closed for the day. As with the adults, most who attended were already in the church, although many of them attempted to bring their friends along. It met with mixed success. The course saw out its duration and seemed to function more like a youth club with many of its usual activities tagged on. Like a number of the churches considered above, those involved here used posters in libraries or schools to attract the young to Youth Alpha. I know of no young people attracted to the course in this way.

Summary

Alpha in the hard places has obviously met with mixed success. To be fair these are early days as far as the respective programmes are concerned and time will invariably see their refinements. Alpha in the prisons certainly has a long way to go, however an adapted version may increasingly appeal to needy men and women in this environment. The youth and student Alpha initiatives will undoubtedly struggle unless they too are able to strike the right chord and mix a meaningful message with the right cultural trappings. It is in dealing with these age categories where Alpha will realize quite how secular a society we have become and the immense difficulty of evangelizing a highly materialistic and worldly culture. There is a long way to go. These categories require niche marketing and the freedom to improvise according to immediate needs. I believe that HTB is aware of the challenge.

I also felt that HTB saw some very real problems with, or at least recognized the uniqueness of, Youth Alpha. In my interview with Mark Elsdon-Dew he indicated that Youth Alpha could work with an inspired youth leadership. Otherwise it was difficult to instigate because of the sensitivity of youth to culture changing so quickly in the contemporary world – youth leaders would have to be aware of such things as the snippets of new films to show, the latest music, and so on. Chris Noble explained how he encountered problems related to gender and age.[7] There were, he claimed, vast differences between 15–16, compared to 18-year olds. The girls showed more maturity and interest, the boys wanting to 'only talk about football'. However, many have developed to lead their own groups which they did more effectively than adults. 'Ministry time' was part of the venture. Noble insisted that in such ministry the young were not surprised to see curious things happening: 'in this post-modern age they were prepared to try it'. The same problems no doubt face student Alpha. For the moment, at least, Alpha does not appear to be a significant vehicle for doing so. This is not good news if Alpha is seeking to win over a new generation of church-goers.

Notes

1   *Alpha News*, November 1999–January 2000, p. 7.
2   Interview with Rachael Robertus, 27 July 2002.
3   *Alpha News*, July–October 2002, p. 8.
4   Interview with Lizi Cope, 2 September 2002.
5   Interview with Mark Elsdon-Dew, 20 September 2002.
6   Interview with Elsdon-Dew, ibid.
7   Interview with Chris Noble, 4 November 2002.

Chapter 13

Is Alpha Homophobic?

The Gay Debate in the Churches

Chapter 5 raised the broad issue as to whether, as some of its critics assert, Alpha is fundamentalist in orientation. In short, the possibility was explored that Alpha constitutes a largely conservative and reactionary programme based upon unswerving dogma put together by a self-assigned Christian elite who insist on their sole interpretation of the Bible as constituting 'basic Christianity'.

I argued in that chapter that Alpha's alleged fundamentalism may be judged by various criteria. I concluded that while it does tend towards a scriptural literalism, a measure of alternative biblical interpretation, usually unspecified, is encouraged at a local level in the churches. Alpha is sufficiently ecumenical as to appeal to all mainline churches with a programme which is by no means all fundamentalist in its theology. At the same time, those who have organized Alpha are inclined to regard themselves as promoting a superior form of faith through a charismatic package of Christianity. Alpha, from this perspective, then, provides the essential 'truths' as interpreted by Holy Trinity, Brompton.

Alpha's attitude towards homosexuality (or perhaps more colloquially 'the gay issue') may reveal much in respect of its fundamentalist or at least conservative outlook. Such possibility is the subject of this chapter. In my brief meeting with Nicky Gumbel he confided in me that gay sexuality had become *the* most controversial issue in the church today and one that Alpha appeared to have particular difficulty in dealing with. This is indicative of the fact that no other current debate, apart perhaps from women's ordination, has divided the Christian community so extensively as the issue of gay rights. In fact, the issue seems to be a fishbone caught in the church's throat that it can neither eject nor swallow entirely. Attitudes towards the gay lifestyle and the lowering of the age of consent now enjoy a greater legitimacy in the secular world. The pressure on the church to embrace a more permissive stance is undoubtedly increasing, while there exists a growing vociferous gay lobby within the churches to parallel the movement in wider society.

Lesbian and gay Christians today can be said to be particularly disadvantaged since the church remains one of, if not the last, great bastions of homophobia (Davies 1975). Even the military, historically that other great bulwark against gays, has sufficiently liberalized its attitudes. Thus it is interesting to see how Alpha handles the subject especially since it appears to

have little problem with women clergy. This chapter overviews the attitude of
Alpha and also includes the testimonies of a number of gay people who have
experienced the course first hand and, as it might be anticipated, where that
experience has proved to be negative.

Firstly, however, the subject of gay sexuality needs to be put into context,
at least as far as the churches are concerned. Certainly, while disagreeing
among themselves on many issues, the controversy of homosexuality appears
to be one where the great majority of more conservative-minded Christians
are united in opposition. At the same time it has to be recognized that within
Christendom the debate regarding the legitimacy of the gay cause is not a
simple polarization of the pros and antis. There are discernibly different
attitudes in the churches today. Indeed, Nugent and Gramick (1989) identify
four basic Christian responses to homosexuality. Between the 'rejecting-
punitive view' of the ultra-conservatives who reject both gay orientation and
behaviour and the 'full acceptance position' of gay Christians and their
sympathizers, are two broad intermediate stances.[1]

One such alternative stance is the 'rejecting-nonpunitive' view which rejects
homogenital behaviour but not the homosexual person. Homogenital acts are
condemned as contrary to human nature. The pastoral response to
homosexual persons includes reorientation where possible, or a life of
complete sexual abstinence. The second mediating stance, 'the qualified
acceptance' view, holds that although a homosexual orientation including, in
some cases, genital expression, can be an acceptable way of living out the
Christian life, it is still somehow inferior to heterosexuality.

The contest between the Christian gay lobby at one pole and their
conservative opponents at the other is significantly more than so much
theological mud-slinging. Influencing this mediating ground and attempting
to forge something of a broad consensus in the churches remains a priority
for both. At the same time, the antagonists attempt to influence the secular
political arena with a discourse that emphasizes 'rights', although these rights
are interpreted differently.[2]

Various conservative Christian groups have organized themselves to
campaign against the extension of gay rights within and outside the churches,
as well as other issues related to what is perceived as the spread of the
permissive society. They include the Christian Institute, Christian Action
Research and Education (CARE), the Maranatha Trust, and the Evangelical
Alliance. Many are frequently registered as companies and charities with a
large and easily mobilized support base. In the UK, at least, some have roots
in the activities of the National Festival of Light that emerged in the 1960s
and condemned what was referred to as 'militant homosexuality' – the alleged
perversion of God-given sexuality.

The language spoken by the conservatives emphasizes liberties, especially in
respect of 'religious freedom under threat', in short, the right to subscribe to a
moral point of view predicated on Christian beliefs. Perhaps more obvious is
a reference to the right of the young to be safeguarded from the 'perversion'

of homosexuality or the rights of the family in terms of the protection of heterosexual marriage. This objective and serious image which the conservative constituency attempts to cultivate for itself is backed up by the quasi-academic use of statistics. For example, 'research' conducted by conservative factions plays down homosexual activity, so that those of the Christian Institute put exclusive homosexual activity at a mere 0.3 per cent of the adult population.[3]

Theologically speaking, gay Christians are, by contrast, largely liberal in orientation. Even before the establishment of a moblized gay Christian movement in the UK those who sought to extend gay rights within the churches found themselves locked in a largely sterile theological debate with their conservative counterparts. Most have embraced a 'higher criticism' with a frequently eloquent theology focusing on Christ's teachings of love and many bring a call to abandon traditional family structures in favour of establishing the more radical community of the church. Much has also focused on an interpretive contextual understanding of the homophobia of biblical times which permits criticism of the conservatives for picking and choosing the sins they condemn. This theological stance, however, has been supplemented by a political activism that seeks to lobby both political institutions and church bodies.

In the UK, the cause of gays within the broad church is largely mobilized by the umbrella organization, the Lesbian and Gay Christian Movement (LGCM). This organization was established in 1976 in order to bring together gay activists from different denominations to ensure strength in numbers and enhance a greater cohesion and focus. Its aims are outlined in its mission statement: to encourage support for Christian gays and lesbians subjected to discrimination within the church; to support the various denominations in re-examining their understanding of human sexuality and to work for the positive acceptance of lesbian and gay relationships; to witness the Christian faith within the gay community at large; and to maintain and strengthen international links with other gay and lesbian Christian groups.[4] There is also a wider agenda which involves a close interface with the secular gay movement both nationally and globally and to advance the cause of promoting gay rights on all fronts. In addition, in the USA and the UK a growing number of 'gay churches' have been established to cater for the needs of gay people.

While the more organized gay and conservative groupings attempt to influence the policies of the various Christian denominations, the position of the churches today regarding the gay issue is a largely ambiguous one. Certainly, the gay cause had made sufficient advance by the late 1990s as to generate something of a backlash. This was epitomized in 1998 when the 750 bishops of the world-wide Anglican church meeting in Canterbury for their ten-yearly Lambeth conference made their harshest condemnation of homosexuality to date. On this occasion a resolution was passed rejecting homosexual practices as 'incompatible with scripture' and that 'abstinence is right for those who are not called for marriage'. The debate was top of the agenda for many participants and was conducted against a background of bitterness and recrimination which one bishop later compared to a Nazi rally.[5]

Despite this backlash, there are fairly frequent reports issued by the major denominations. The great majority have tended to be unclear in their recognition of the value of a gay orientation but at least acknowledge that the controversy cannot be ignored and will not go away. Nonetheless, there has been some mellowing in the attitude of many Christians including a number of conservative factions so that the 'rejecting-nonpunitive' stance has become something of an orthodoxy. Hitherto both homogenital expression and the homosexual condition/orientation were regarded as sinful and prohibited by God. This judgment relied heavily on biblical texts that were conventionally understood as clearly and unequivocally condemning homosexuality. Thus the conservative constituency has historically focused on the significance of a small number of biblical passages related to homosexuality, the meaning of which they regard as clear and whose moral imperatives are asserted as binding on the church today. For the conservatives the emphasis was once based on a moral absolutism. The truth is self-evident and immutable. This position has, however, weakened more recently and a number of conservatives hold that while homogenital expression remains a sin, the homosexual condition/orientation does not. As we shall see, this latter stance is largely that taken by Alpha.

Alpha's Attitude to the Gay Issue

Alpha does not deal so harshly with the subject of homosexuality as some groups that wear the conservative badge. At the same time, those who put the Alpha course together identify the topic as one of the most common objections to following the Christian faith: that homosexual behaviour must be condemned as a 'sin' even if gay people may be treated with sympathy. As we have already noted, the Alpha booklet which engages with such controversies, *Searching Issues*, underlines homosexuality as one of the principal stumbling blocks to the faith. We have also noticed (Chapter 8) that over 6 per cent of respondents in the national survey raised the churches' attitude towards the gay issue as their major objection to accepting the Christian faith.

In the section of *Searching Issues* on homosexuality, 'What is the Christian Attitude to Homosexuality?', Nicky Gumbel presents a statement espousing Alpha's generalized view of the gay issue:

> ... I am conscious of the agony that exists for many people in this area
> ... the Christian community needs to show sensitivity towards those for
> whom their homosexual orientation is a daily struggle and to affirm them
> as human beings loved by God.
>
> (Gumbel 2000, p. 20)

Elsewhere Gumbel says:

> Many ('guests') are still a long way off (a real experience of God) when they began Alpha. Some are convinced atheists, some are New Agers, some are adherents to other religions or cults. Many are living lifestyles which are far from Christian. Some are alcoholics, others are compulsive gamblers, many are living with partners to whom they are not married and some are homosexual in lifestyle.
>
> (Gumbel 2000, p. 26)

As with other conservative-minded evangelicals, those who put Alpha together approach the subject of homosexuality by utilizing both theological and what might be termed 'genetic' arguments. Theological prohibitions and scientific evidence thus become powerful dual planks against homosexual activity (rather than orientation). On the first ground, homosexuality (lesbianism is not mentioned at all in the discussion) is measured in a negative way against the life-long commitment of a man and a woman in an idealized marriage. All sex outside of marriage, whether homosexual or heterosexual, is regarded as a sin.

Searching Issues takes the broad gay liberation movement to task for claiming that gayness is as natural as being left-handed and, without explicitly naming the gay Christian movement, quotes some unnamed source as stating that homosexuality 'is well within the purpose and will of God' (Gumbel 2000, pp. 19–20). The booklet insists that there is no conclusive evidence that genetic or hormonal factors are causative in homosexual behaviour, neither, we are told, is the human body 'designed for homosexual intercourse'. Thus homosexuality is deemed as generally acquired or learned. This does not mean, it is subsequently argued, that the blame lies with the individual: (it is) 'almost certainly not that person's fault' (Gumbel 2000, p. 20).

This line of argument thus plays down moral responsibility as least as far as gay orientation is concerned. The sin is, rather, an 'indirect' result of a fallen world where people are abused and models of homosexual behaviour are increasingly rampant. At the same time gayness is practically designated a 'disease' in that it is in need of 'healing'. Quoting Romans 8:23, it appears that this healing occurs for some in this life and for others in the next:

> ... but we ourselves, who have the first fruits of the spirit, groan inwardly as we wait eagerly for our adoption as sons, the redemption of our bodies.
> (*New International Version*)

Such an interpretation might suggest that some will never be 'healed' of homosexuality in this world. The only alternative, therefore, is to lead a celibate life.

There is a differentiation between gay 'orientation' and 'action' to be found in the Alpha literature. *Searching Issues* points out that nowhere does the Bible condemn homosexual orientation, feelings, or temptation. However, it does condemn the practice. The pamphlet nonetheless distances itself from that argument typical of New Right Christians in the USA that AIDs is a punishment for sin, especially the act of homosexuality (pointing out that 90 per cent of AIDs sufferers are heterosexual). To be more specific, AIDs is not God's personal judgment on sin, rather it is a consequence of sin and stepping outside of God's natural order. Thus, the 'Best way to stop (the) spread of AIDs – (is to) return to biblical standards' (Gumbel 2000, p. 20).

What should the correct attitude of Christians be towards homosexuality? *Searching Issues* argues that homosexual behaviour must not be condoned. Yet, like all other sinners, homosexuals should be welcomed into the church, and someone found with whom they can talk frankly and pray. It follows that they would be welcomed onto Alpha courses. That is about as far as *Searching Issues* goes. The assumption is, however, that active gays and lesbians should renounce their sin and seek healing. Presumably, if healing is successful, then subsequent sexual activity will be heterosexual and within the framework of marriage.

This attitude, as played out in Alpha courses in local churches, has proved to have at least some negative consequences. In my interview with Mary Robins, the 'spiritual director' of St James', Piccadilly, London, she claimed that it was not Alpha courses per se or its content that she was most concerned about and conceded that a great deal within the programme was beneficial especially in terms of introducing people to the faith. Moreover, she related, HTB was evidently aware of how damaging a dogmatic approach could be to the subject of homosexuality. Yet it was how Alpha was carried out on the ground by particular churches and course leaders that could prove particularly harmful. Dogma at worse, and insensitivity at least, invariably caused problems over controversial issues such as homosexualty. Apparently, St James' frequently heard from gay people attending an Alpha course who had been informed that their sexual orientation was unacceptable and should be changed if they wished to become 'true' Christians.[6]

Further evidence arose in another interview with Richard Kirker, the chairman of the Lesbian and Gay Christian Movement. Kirker explained to me that he had received 'a fair number of complaints' regarding their members' experience of Alpha courses.[7] The great majority of those in contact had objected to the harmful homophobic stance taken on the course, not just of the explicit or implicit teachings but the way they were treated as individuals regarding their sexuality.

Case Studies

Throughout the duration of my survey I spoke to several people (all men) who were active homosexuals. They had all been involved with Alpha at one level or another and, interestingly, were all committed Christians and already attended church on a regular basis. They were reached via a notice in the LGCM's magazine. The experiences of three are explored below. Not all were members of the organization. Their names have been changed in order to protect their anonymity.

Case no. 1   Colin is frequently active in administering an Alpha programme. He had his first experience of Alpha having sat through a course several years ago as a guest even though he was a member of a church. Since that time he had helped out on subsequent courses by overseeing the refreshments and conducting other work behind the scenes. Colin is largely in agreement with the aims, teachings and ethos of the Alpha programme although he admitted that he had some major objections to it besides its attitude towards homosexuality. He had attended many 'introduction to Christianity' courses over the years and, by comparison, he maintained that Alpha was too advanced for some people. What was needed was a pre-Alpha course to deal especially with theological issues a little more broadly. Neither did other Christian courses approach issues such as homosexuality with such dogmatism. Colin found Alpha unnecessarily doctrinaire and that one of its drawbacks was the strategy of setting the agenda – treating all subjects in black and white, as so many rights and wrongs.

   Colin is a self-confessed gay Christian but does not make a point of telling the world about it so, as he explained, 'has not really come out' and is certainly not a campaigner for gay rights. He also calls himself a 'fundamentalist' in that he believes in the 'fundamentals' of the faith but is not a literalist in that he fails to subscribe to the view that every scriptural word is infallible. Even though he had undertaken the Alpha course it was not immediately obvious to him that homosexuality was designated a 'problem' area by Alpha leaders. Neither was he aware of it being ever mooted in Alpha courses at his church. He was not sure, however, if the subject was deliberately avoided. In Colin's view topics such as homosexuality should be discussed as a matter of course, not because they may simply arise in conversation in small group discussions.

   The 'left-handed' argument (refuted by *Searching Issues*) was readily utilized by Colin. Gayness, he explained, is no more dysfunctional than being right-handed. As in the instance of being left-handed, a gay orientation could be attributed to many complex factors including genetics and the environment: 'Gay people cannot help themselves', he explained to me. Attempts to 'heal' gayness, he further maintained, were misguided, invariably failed, and were potentially damaging. For many years he had prayed to God to make him 'straight' as a result of the broad church's attitude towards homosexuality and the burden of a felt sense of guilt and sin. God had not answered his prayers so he was left to surmise that 'gay was how God wanted him' and that there must be a divine purpose behind it. Now he simply feels that he has to 'get on with it' as a gay man within the church.

   Colin's recommendation was that Alpha should openly and systematically discuss homosexuality and include the gay point of view. Sex, he explained, is God-given for enjoyment – including gay sex. Persecution of gay people, in his view, tends to make people introvert and neurotic, and alienates them from their faith. In short, the attitude of the church was unsympathetic and harmful. As far as Alpha was concerned, Colin suggested that there should be an opportunity to invite marginalized people along including gays and single parents to put forward their point of view and to achieve a balanced appraisal. This he had experienced on other Christian courses, Alpha was excluding them. He conceded, however, that the organizers of Alpha were unlikely to do this.

Case no. 2   Roy took the Alpha course in the autumn of 1999 as a member of an Anglican church. At the time he felt very positive about the programme and claimed that it helped him understand more of the Christian faith and enhanced his spiritual growth. However, it had a negative effect on how he felt about his sexuality as a gay man. Roy explained that the references to homosexuality in the Alpha courses he undertook were fairly subtle but he picked up on them instantly and they made him feel that his sexuality was wrong. The implicit pressures on him to change his sexual orientation he felt were overwhelming. He even considered speaking to the leader of the course about it and asking for him to pray to become 'normal'. Yet, as Roy explained, he thanked God that he did not go through with this, even if for a time after taking the course he did pray for his gay orientation to be taken away from him and that his 'sinful' inclinations would cease.

After a while Roy sensed that this was not going to happen, so he just prayed for help in dealing with his sexuality, although he admits that he did not really know what he was supposed to have help with. Early in 2001 a series of contacts, via the LGCM, put him in touch with some gay priests in his area who were sympathetic towards his plight. With their help he gradually came to terms with, and then fully embraced his sexuality. Roy explained in his own words that:

> I sensed that God was involved with the acceptance of my sexuality in ways that would be completely contrary to the view put forward by those leaders of the Alpha course.

In January 2001, to coincide with his 'coming out', Roy was confirmed by an Anglican priest who knew he was gay. In his own words Roy claimed that he thanks God for the help that he had received from some people in the church who convinced him to fully accept himself as a gay Christian man:

> I also thank God that the negative aspects of the Alpha course only had some short term effects on me and I did not get dragged into a process of trying to change my sexuality, which of course, would have been very damaging.

Case no. 3   Case no. 3 highlights a research dilemma. I had placed a notice in the LGCM magazine asking for the experiences of gay people on Alpha courses. In one instance this had the effect of influencing the people that I wished to study, rather than recording their views. George, a manager of a Christian bookshop, contacted me by phone. He was about to join an Alpha course but had heard about its attitude towards gays and this was enforced by my research request. A practising Christian, he also has a male partner and was a subscribing member of the LGCM. George is divorced with a young son. He had separated on good terms with his wife when he was honest with himself about his sexually. George's church, of High Anglican tradition, promotes the Alpha course which was held jointly with a Methodist church in the village in which he lives.

George explained that his church was temporarily without a vicar. In the resulting vacuum a charismatically-oriented individual had become increasingly influential and was exploiting the lack of headship and guidance, as well promoting the Alpha course against the wishes of some in the church. George was thinking of joining the course organized at the church but had heard through the grapevine that this particular church member had intended to take an aggressive stance on the gay issue by roundly condemning gay orientation and behaviour. This brought matters to a head for George. He explained to me that he had no desire to be condemned for his orientation and would reject any attempt to 'heal' him. Yet he feared that he might be traumatized by the Alpha course. For the moment he vowed that he would keep quiet until the matter was raised. He finished our conversation by objecting to the fact that there is no mention of the gay Christian movement in the Alpha programme and the alternative theological arguments that it advances. The course is, therefore, essentially unbalanced.

Summary

It is not just some of the guests of Alpha that have difficulty with the way that it deals with gay sexuality. A number of course leaders that I spoke to, if not finding it something of a dilemma, were outrightly opposed to Alpha's approach. An Anglican minister confided in me that it was in dealing with such issues as gays that had turned him against Alpha. Initially, he had warmed to the course since it taught the basics of the faith, but in many respects was illiberal and insensitive. In his words:

> We should not be concerned with whom who is sleeping with whom. Take the issue of gays. I know many gay priests. I am sure that they are born that way. They are lovely people. However, Alpha seems to encourage a kind of evangelical thought police, persecuting those who do not fit in. I am not a gay myself but many gay priests are good friends and colleagues, and good priests too. I do not have a problem with them.

Another clergyman that I spoke to had similar views. He was well placed to talk about the subject of sexuality since he was the chaplain of one of the prisons discussed in Chapter 12, one that dealt with sex offenders. 'It was not so long ago', he explained, 'that practising homosexuals would have found themselves behind bars. We have no one here now in this prison who has been locked up simply because they are a practising gay. The subject of gays is sidestepped by Alpha, as are many other issues. Alpha does not recognize that "Gay is what I am".' The chaplain subscribed, after what he claimed was much study, to the complexity of the genetic viewpoint – arguing that the scientific evidence suggests that 15 per cent of men and 5 per cent of women are gay. This conviction led him to explain to the inmates of his jail that those who put Alpha together had their own view on a delicate subject and that much was open to debate.

How might we conclude on this sensitive subject? To be sure, it is very difficult to sum up since gay sexuality remains a topic of continuing debate in the churches. As far as Alpha is concerned, the programme clearly advocates a sensitivity and understanding towards those with a gay orientation, although it is suggested that, on courses, leaders should 'speak out where appropriate'. Yet its approach is both restricted and simplistic. Advancing a crash course in Christianity for the unchurched may be commendable but in the rush to win souls there is a danger that complex moral issues may be treated in an unsophisticated and hurried way at best, and with bigotry at worse. Dealing with issues in unthoughtful 'packages' may ultimately be damaging to the cause. The above examples are the experiences of those already in the church. There are clearly further difficulties in dealing with non-churched gay people who are seeking to know more about 'basic Christianity'. They may encounter the programme in a local church which lacks a sophisticated, balanced, and tolerant approach. Given the scale of Alpha there are obvious implication here which call out to be addressed. Not all the difficulty, however, rests with Alpha. The attitudes of wider society also have an impact. A course leader related his experience of the gay issue:

> We had a discussion on gays. Some were arguing what difference does it make if you are born that way? Other guests held contrary views. Two older ladies did not like the discussion and refused to talk about the subject at all. They decided to go home early.

Notes

1   There are variations even on these four responses. For instance, many Christians have taken the view that there should be a distinction between what the secular law permits and what the church considers morally acceptable. Others believe that gay Christians should not be excommunicated and that the issue is one upon which Christians can honourably disagree.

2   For an outline of the development of the wider gay movement in the UK see Shepherd and Wallis (1989); and Weeks (1977).

3   Christian Institute, *Bankrolling Gay Proselytism: The Case for Extending Section 28* November 1999.

4   By far the best account of the movement in the UK is Sean Gill's *The Lesbian &
    Gay Christian Movement* (1989). Most of the major denominations in the UK have
    their own caucuses advancing the cause of gay rights. For instance, the Anglican
    church has the Changing Attitude network and the Alliance of Lesbian and Gay
    Anglicans. There are also autonomous church-based organizations such as Safety
    Net – a website offering support for gays, lesbians, bisexual and transgendered
    Christians. Of a similar function is Safe Space that operates at the annual
    Greenbelt Christian Arts Festival.

5   Quoted in *The Guardian*, 11 November 2000. The LGCM's own conference in 1999
    called 'After Lambeth' attracted 270 people including 12 bishops and official
    representatives of 32 dioceses. The conference was intended to act as a spur to
    further action within the Anglican church (*Church Times*, 12 February 1999).

6   Interview with Mary Robins, 8 October 2001.

7   Interview with Richard Kirker, 13 May 2001.

Chapter 14

Holy Spirit Weekend

The Holy Spirit weekend is in many respects the centrepiece of the Alpha programme.[1] It has two principal functions: firstly, to bring a greater integration to the Alpha group which is attempted through a round of pre-organized activities; secondly, to provide a series of teachings on the Holy Spirit which emphasize the charismatic core of the Alpha course. Yet these two days are not limited to the instruction of doctrine since the Holy Spirit is meant to be 'experienced' in a profound way. The weekend is, therefore, deliberately planned, at least ideally, to be held at a particular stage of the course and to coincide with teachings on the Holy Spirit and, as one clergy interviewee suggested to me, 'it brings the course alive'.

By the time the guests are invited on the Holy Spirit weekend they would have had a basic introductory talk on Christianity, teachings on Christ and the atonement, the significance of the Bible and how to read it, how to pray, and how God guides and communicates with the believer. The teachings on the Holy Spirit come next in the form of three talks on overlapping themes that are the real theological substance for the weekend. The programme can, however, be concentrated into just one day's activities, usually a Saturday, as was the case with the majority of the churches where I attended Alpha. In most instances this was because overnight accommodation frequently proved costly, while few people could afford to have an entire weekend free from family or even work obligations. The Holy Spirit day or weekend is also sometimes organized to coincide with later course teachings on healing since some churches believed that it was either a more relevant teaching for the occasion, or that the group needed more instruction and time to bond. The intended effect, however, is the same: to turn some of the theory into practice.

I have attended several Holy Spirit days or weekends. Below is my experience of what was billed as the 'Holy Spirit away day' by the group that I accompanied in 2002. The day brought together all those churches in the town involved in Alpha. It was planned for the first Saturday in November, and seemed to coincided with similar events held up and down the country. The day was built up by course leaders from the very beginning of the programme and was awaited with some anticipation by all those involved. 'This is kind of what it is all leading up to', Mary the course leader had explained a couple of weeks prior to the Holy Spirit day. These are merely my experiences of the day's events, although I did include some feedback from others who attended as guests.

Welcome and Songs

I had told the course leaders that there was a good chance that I could not attend the Holy Spirit day because I was hosting a family visit, however, I informed them that I would let them know either way as a matter of courtesy. This I had neglected to do. Nonetheless, there was a beaming smile and a wave from Mary as I accepted a lukewarm cup of tea that was handed to me when I walked into the church. I fumbled through the printed programme for the day. At the top it read 'Arrive 9.15am for tea and coffee' – I was 25 minutes late. Mary was leading the worship that was already well under way. She beamed at me again. Why she did so in quite the way she did I was later to discover – I had answered her prayers.

The rain had become almost torrential as I travelled in for the day and I thought of several reasons why I should go home. One was that the temperature on the gauge of my car was dangerously high. Then there was the thought of having to deal with 'ministry time' – the centre of the day's events. I had encountered ministry at a personal level on several occasions and had developed something of an aversion to it. Even though I was conducting research as an 'outsider' I knew that I was going to be asked to participate. A refusal would be awkward and embarrassing.

The Holy Spirit day began with an official welcome and I had missed it. Hence, I crept in sheepishly and was just in time for the last praise song that the small gathering of some thirty people were hammering out. I found a chair at the back of the church. The chorus being sung was familiar to me: it was an old charismatic favourite. I knew the words but since singing is not one of my gifts I made little effort to pretend that I could. It probably appeared as if I felt uncomfortable with the proceedings, seemingly cast into this environment for the first time. Unlike many Alpha groups, the one I belonged to did not begin the mid-week evening session with worship thus, so it struck me, the uninitiated Alpha guests would have been thrown into the charismatic worship mode quite unprepared and perhaps alienated.

I looked around me; taking a pencil from my pocket I sketched the layout of the building. This was something that I frequently did as part of my fieldwork. I find it useful to note objects, spaces, and the general layout of a building, which was something that I had learned from a study of anthropology rather than sociology. My neighbour, a large woman dress in a pleated skirt and pink cardigan, was in full voice – watching me with a sense of unfamiliarity and curiosity out of the corner of her eye. I scribbled away on the inside cover of my Alpha manual.

Locations for the Holy Spirit weekend differ considerably from course to course. In my experience they vary from a weekend away at a rural church at the invitation of church members, to a small hotel, or even an animal sanctuary. Wherever it is held, however, the core principle is the same: to have relative seclusion from the outside world. Meals, sleeping arrangements (if over a weekend rather than a day), and all other necessities are usually on site even if there is the odd short excursion to the local pub. For this particular event, the church building of another congregation was selected, but only for the day. Tucked away on the fringes of a small village, the site was both isolated and secluded. The church provided all the necessary conveniences for the event including cooking facilities, rest rooms, and so on.

From my vantage point at the back of the assembled gathering I jotted down a few notes. The OHP projected the words of the songs onto the wall to the left of a large wooden cross. The walls were painted a milky white colour – all the way up to the open ceiling that was supported by polished dark wooden beams. There was an open fresh look about the interior of the building – creating a feeling of space in a rather small chapel. Later I was to discover that it was once the old church school for the Anglican parish. It had very recently become Down Hill Christian Centre – a designation proudly placed across the front door with a New Testament quote beside it. The church was now used by the Christian community in the small village and only had as its rival, the tiny and dilapidated Methodist chapel at the end of the road. The centre appeared to be the only hive of activity in this quiet almost lifeless village.

Having something of an interest in church architecture, I took notice of the main features of the interior. There was not too much to note in this small compact building. Obviously it served various activities. To the left front of the church were the play objects of the village nursery group (providing such facilities was a familiar way of trying to encourage local women into the church). To the centre was the wooden podium where the lay preacher would stand every Sunday morning. To the right was a piano set at an acute angle from the wall. Along the wall were large windows which allowed a glimpse of the grey skies as the rain heavily battered the panes. On the opposite bare and plain walls was displayed a colourful wall hanging claiming 'Blessed be the name of the Lord'.

I sat in the back row of the chairs that were organized in two banks of five rows – some forty chairs laid out with a gangway between them. They were angled slightly inwards so that everybody was able to get a good view of the small television screen. Behind the chairs were laid tables in preparation for lunch, plastic table clothes, untimely Christmas decorations and jugs of water. At the back was the kitchen where three women beavered away behind the closed hatches, and there they stayed for the rest of the day. I counted the people present – twenty-nine in all. Apparently it was a disappointing turnout, at least according to the leaders. Illness and family commitments had taken their toll. I did not know the members of the other two Alpha groups that had joined us. Over two-thirds were women. There were few under thirty years old. No children were brought along. Gathered together were the town's Anglicans, Methodists and Baptists all mixing freely together. The Roman Catholic group did not come along for some reason best known to themselves. They were believed previously to have run their own, exclusively Roman Catholic, Holy Spirit days. Present today were a few people who came from these churches but were not part of Alpha groups. As far as I could judge, there was no one representing the congregations of the local village. The assembled were a uniquely Alpha-oriented gathering.

There were no church ministers present, only a handful of church deacons or the equivalent. The group leaders each organized the activities for the day. Two of them led the worship, a third person, a woman sitting in the front row, would occasionally step up to accompany them for the singing. All in all, the gathered were an outgoing and genuinely friendly bunch of people who obviously all knew each other well. They were mild-mannered in disposition, tempered by an attempt to be rather wacky. Most wore causal dress; many men and a few women wore jeans, others dressed up for the occasion. One middle-aged man sported a black tee-shirt on the back of which there was a depiction of a white dove and the legend 'Free Your Spirit' – very apt for the occasion.

What Does the Holy Spirit Do?

After the singing and short announcements came the first of the four Alpha videos on the Holy Spirit. This was the 15-minute 'Introductory video' in which Nicky Gumbel welcomed those participating and broadly outlined the events for the day. The background against which he spoke was different from the earlier video presentations and was obviously the site of one of HTB's own Holy Spirit weekends. The talk was short and to the point but nevertheless seemed to allow Gumbel to cast his mastery over the events that followed.

Tea and coffee were then served. Many of those present took the opportunity to welcome me, especially if they had not come across me previously. There was no doubting the hospitality. I talked frankly about my research, enquiring who had been to Holy Spirit days before and what people thought of them. The great majority claimed to have already experienced such events, enjoyed them, and were more than happy to be there on this occasion. I also spent some time looking through the literature on the bookstall. Mary, who was thumbing a number of books, recommended those she said were 'more intellectual for clever people like yourself'. My money remained in my pocket since I decided not to buy volumes that I would probably not get around to reading and would just take up space on the book-shelves at home.

We were then called into church by the organizers of the weekend to watch the second video presentation entitled 'Who is the Holy Spirit?'. I had previously noted its content throughout. Doctrinally there was not too much to object to even by the most conservative Protestant or Catholic, or the liberal-minded, but it did seem rather incongruous with the rest of the course, an over-emphasis on one person of the Trinity. The key question for me was, why an entire day set apart to discuss the Holy Spirit?

The video began with a timely reminder of how the Holy Spirit had been neglected by the church in the past. It concluded with the suggestive statement by Gumbel that:

> We live in the age of the Spirit. God has promised to give his Spirit to every Christian.

This followed an account of Pentecost in the early part of the Acts of the Apostles, as if it were all relevant today. At this point teaching on the Holy Spirit took a distinct twist – one to which at least some Christians might object. The personality of the Holy Spirit was given particular stress, so were teachings alluding to His constant activity and irresistible 'power'. As the Alpha manual accompanying the video put it, 'He wants to take control'. In the manual, accompanying the text, there is a cartoon of a man with his arm outstretched, trying to resist an invisible force without apparent success.[2]

The manual also teaches how, in the Old Testament, 'He (the Holy Spirit) came upon particular people at particular times for particular tasks'.[3] In the New Testament, we are told, '... there is a great activity of the Spirit' and that 'At Pentecost the disciples were filled with the spirit and received – new languages – new boldness – new power'. The conclusion was that 'We live in the age of the Spirit'.[4] The emphasis was upon the 'new languages – new boldness – new power' that is available to every believer.

That was about it. Much was rather matter-of-a-fact and doctrinaire. To my surprise and disappointment, there was no discussion group afterwards. Another round of tea and coffee followed and an opportunity to wander around and mix with the group and talk particularly with those that I had not met earlier. At this point I related the story of my late arrival to Mary; how I had problems with the thermostat of the car and how I nearly did not turn up at all. I should have known better. There was a miraculous element here she explained. The entire Alpha group that I belonged to were praying that I would come for the Holy Spirit event. Mary had even fasted the entire previous day – this from a rather oversize lady who admitted to 'liking her food'. I was touched with not a small twinge of conscience. I was destined, with the help of God, to make the journey. This only led, it seemed to me, to increasing pressure to respond to the day's events in the appropriate way, not least of all 'ministry time'. With these thoughts I took my seat and awaited the next video presentation.

Departing from the HTB recommended way of doing things, the third video was shown before the lunch break rather than afterwards. By this point the events, which were concentrated into one rather than two days, all seemed a little rushed and all too much for some people to take in. In terms of the content of the video, there was not a great deal that was controversial, at least until towards the end of the talk when the topic of the charismata was explored – the possibility of speaking in tongues, prophecy and so on which, it was assumed, are part of the normal Christian experience.[5] At this point, as with most of the previous talk on the Holy Spirit, there is a certain amount of suggestibility woven in, particularly the notion that the Holy Spirit is constantly active and hard to resist. This was to be significant for what followed later in the afternoon.

One interesting aspect of the presentation was the short element supporting ecumenism. Within the context of the Holy Spirit Gumbel spoke about unity in the Spirit and that it filled all Christians, whether Protestants or Catholics, Anglicans, Baptists, Methodists, or Pentecostals. To illustrate his point Gumbel related a story (it was not clear if it was true or not) of a bigoted Baptist minister who shared no such ecumenical sentiment. He found an old lady he did not know sitting on her own in the front row of seats in his church. He asked all those there to put up their hands if they were not a Baptist. Bravely she raised hers and was the sole person to do so. He scowled at her and enquired what denomination she came from. She told him that she was a Methodist. 'Why?', he asked rather irked. 'Because my father and grandfather were Methodists', she answered. Still annoyed, he then asked her the following question: 'If my father and grandfather were Baptists what does that make me?' 'A moron?' she replied. The apparent moral of this story was that all those who do not have the ecumenical spirit, and by way of argument, a particular view of the Holy Spirit, are dogmatic and ignorant.

Discussion Groups

After the video presentation there followed the first of two periods set aside for discussion. We divided into four groups based around our weekly meetings. It was decided that this would work better since a greater familiarity had already been achieved and people would feel free to speak openly. One group took to an upstairs room, another to the kitchen. The other two groups, including mine, remained in the church. We gathered around the radiator since the hall was rather cold. Some complained of the low temperature. These dissenting voices were interrupted by Mary's insistence that I once more related the story of the near-overheating car and the miraculous way that God had made it possible for me to attend the day's events.

The content and direction that the discussion group took was a surprise to me. I had expected a broad debate around the earlier videos that we had seen, thus following the standard procedure. Instead, after asking if anyone was 'burning to say anything', which no one was, Mary focused on the spiritual gifts, sticking closely to the script in the Alpha leaders' manual for the Holy Spirit weekend. She insisted that the group would concentrate on 1 Corinthians, chapter 12. 'We are going to do something radical', she told us, 'We are going to read from the Bible'. Evidently we were all to relate a couple of verses from this chapter. Bibles were distributed.

Two people read their sections and that was about as far as the planned readings got because the discussion was taken over by the issue of miracles which then occupied the remaining twenty minutes. I was the culprit in raising this topic, but people seemed to like the opportunity of joining in. All bar two of us, the non-churched, discussed their spiritual gifts and the dangers of misusing those such as healing and prophecy. Two in the group claimed to speak in tongues, others related stories of healing, their own and others. Finally, as the time approached 12.30 we were told to wind down for lunch.

The meal lasted for almost an hour. It comprised baked potatoes with either a vegetarian or meat chilli dish, followed by apple tart or fruit, or yoghurt, then cheese and biscuits. It was all rather good. There was plenty of food. Obviously no expense was spared although an offering of £5 per person was suggested. I selected my table and hoped to speak to people about their experiences of the day so far. It was an opportunity to talk to the one or two genuine guests, to gauge their opinion of Alpha and the Holy Spirit day. However, since I found myself with people from other groups that I did not know, they proceeded to bombard me with questions about myself. In that sense it was not a fruitful lunch hour, although I did get to know more about the church 'scene' in town – how the churches worked closely together and had put joint effort into running a café as a centre of outreach. The ecumenical co-operation of most of the local churches was evident and Alpha was only one such event. Most, it seemed, embraced a rather diluted charismatic-oriented culture and, as with many small towns, those who attended church knew each other with a well-worn familiarity.

Afternoon Events

'Walk or Social Activity' – that was how the hour after lunch was billed. Since no one had another alternative activity organized we set off in the rain which had eased by this time. I joined the party unprepared, without walking boots or suitable attire but with my usual enthusiasm for a ramble. In total, 17 of us emerged rather sheepishly from the confines and warmth of the church, leaving some of the older members behind, along with six women who had volunteered to do the washing and clearing up.

I decided that on the walk, about a mile and a half gentle ramble around the village, I would catch up with two of the three unchurched people in the group to gauge their opinion of Alpha. One, a rather large gentleman, while not claiming a conversion as yet through Alpha, was well on the way and was something of 'a star' in the group. He had bravely ventured into the unknown by saying grace at lunch-time as we all held hands around the table in prayer. I never did get to speak to him.

The second unchurched person was Robert who proved to be an interesting character. On my weekly group he was known as something of a thinker. On talking to him I discovered that he had fairly recently begun a philosophy degree at a Welsh university before his financial situation forced him to give up. He was a psychiatric nurse and due to work that night. He admitted to being a depressive, largely as a result of his marital break-up some fifteen years before. His daughter, also in the group, attended a large local church and had encouraged him to come along to Alpha. He had a good general knowledge of world religions, being particularly impressed by Jainism and other minor religions of the Indian subcontinent.

I pressed Robert on his thoughts and experiences of Alpha as the walk came to an end. We stood outside the church in the rain, as he puffed at his cigarette. Apparently, he had once belonged to a High Anglican church for many years. Then, some five years earlier, it had taken a charismatic direction. He disliked this reorientation intensely and sought out a church that he said was open to eastern mysticism and 'New Ageist' in orientation, although he admitted, 'I have reservations about some of that stuff'. Robert objected, nonetheless, to the way that his Alpha group had so easily dismissed it. This had not, however, alienated him from the church members that comprised it. They had become part of his social life. Having recently moved to the town he would often meet up in a pub with the group leaders and one or two others after the evening church service which he occasionally went along to.

I pressed Robert for his further thoughts of Alpha. He replied that he was 'pleasantly surprised'. He largely liked the content, and was very much endeared to the people. 'Lovely folk', he called them, 'but they do tend to be a bit narrow-minded'. He claimed that he would see out the course but was unsure where he would go next. He trampled his butt end into a puddle as he thought and looked up to the heavens. We decided that, as interesting as the conversation was, we should seek shelter from the rain that now poured down, while it was likely that others would be wondering where we had got to.

We stepped into the church as the worship group lazily played a few songs. People helped themselves to even more tea, coffee and cakes. It was obvious that we were supposed to be in a relaxed mood and suitably endeared to each other. I stood at the back of the church carrying on my discussion with Robert, watching the assembled sing with some detachment. Mary, however, had wandered over towards us and stood close by. I thought that she was listening to our conversation of our experiences of church life. She appeared to be waiting for a moment to interrupt. Handing me a book that I had earlier thumbed through, she explained that she had bought it for me. I was slightly embarrassed and offered to buy it. She refused. Then I offered to read it and give it back to her, but she insisted. This, along with her fasting in prayer for me, was genuinely touching. I was aware however that emotional weakness was not a front that I should be displaying as 'prayers' were now on the agenda. Indeed, my short conversation with her was interrupted by the call to be seated for the last video presentation.

'Ministry Time'

I sat at the back next to Robert. The video was already running. This fourth and final talk, 'How can I be filled with the Holy Spirit?', began by building upon the earlier teachings. Gumbel asked and answered his own question of what it was liked to be filled with the Holy Spirit. All the key New Testament passages were looked at. Much was made of speaking in tongues – that when the Holy Spirit arrived this often happened, especially with new converts to the faith. There was much talk about 'the power' of the Holy Spirit. Gumbel warned beforehand not to be alarmed. He said that he was not suggesting that things would happen, but only that it was right to let people know what *could* happen. There might be those who shook, fell over, or cried, or felt sensations like a warm feeling going up the arm. These were the 'physical manifestations' of the Holy Spirit. As the video came to an end there was a great sense of expectation. I anticipated what would come next. What followed was billed in the programme as 'prayers' but it was 'ministry time' by any other words and as I knew it.

So-called 'ministry time', primarily associated with John Wimber's Vineyard churches, has been one of the principal pastoral events in contemporary charismatic movements for several years. Its attempt at healing has usually been of an emotional form, although physical healing is sometimes addressed. It is the healing component which has survived in popularity while the rest of Wimber's 'power evangelism' is now somewhat discredited. In Alpha, however, 'ministry time' continues to offer divine 'power' and the necessary demonstration of God's presence.

'Ministry time' means administering to the needs of individuals. This frequently involves dealing with spiritual, emotional, and psychological problems. A gathered group of believers (perhaps with non-believers), led by a team of 'experienced' Christians, evoke the Holy Spirit. After a period of time, there will be, more often than not, various apparently supernatural phenomena to be observed – perhaps physical shaking, speaking in tongues, weeping, and claims to healing. In the more spectacular manifestations people may cry, fall to the floor – 'resting in the spirit' – or scream with apparent demonic deliverance.

In order to understand some of the rationale behind the structure and events of the Holy Spirit weekend, particularly its climax in 'ministry time', it is necessary to take in a broader understanding of the thinking behind it. In the first place, there is much that happens in 'ministry time' which should not surprise anyone who has been familiar with the charismatic movement over the last decade or so. In Chapter 2 we noted the late John Wimber's influence on the movement. At the core of Wimber's teachings was the emphasis on 'living out' the acts and commands of Christ through the experiences of the Holy Spirit, including healing the sick and casting out demons. These were the visible 'signs and wonders' that could convince the disbelieving world and bring church growth. This idea was not entirely original since the teachings had long been developed at the Fuller Seminary where Wimber taught and trained. However, he took some of the doctrines and practices further, to the point where he was effectively disowned by Fuller.

Wimber believed that supernatural phenomena could be manifest if God was given room to act via the faith of believers. This was 'a theology of power' that was furnished with a practical expression through 'power evangelism'. He also developed the notion of 'the divine appointment' which means the appointed time at which God reveals His power to an individual or group through the spiritual gifts or other supernatural phenomena. The Holy Spirit could bring signs and wonders, healings, miracles and other manifestations if people were open to them. The secret therefore, is to create the right psychological environment for the Holy Spirit to work. This kind of strategy became very popular in many UK charismatic churches in the 1980s. While the emphasis upon 'power evangelism' and signs and wonders has declined considerably, the pastoral and emotionally healing element remains. So has the practice of evoking the Holy Spirit in which God is asked to minister to those present. It is a practice which engenders a great degree of suggestibility and anticipation.

One of the most vehement critics of Wimber's theology and praxis is Martyn Percy (1996). The main objection advanced by Percy is that Wimber (and those inspired by him) has a rather mechanistic approach to the Holy Spirit, that is, that if certain procedures are followed, then God is expected to work as if He is some intangible force at the beck and call of believers. Moreover, that in preparing the 'divine appointment' – the conditions in which the Holy Spirit works in a human environment – there are various aspects of suggestibility to be considered. This suggestibility is largely observed through the lyrics of songs and choruses (and their mantra-type form), group conformity, and the influence of charismatic leaders which all create an atmosphere which precipitates alleged ecstatic and esoteric manifestations (much of which was typified by the Toronto Blessing). In turn, these 'signs' feed back as a confirmation of the faith of believers and the authority of church leaders.

The church members that I interviewed generally spoke well of 'ministry time' within the context of the Holy Spirit weekend. However, a handful that

I had spoken to on earlier occasions believed that they felt compelled to attend the Holy Spirit weekend and pressurized into responding to 'ministry time'. Others complained of attempts to heal them of emotional problems that they felt did not need to be brought to the surface in public. For some, the Holy Spirit weekend was the point where they had opted out of the course.

On the more positive side, a number of individuals laid claim to receiving spiritual gifts, experiencing healings of an emotional kind and, for one, the claim to a physical healing in the form of a life-long stammer being overcome. One woman maintained that she had conquered her severe jealousy problem and quite a few believed themselves to have been healed of negative memories of the past. However, not all Holy Spirit weekends are so spectacular or noteworthy. Some are quite low key and may be deliberately aimed at being so on the recognition that emotional outbursts and strange manifestations may be alienating to guests from outside the church and those who have not witnessed them before.

Such experiences observed on the weekend away are frequently very personal and subjective. Judgements as to its interpretation and benefits remain equally personal and subjective. Certainly, church leaders and course leaders know what to expect and 'ministry time' was calculated to have impact. As an Anglican clergyman I interviewed explained, ministry time is:

> ... deliberately aimed at getting a feeling of closeness of God. It makes the course mean something – the 'heart stuff' ... it relaxes people, but can frighten others ... it is the core of the course and brings it to life. People are ministered to and God is present. They have a strong sense of being cuddled. The Holy Spirit comes in a special way, usually a gentle way. But what is being said however, is 'you've had the theory of Christianity, now here's some of its proof'.

In fact, what is to be expected may be sown into the minds of those present long beforehand. As one course organizer told me:

> We are always a bit worried about how people will see things .... Before the weekend we give the 'guests' a knowledge of what is likely to happen.

As the prayers finished in our particular group, Mary spoke of what would occur next. She spoke of 'filling' and how this happened when the Holy Spirit was called upon. Two songs were gently sung followed by more prayer. A worship leader spoke quietly: 'Come Holy Spirit'.[6]

We were all seated apart from those people in the back row who stood up with their hands in the air. Most of those sitting down closed their eyes and held out their hands, palms upwards, in anticipation. I noticed how boxes of paper handkerchiefs were strategically placed on the window sills and the alcoves opposite, in case some people felt tearful. The last time I had seen this was during a deliverance ministry several years ago. We waited for what felt like a long time. Quarter of an hour passed. There was great expectation but nothing happened. I could sense the disappointment. There was no calling out, no crying, or physical manifestations, no tongues.

Then a young man in the front row begun gently weeping. Someone ran over to his side, spoke and prayed for him. Others followed with some excitement. He became very upset but was now the centre of attention. Then on the opposite front row one of the female worship leaders reached for the tissues and dabbed a tear from her eye. I reflected on what I knew were her difficult personal circumstances. Meanwhile the young man and three women were in a circle, on their knees, and holding hands. Two or three groups of people were standing in other huddles hugging each other, some in tears.

The male worship leader came across and asked Robert if he wanted prayer. This he did by standing over Robert with outstretched hands and speaking in tongues, although the latter appeared to show a certain amount of detachment. He later told me that he felt obliged to respond to the request for prayer and had no real need. I was asked if I required prayer but quite firmly but politely declined. 'That's OK. That's fine', said the worship leader. Ten minutes later he was back and it was all repeated again. Soon after another person asked me. I politely refused once more.

Finally, as it all began to peter out, I was joined by Mary and two others. I was cornered and surrounded. I was asked if I wanted prayer. I thanked them and declined once more. I think that they felt slightly snubbed. They began to ask questions about my personal circumstances. Obviously, they were trying to solicit some emotive reaction. Was I facing any emotional difficulties? Did I have bad memories of the past? Was I resentful and bitter about things that had happened in my life? I gave them a few details of some practical problems but I gave no emotional response. We talked out the rest of the time and finished on the dot at 4 o'clock. It had all been a bit of an anti-climax. No one was on the floor lying 'resting in the spirit' as often happened in 'ministry time', although the group on their knees continued to 'pray over' each other.

John, a Scotsman in his sixties, sat in front of me slightly to the left. He was the third unchurched member, describing himself as an agnostic. Occasionally he joined his wife at a church service, usually under sufferance. He was sceptical at this point and called prayers no more than 'psychotherapy for those who don't really need it'. His wife, sitting next to him, walked off in a huff and joined the women in the kitchen who were clearing up.

There was a sense of disappointment. Slowly people pulled themselves together, and sat in silence. 'Ministry time' was coming to an end, and so was the Holy Spirit day, apart of course from another cup of tea before we made our way home.

Is Alpha a Cult?

At this point I would ask the question whether Alpha is a cult, especially on the evidence of the Holy Spirit weekend. It would perhaps seem an odd question, but one which is sometimes advanced by its critics – at least by some church leaders whom I have spoken to. But does this claim stand up to scrutiny? The answer is again perhaps 'yes' and 'no', depending on the definition of 'cult'.

Perhaps no category of religion has created so much confusion as the definition of 'cult'. Frequently it is a term interchanged freely with that of 'sect' or a variety of other labels most of which have negative connotations. All such classifications of cults are usually associated with deviant forms of religiosity which, more often than not, are in conflict with their social environment. This generalized appraisal results partly from a widespread public ignorance which associates the cult with dangerous religious movements that embrace a bizarre set of beliefs, and are led by unscrupulous, often psychologically disturbed individuals. Media sensationalizing stories of so-called 'brain-washing', financial extortion, and abduction of members, all add to this rather disparaging picture. While there are certainly cults that may display at least some of these characteristics, they are relatively few. The whole area of cults therefore deserves clarification and a broader assessment.[7]

To some extent the confusion as to the definition of a cult has not been aided by the sociological enterprise. Sociology has defined and accounted for cults in very different ways, largely because they are extremely complex religious phenomena, and not infrequently sociologists appear to be discussing different things. A wider sweep of analysis would however suggest that there is much in the contemporary charismatic movement that is cultist in terms of popular designations.

One element of a cultist tendency of the charismatic movement could be said to be the high profile of many of its leaders who expected, if subtly, loyalty to themselves as well-known personalities on the charismatic circuit. While many of the leaders of the Alpha programme have not enjoyed quite the same personal impact as those such as John Wimber, many have inherited his theology and praxis.

It could be argued that Alpha takes people out of their natural environment, plies them with food and personal attention, and then subjects them to systematic indoctrination over a period of weeks – in short, that it exposes them to manipulation in much the same way as, so it is often alleged, do cultist forms of contemporary religion such as Scientology and the Unification Church ('Moonies'). Certainly this is something that the Holy Spirit weekend would seem to do. The fear is that people are removed from their usual personal networks and familiar environment and are subjected to indoctrination and what has come to be known in anti-cultist circles as 'love bombing' – where potential converts become the focus of relentless attention and affection. In the eyes of its critics, Alpha, in this context, brings undue coercion to bear on believers and non-believers alike – at least to be become involved in activities they would not usually consent to.

The dangers of the Holy Spirit weekend were put across in no uncertain terms by an Anglican woman that I interviewed who complained that she felt she was being brainwashed and that if people did not display manifestations of the Spirit such as speaking in tongues and healing, then the weekend had not been successful. The Alpha classes hitherto had been organized to lead up to this 'climax' of the 'proofs' of God:

> My biggest argument against Alpha was a general feeling that if you hadn't witnessed the Holy Spirit on the appointed weekend then you weren't worthy enough. The weekend was an intense day of being brainwashed. That was the day that it was all leading up to and if you didn't perform then they (the course leaders) thought they had failed. The type of pressure they put on you is like being with the Jehovah's Witnesses. Then they laid hands on me for healing. I was due to have a minor operation on my leg and they thought that I wouldn't have to go. I took it as bit of an insult.

The following interpretation of the Holy Spirit weekend is possible in suggesting cult-like tendencies:

- Individuals are taken away from their environment into an unfamiliar situation.
- Indoctrination through the charismatic explication of the works of the Holy Spirit. This might include heightened suggestibility of what the Holy Spirit can do and characteristic manifestations of his presence in the individual/group.
- Constant references to past visitations and powerful acts of the Holy Spirit, such as healing and 'falling in the spirit'.
- The singing of selective choruses referring to God's love and power, accompanied by singing in tongues enhancing a suggestibility that the supernatural is present.
- That expectations of supernatural activity enhance the personal authority of Alpha group leaders.
- Implicit expectations of a high level of group conformity.
- Three video presentations of a talk by a 'celebrity' charismatic leader.

Is Alpha a cult? While the Alpha course, including the weekend away, can encourage a good deal of conformity it is in reality, I would suggest, far from cult-like. There is little to compare with the systematic brainwashing techniques that some of the cults employ (and even in these cases are often exaggerated). However, those of us who have observed charismatic circles for long enough are aware that undue coercion might be brought to bear on believers and non-believers alike especially in the context of the weekend away. In the case of Alpha, this remains a possibility, but there is a great danger in overstating the case.

Notes

1 Peter Cook, in his article 'Alpha Courses: Some Observations and Misgivings', *Challenge Weekly*, 27 November 1999) presents a useful criticism of the weekend away, especially the emphasis of waiting on the spirit and speaking in tongues.
2 Alpha manual, p. 30.
3 Ibid., p. 31.
4 Ibid., p. 32.
5 Ibid., p. 35.
6 Among Roman Catholics there may be prayers of confession (in Roman Catholic circles the weekends are often run by a priest) during 'ministry time'.
7 Perhaps the most accepted definition and classification of cult is that of Stark and Bainbridge. Their three-fold definition of 'client', 'audience cults' and 'cult movement' do appear limited in that they seem to be describing New Religious Movements (see Chapter 8 of this volume). Stark and Bainbridge see the cult as an innovating and uniquely contemporary form of religion. They are generally free of the deficiencies of the older religious traditions and in line with the needs of individuals in Western societies. The charismatic movement, it might be argued, is an innovating form of religion that departs from traditional Christianity and offers new wares in the marketplace. If we accept these propositions, Alpha could be said to be a means by which the movement carries out its cult-like activities in the spiritual marketplace. Subscribing to an introductory course into Christianity, exemplified by Alpha, is almost unprecedented in the mainline churches, although frequently used by other successful movements ranging from Jehovah's Witnesses (free of charge) to Scientology (very expensive).

Conclusion

Alpha – A Sign of the Times?

This book has sought to describe, account for and analyse the Alpha programme, hopefully in a constructive and impartial way. In concluding, I will allow myself a little more subjectivity; expressing some views and even the indulgence of outlining an 'alternative Alpha course'. In moving towards a conclusion, however, I will first draw together a few themes.

The findings of this volume are based on a nationwide survey which has taken into account the different contexts in which Alpha is applied: in the churches, the prisons, the universities, and among young people. Such a survey admittedly has its limitations. While it has included a historical dimension, the net result is a 'snap-shot' since it constitutes a picture of Alpha over three or four years as experienced in different environments in respect of its 'supply-side' and a corresponding 'consumer demand'. It may yet be far from a complete picture. There is undoubtedly room for further research. Some of the themes discussed in this book, including Alpha's theological leanings, the dynamics of Alpha groups, and its application in the non-church setting, all need further exploration. The programme has also made an international impact, thus research needs to be conducted in other cultural contexts.

In all probability, the story of Alpha is far from over. Yet given the evidence of the number of churches subscribing and people attending, it may have reached its apogee in the late 1990s, certainly this is probably the case in the UK. Indeed, Alpha may be approaching a 'critical mass' – there is a limit to the times church members can go through the course and, given that the great majority of genuine 'guests' who attend do so through social networks, there must also be a limit to the number of people who can be asked to enrol.

My own view is that Alpha will continue to develop and its utilization worldwide will continue to spread for some time yet. Clearly Alpha has made waves and these waves are global. The sheer scale, direction and working philosophy of Alpha are noteworthy. Evangelizing initiatives come and go, yet Alpha deserves and calls out for attention. It is more than a passing phase or craze in the churches. It is not the 'here today and gone tomorrow' of the Toronto Blessing of the mid-1990s. Alpha has been around for some time and will continue to be so. At the very least it has put one London church, Holy Trinity, Brompton, firmly on the map.

Alpha is thoroughly modern or, if one perfers, post-modern. In many respects it is a barometer of developments and thinking in the contemporary church. It utilizes the insights and experiences gained by the churches in a secular world over many years, if not decades. In engaging with secularity, it uses secular tools, applying sociology, psychology, business and organizational studies. It recognizes cultural and social change, while appreciating individualism, consumerism, and the need to be relevant in a relativizing culture. Alpha attempts to be 'safe' and non-threatening but boldly proclaims what it has to offer. It is consumer-led to a degree since it takes into account people's experiences and views, whether guests or church leaders. It is also user-friendly in the sense that it is ecumenical and is popular across the denominations. Of course, Alpha will not be to the liking of the conservative-minded Christian (nor for that matter the liberal) but it is in step with much current evangelical thinking.

Alpha is a programme aimed at the twenty-first century. It would seem to fit well into the contemporary spiritual marketplace. It has a powerful supply-side that has produced a standardized package supported by a £ million industry. It attempts to appeal to the 'consumer-side' and the spiritual seeker – the Alpha 'guest'. Alpha, then, constitutes a very vibrant area of the Christian market, at least within the churches themselves and appeals mostly to the already convinced. At the same time, the programme is a testament to an ever-increasing secular society. Alpha is designer Christianity even if on the ground, in the local church hall or somebody's home, it is still subject to the rather archaic traditions and culture of many churches. Moreover, while Alpha at HTB is undoubtedly a very slick model, driven according to the manual, in the provinces it is often difficult to get on the road and may be subject to considerable customization in terms of organization and doctrine.

Contemporary evangelism, as evident in Alpha, is forced to appeal to 'common man' (and woman) in a user-friendly way, practically without the outright condemnation of sin. At the same time that it engages with secularity, however, it has not lost sight of a 'basic Christianity' and is recognizable for the most part as historical Christianity. It can scarcely be seen as a resurgence of fundamentalism in the church despite its stance on some issues. Having said that, there is an imbalance in this 'basic' Christianity. The over-emphasis on the Holy Spirit is there for all to see, while the time and energy (through the Holy Spirit weekend) spent on one person in the Trinity, gives away Alpha's charismatic credentials. Theologically speaking, there are those who object to this emphasis and the teachings contained in this section of the course. Nonetheless, my survey has shown that this is the part of the programme that guests most appreciate – at least those within the church. It is the teachings on the Holy Spirit which take many on in their Christian faith. To dilute it might be to reduce Alpha's appeal in the churches. Whether this aspect needs to be toned down for a wider public consumption, is ultimately a matter of opinion.

Alpha – A Success Story?

Is Alpha a success? Again it depends what criteria are being used. Some might argue that there is much which it leaves out in terms of 'basic Christianity'. While for some Alpha is too long and rather dull, there is a great deal that it omits: church history, personal experiences, and elements of a social gospel. It would also seem to fail to recognize the rich diversity of expressions of the faith. Yet if it includes too much it may fail to be 'basic' in any meaningful way. As I will suggest below, perhaps more should be arranged post-Alpha, or maybe there should be a series of courses which addresses these issues. Post-Alpha courses currently do run but most appear to take conversion through Alpha for granted rather than allow the unchurched 'seeker' to seek some more.

Alpha is a cheap and standard package. It has an advantage for the churches because it easy to set up and administer. Once the tapes and books are bought, the investment can go on indefinitely as courses are run over and over again. The supportive literature is easy to understand and is pleasing to the eye. In the courses that I engaged with Alpha was generally conscientiously run by diligent and responsible church leaders. It is also based in the locality, in neighbouring churches with the advantages of familiarity and of setting up networks and sustaining them. Alpha does not have the remoteness of tele-evangelism or the itinerant ministry: the informality, emotionalism and temporary nature of the rally and visiting evangelist.

Alpha's standardization is, however, not without its problems. In some respects the course is too structured. Alpha sets its own frameworks, asks its own questions, and provides relatively fixed answers. One could say that it was hermetically foolproof. Alpha is sufficiently more than just propagating a belief system. Through the Holy Spirit weekend it offers 'experience' and as a broad package it advances a distinct sub-culture, which helps forge an identity, and a particular Christian identity at that, in a world where it is difficult to claim one.

In many ways, as we have seen, Alpha exemplifies the tendency in the contemporary church to express aspects of McDonaldization. It would seem to standardize views and attitudes, such as the 'gay issue', perhaps to detrimental effect. Yet it is sufficiently wide in scope to cater for the pastoral and spiritual needs of the churched and unchurched, although it is perhaps pitched a little high for some. The meal, the video, the discussion are highly praised by most guests but they are not without their difficulties.

How has Alpha faired in terms of converts? I have argued throughout this volume that the evidence suggests Alpha appeals mostly to those already within the church, revitalizing some churches, dividing others. I believe that very few converts are being made. But perhaps we have to look at the long-term picture. Perhaps the seeds are being sown, with the harvest to come at a later day. After all, Alpha is supposed to be only part of the journeying for

the spiritual seeker. Personally I doubt it. Global catastrophe or environmental disaster apart, I cannot see a prospect for a nationwide revival, at least
in the UK. The bottom line may be that Alpha's inability to reverse church
decline may suggest that the best has been tried and largely failed, especially
in those 'hard places'. However, the USA may prove a different prospect, as
may Alpha's application in many countries in the Third World.

Does Alpha do enough to exploit the spiritual marketplace? It largely
works through networks spreading out from the churches. This is important
to the programme since cold advertising does not work. It brings in those on
the fringes, perhaps converting them. Family, friends and associates of church
members may be persuaded to participate but they are a small catch. Perhaps
a greater take-up rate may come with the door-to-door salesman. This is what
the Jehovah's Witnesses do and it has worked in part for them. The personal
touch is important even if it means some Christians leaving their comfortable
pews.

The drop-out rate on Alpha is also worth considering. It is one thing
getting people to the course, it is another keeping them there. Most who leave
do so within the first few weeks. What alienates them? If held in church
surroundings Alpha can be off-putting. Other aspects of the course can also
be a problem. I do not think that most unchurched guests have a difficulty
with the meal and this remains a successful part of the programme. The video
is too long, and often uninspiring. It makes Alpha something of an endurance
test for those who have had a long day at the office, factory or looking after
the family. More generally, Alpha may be all too biblical for some, failing to
ease people into a distinct Christian culture. Also, the discussion groups can
be intimidating for a few guests. The emphasis on small group evangelism
recognizes the impact of group dynamics but there are also some
unanticipated consequences, not least of all in terms of those who become
disenchanted with the lack of open discussion.

Despite its success Alpha needs to be put in perspective, especially against
the background of church decline. At the time of writing Alpha has become
almost a compulsory church activity. It *is* what is going on in the churches.
There is precious little else to report upon – no new major movement and no
issues other than the ordination of gay priests appear to be to the fore. A
broader historical sweep might locate Alpha at the fag-end of charismatic
renewal, Toronto Blessing et al. I have conjectured above that the net result
of Alpha is of an 'internal revival' – largely impacting church members rather
than the non-churched and exposing ever more churches to the theology,
praxis and culture of the charismatic movement. Yet it is very much a diluted
version of charismatic renewal that is being spread. In fact, Alpha would seem
to indicate that the charismatic movement has, after some forty years, finally
blown itself out.

This may be interpreted as good or bad news, depending on your theology
or churchmanship. The reality however, is that the renewal movement has
proved to be the only vibrant movement in the churches, warts 'n all. Yet now

we may be looking not just at post-Christian society but a post-charismatic church. There is evidence that contemporary Christians, perhaps in post-modern style, are looking elsewhere – perhaps at more traditional forms of Christianity. There may now be discernible what Andrew Walker has called the 'Catholic turn' and he has pointed out that many of HTB's church plants have refused, ironically, to endorse Alpha and are seeking a more traditional expression of the faith.[1]

The Alternative Alpha Course

Another key question is whether Alpha is meeting the needs and expectations of its guests. Ultimately there may be a mismatch between what the supply-side delivers and 'consumer' expectations. 'True guests', the unchurched, would want to know about Christianity. They may want to know 'the basics'. At the same time they will undoubtedly have 'searching issues' to raise – suffering, other religions, sex, science versus faith, readily come to mind which may or may not come up during an Alpha course. However, perhaps they should stand as discrete topics in their own right and be incorporated into the structure of the course – bite-sized chunks in a programme which now stands a little on the long side.

Perhaps any 'introduction to Christianity' needs to strike a balance. Of course it must instruct and set down basic Christian dogma, but in these times people also want to be entertained. This does not have to mean superficiality, commodification or all the trimmings of Disneyization. It can however mean innovation, enterprise and, above all, imagination. What is needed is variety and flexibility.

Perhaps the greatest difficulty I have is that Alpha sets the agenda to a far greater extent than necessary. Each week presents its own theme from a Christian point of view which is held, by definition, to be invariably true. The onus is on the guests, should they wish to participate in discussion, to disprove the evidence or enter into contention by forceful argument. In the first few weeks this type of approach can be intimidating and probably explains the high drop-out rate at this stage. This is particularly the case in churches where the enquiring guest is in a discussion group comprised largely of leaders of the course plus church members who have enrolled.

Alpha, in my opinion, also assumes too much knowledge. Since, at least in the churches I initially surveyed, most of those on the course were already committed Christians, they would not have the difficulty of following the arguments or finding the relevant biblical passages. A course for beginners, however, has to be a little more basic and use a few more imaginative ways of exploring what Christianity is all about. Forty minutes of Nicky Gumbel dictating what is self-evidently true is not always helpful. Moreover, over-long video presentations are not the only medium which could be used. Variety would add to the attraction of the course. However, there may be dangers in leaving innovation to individual churches. Above all, it would disturb the standard product of Alpha which is partly one of the reasons for its appeal. At the same time, to encourage innovation may mean that HTB might lose its control over the course and hence its high profile.

Sandy Millar at HTB has stated:

> Without taking anything for granted, stripping the gospel down to its bare essentials, he (Gumbel) has made Christianity accessible to this generation.[2]

I think this claim is a little too optimistic. In providing the quintessential 'Introduction to Christianity', Alpha still has some way to go.

Ultimately, perhaps, Alpha should decide who it really wants to appeal to, the churched or unchurched. If it opts for the latter it should, to my mind, be broken down into more manageable parts. The meal and the discussion groups should be kept. The video presentation should be used among other means of putting the message across. My suggestion is that there should be a pre-Alpha course which discusses broad issues of morality, with C.S. Lewis's *Mere Christianity* providing the ideal text. Give people something to read. As part of this alternative introductory course Christianity can be compared to other faiths. Let it win its case by a simple exploration of a simple faith. A few testimonies, thoughfully given, might enhance the cause.

A much reduced Alpha course which people may wish to move on to, minus the Holy Spirit weekend (of course, a retreat of some kind might be a good idea), would develop some of the key doctrines of faith – again with suitable and varied material. For those who wish to go on in their spiritual searching, perhaps a further course on the 'searching issues' would be a good idea.

The Pre-Alpha Course
   A moral law?
   Christianity and no-faith
   Christianity and other faiths
   Christianity in a nutshell
   Testimonies

Alpha Basic Teachings
   The relevance of Christianity today
   Jesus – who was he?
   The Trinity
   Eternity
   Repentance
   The Christian life
   The Bible
   Prayer and relationship with God

Other Issues
   Suffering
   Sexualities
   Church history
   Denominational differences
   Why Christians disagree
   The social gospel

These are my thoughts as an 'outsider' who knows Alpha through personal experience. Yet such a programme lacks the simplicity of Alpha and would not travel so well. This is the genius of the course. Anything else simply wouldn't be Alpha.

Notes

1   Interview with Andrew Walker, 10 May 2003.
2   Quoted in Gumbel (1994), p. 14.

Appendix

Is Alpha Working?: HTB's View

In order to supplement and enhance the discussion as to whether or not Alpha is working, I shall briefly explore the findings of a report passed onto me by HTB entitled *Alpha Initiative Highlights Report*. The report is based upon a survey which sought to generate information regarding guests' locations, denominational participation, publicity and impact of the Alpha initiative begun in 1998. The report was seeking to establish whether to move ahead with another Alpha initiative in 1999. It does, however, provide significant broader insights into the Alpha programme.

Each of the 4,157 churches and church groups that participated in 1998 were sent feedback questionnaires, the findings of which formed the basis of the report. A total of 2,036 were returned. The report claimed that the questions were to be answered with quantitative data but that there should be an opportunity to give written commentary. Some 64 per cent indicated that they would be involved in another initiative in 1999; a further 26 per cent 'possibly'; 10 per cent would definitely not. Of those that responded 'No' to this question, 'many' said this was because they stipulated that 1999 was too early; others said they felt that their own activity was sufficient and that Alpha only duplicated efforts. The fact that 1999 was perceived as 'too early' may suggest that the 'demand' simply was not there to justify running another programme a year later.

The second set of questions was related to 'guests'. The report claimed that the average number of guests attending Alpha in any given course in 1998 was 18, a rise of 7 on the previous course (or 61 per cent). The total numbers, extrapolated over the full 4,150 courses, was approximately 75,000 guests. Assuming one helper or leader for every three guests, this suggested, at least for HTB, 100,000 'true' guests on the courses nationwide. The increase of almost two-thirds in numbers over two consecutive years includes those attending for the first time. If these 395 courses are excluded then the increase in numbers remains 'very marked' at 32 per cent, which allegedly 'replicates the experience at HTB once the course had "settled"'.

Since Alpha, the report pointed out, 'is aimed primarily at the unchurched', respondents were asked to approximate the number of unchurched guests (see Table A.1).

Extrapolated to the full number of churches in the initiative, the total of unchurched attendees becomes almost 26,000. It was stated in the report that

Table A.1   Number of unchurched guests

	Average	Total
Number of unchurched guests attending current course	6	12,525
Number of unchurched guests attending last course	3	6,069
Increase	3	6,456
Percentage increase	106	

Source: Alpha Initiative Highlights Report, HTB

the national initiative reached more than twice as many unchurched people as had the pre-initiative courses. Moreover, the report stated that the ratio of unchurched to churched rose from 2.7 to 3.5 for each ten churched. On repeated courses the ratio rose from 3.3 to 4 for each ten.

The HTB report claimed that there was a very even spread of courses in the different locations, with the exceptions of the inner-cities, where there were notably fewer courses (see Table A.2).

It was interesting, the report noted, that the average number of guests was uniform but that the initiative had impacted each location differently in order to reach that uniformity; for example, that rural numbers had risen 45 per cent to an average 18, whilst inner-city numbers had risen 88 per cent to reach the same total. No explanation was given as to why this was the case.

The relevance of denominations was also examined. The greatest increase in overall numbers was in the New Churches of The Pioneers (156 per cent); New Frontiers International (150 per cent); independent churches (108 per cent); and Vineyard churches (104 per cent). This cluster of churches also experienced the highest increase in unchurched guests and the highest ratio of unchurched guests. In the more traditional denominations, the six Presbyterian churches surveyed showed the worst movement. Anglican churches had the greatest number of respondent churches (36 per cent of the total). The

Table A.2   Locations of courses

	Number	% of total	Average number of 'guests'	% Increase over course	Average unchurched 'guests'	Percentage increase over last course
Rural	458	23	18	45	5	93
Small town	463	23	18	71	6	131
Town	512	25	19	64	7	98
Suburban	436	22	18	54	6	97
Inner-city	167	8	18	88	7	127

Source: Alpha Initiative Highlights Report, HTB

report stated: 'They are clearly motivated to respond as they represented only 25 per cent of the participating churches' (p. 3). Of the comments coming back from the churches the report said:

> There is also a great deal of comment to show that after the third or fourth Alpha there is a wall which is, in effect, the result of running out of people to invite. (p. 3)

The respondents were asked to grade the various materials and media used to publicize the initiative with '1' being the most ineffective and '5' the most effective. The middle range proved to be '3' which suggested that the media was 'neither effective nor ineffective' (p. 4) (see Table A.3).

As regards reaching the unchurched with the Alpha message, the report stated:

> The materials which had a more local effect, and were under the control of the local co-ordinators, the invitations, notice board posters and, above all, word of mouth were all perceived to be effective ... This set of responses can be viewed alongside the very common comment which was that 'word of mouth is best' or 'friendship is the key to inviting people successfully'. (p. 4)

The impact of the initiative as measured in terms of a felt improvement of awareness and co-operation in the area within and between churches in Table A.4 is shown. The grades of 1 to 5 represented 'least beneficial' through to 'most beneficial'.

However we might interpret these findings, HTB saw them in a positive light. This was especially true of Alpha's perceived impact on the community as 'a very strong base to progress from'.

Table A.3 Effectiveness of course publicity

	Average rating excl. zero	Number of N/A responses	% Giving N/A
Invitation	3.6	130	6
Noticeboard posters	3.6	107	5
Billboards	2.9	422	21
'Songs of Praise'	3.7	243	12
Other TV/radio broadcasts	2.8	700	34
Local editorial	2.7	701	34
National editorial	2.8	643	32
Locally organized advertisements	2.9	587	29
HTB-organized events	2.7	637	31
Word of mouth	4.3	214	11

Source: Alpha Initiative Highlights Report, HTB

Table A.4 Impact of the initiative

	Average excl. zero	Number of N/A responses	% Giving N/A
Links with other denominations	3.1	212	10
Awareness of Alpha in church	3.8	91	4
Awareness of Alpha in community	3.1	137	7
Awareness of church in community	2.9	221	11
Effect of Alpha on church	3.6	153	8
What is overall effect of initiative?	3.5	207	10

Source: *Alpha Initiative Highlights Report*, HTB

Comments from the churches were felt by HTB to fall into a number of broad categories although it is not clear whether the following was in any particular order:

1 Word of mouth not advertising is 'the key for invitations and that friendship-building ... is the most important activity to be engaged in'. (p. 5).
2 More time to prepare for new courses.
3 Disappointment over leaflet drops and advertising which raised church members' expectations unrealistically.
4 Further-ranging style of posters. It was argued that '9 to 5 did not go down well in the unemployment high spots'.
5 Local church co-ordination was perceived as important.
6 There were calls for greater use of testimonies in the press releases and more use of 'senior figures' in the commentaries.

References

Abdulla, M. (1995) *Muslim Minorities in the West*, London: Grey Seal.
An Introduction to Alpha for Prisoners and Caring for Ex-Offenders (undated), HTB.
Anthony, D. and Robbins, A. (1982) 'Spiritual Innovation and the Crisis of American Civic Religion', in M. Douglas and S. Tipton (eds) *Religion and America: Spirituality in a Secular Age*, Boston: Beacon Press.
Asch, S. (1952) *Social Psychology*, New Jersey: Prentice-Hall.
Barker, E. (1984) *The Making of a Moonie*, Oxford: Blackwell.
—— (1992) *The New Religious Movements: A Practical Guide*, London: HMSO.
—— (1999) 'New Religious Movements: Their Incidence and Significance', in B. Wilson and J. Cresswell (eds) *New Religious Movements: Challenge and Response*, London: Sage.
Bauman, Z. (1992) 'Postmodern Religion', in P. Heelas (ed.) *Religion, Modernity and Post-Modernity*, Oxford: Blackwell.
Bebbington, D. (1998) *Evangelism in Modern Britain*, London: Cambridge University Press.
Beckford, J. (1975) *The Trumpet of Prophecy: A Sociological Study of Jehovah's Witnesses*, Oxford: Blackwell.
Bellah, R. (1964) 'Religious Evolution', *American Sociological Review*, 29 (3): pp. 358–74.
—— (1976) 'New Religious Consciousness and the Crisis of Modernity', in C. Glock and R. Bellah (eds) *The Consciousness Revolution*, Berkeley, CA: University of California Press.
Berger, P. (1970) *A Rumour of Angels: Modern Society and the Rediscovery of the Supernatural*, London: Allen Lane.
Berger, P. (1973) *The Social Construction of Reality*, Harmondsworth: Penguin.
Bibby, R. (1993) *Unknown Gods*, Toronto: Toronto University Press.
Bird, F. (1978) 'The Pursuit of Innocence: New Religious Movements and Moral Accountability', *Sociological Analysis*, 40 (4): pp. 335–46.
Bonnett, K. (1994) 'Power and Politics' in M. Haralambos (ed.) *Developments in Sociology*, 10, Ormskirk: Causeway Press.
Brierley, P. (1992) *Christian England: What the 1989 Church Census Revealed*, London: Marc Europe.
—— P. (2000) *Religious Trends*, London: Marc Europe.
Bromley, D. and Shupe, A. (1979) 'The Tnevnoc Cult', *Sociological Analysis*, 40 (4): pp. 361–6.
Brouwer, S., Gifford, P. and Rose, S. (1996) *Exporting the American Gospel*, New York: Routledge.
Bruce, S. (1988) *Rise and Fall of the New Christian Right in America*, Oxford: Clarendon Press.
—— (1993) 'Religion and Rational Choice', *Sociology of Religion*, 54 (2): pp. 193–205.
—— (1997) 'The Pervasive World-View: Religion in Pre-Modern Britain', *British Journal of Sociology*, 84 (4): pp. 667–80.
Campbell, C. (1987) *The Romantic Ethic and the Spirit of Modern Consumerism*, Oxford: Basil Blackwell.

Carey, G. (1990) Foreword, *The Church in the Marketplace*, Eastbourne: Kingsway.
Cartwright, D. and Zander, A. (eds) (1960) *Group Dynamics: Research and Theory*, Evanston, Ill.: Row.
Cook, G. (2000) *European Values Survey*, London: Gordon Cook Foundation.
Cox, H. (1994) *Fire From Heaven*, Reading, MA: Addison-Wesley.
Cupitt, D. (1998) 'Post-Christianity' in P. Heelas (ed.) *Religion, Modernity and Post-Modernity*, Oxford: Blackwell.
Davie, G. (1994) *Religion in Britain Since 1945: Believing Without Belonging*, Oxford: Blackwell.
Davies, C. (1975) *Permissive Britain. Social Change in the Sixties and Seventies*, London: Pitman.
Delamont, S. (1984) *Appetites and Identities: An Introduction to the Social Anthropology of Western Europe*, London: Routledge.
Demerath, N. (1965) *Social Class in American Protestantism*, Chicago: Rand McNally.
Douglas, M. (1978) *Constructive Drinking*, Cambridge: Cambridge University Press.
Downton, J. (1979) *Sacred Journeys*, New York: Columbia University Press.
Dreitzel, K. (1981) 'The Socialization of Nature: Western Attitudes Towards Body and Emotions', in P. Heelas and A. Lock (eds) *Indigenous Psychologies: The Anthropology of the Self*, New York: Academic Press.
Ellwood, R. (1979) *Alternative Altars: Unconventional and Eastern Spirituality in America*, Chicago: University of Chicago Press.
Exline, R. (1957) 'Group Climate as a Factor in the Relevance and Accuracy of Social Perception', *Journal of Abnormal and Social Psychology*, 55: pp. 382–88.
Festinger, L. (1950) 'Informal Social Communication', *Psychological Review*, 57: pp. 271–82.
Fiedler, F. (1967) *A Theory of Leadership Effectiveness*, New York: McGraw-Hill.
Finke, R. and Iannaccone, L. (1993) 'Supply-side Explanation for Religious Change', *The Annals*, 527: pp. 27–39.
Fischler, C. (1990) 'Food Habits, Social Change and the Nature/Culture Dilemma', *Social Science Information*, 19 (6): pp. 937–53.
Fry, C. (1965) 'Personality and Acquisition Factors in the Development of Coordination Strategy', *Journal of Personality and Social Psychology*, 2: pp. 403–407.
Gerard, D (1985) 'Religious Attitudes and Values', in A. Abrams, D. Gerard and N. Timms (eds) *Values and Social Change in Britain*, Basingstoke: Macmillan.
Gerard, H., Wilhelmy, R. and Conolley, E. (1968) 'Conformity and Group Size', *Journal of Personality and Social Psychology*, 8: pp. 79–82.
Gill, S. (1989) *The Lesbian and Gay Christian Movement: Campaigning for Justice, Truth and Love*, London: Cassell.
—— and Bellah, R. (eds) (1967) *The Consciousness Reformation*, Berkeley, CA: University of California Press.
Glock, C. and Stark, R. (1969) 'Dimensions of Religious Commitment' in R. Robertson (ed.) *Sociology of Religion*, Harmondsworth: Penguin.
Gordon, M. (1964) *Assimilation in American Life: The Role of Race, Religion and National Origins*, Oxford: Oxford University Press.
Gray, R. and Moberg, D. (1977) *The Church and the Older Person*, Grand Rapids: Eerdmans.
Green, M. (1990) *Evangelism Through the Local Church*, London: Hodder & Stoughton.
Greil, A. and Rudy, D. (1984) 'What Have We Learned From the Process Models of Conversion? An Examination of Ten Case Studies', *Sociological Focus*, 17 (4): pp. 305–21.
Gronow, J. (1997) *The Sociology of Taste*, London: Routledge.
Gumbel, N. (1994) *Telling Others: The Alpha Initiative*, Eastbourne: Kingsway.

—— N. (2000) *Searching Issues*, Eastbourne: Kingsway.

—— N. (2001a) *Challenging Lifestyle*, Eastbourne: Kingsway.

—— N. (2001b) *Alpha for Prisons Training Manual*, London: HTB.

Hadaway, C., Marler, P. and Chaves, M. (1993) 'What the Polls Don't Show', *American Sociological Review*, 58, December: pp. 741–52.

Hammond, P. (1988) 'Religion and the Persistence of Identity', *Journal for the Scientific Study of Religion*, 27 (1): pp. 1–11.

Harding, S., Phillips, D. and Fogarty, K. (1986) *Contrasting Values in Western Europe*, London: Macmillan.

Hearne, G. (1957) 'Leadership and the Spatial Factors in Small Groups', *Journal of Abnormal and Social Psychology*, 54: pp. 269–72.

Heelas, P. (1996) *The New Age Movement*, Oxford: Blackwell.

—— P. (1998) 'Introduction' in P. Heelas (ed.) *Religion, Modernity, and Post-Modernity*, Oxford: Blackwell.

Hinchelwood, R. (1987) *What Happens in Groups. Psychoanalysis, the Individual and the Community*, London: Free Association Books.

Hocken, P. (1994) *The Glory and the Shame*, Surrey: Eagle.

Hoffman, L. (1959) 'Homogeniety of Member Personality and Its Effect on Group Problem-Solving', *Journal of Abnormal and Social Psychology*, 58: pp. 27–32.

Homans, M. (1975) *The Human Group*, New York: Harcourt, Brace & World.

Hunt, S. (1995) ' "The Toronto Blessing". A Rumour of Angels', *The Journal of Contemporary Religion*, 10 (3), pp. 257–72.

—— (1996) '*A Holy War at St James*', paper given at the 10th Congress of CESNUR, Montreal, Canada, 16 August 1996.

—— (1998) ' "Christianity Versus the New Age": The Dimension of Boundary Maintenance Among Neo-Pentecostal Healing Groups', in M. Bowman (ed.) *Healing and Religion*, Hisarlik Studies in Contemporary Religion, 1, London: Hisarlik Press.

—— (2000) 'Winning Ways: Globalisation and the Impact of Health and Wealth Ministries', *Journal of Contemporary Religion*, 15 (3): pp. 215–30.

—— (2001) *Anyone for Alpha?*, London: Darton, Longman & Todd.

Inglehart, R. (1997) *Modernization and Post-Modernization*, Princeton, NJ: Princeton UP.

Kelley, E. (1952) 'Two Functions of Reference Groups', in G. Swanson, T. Newcomb and E. Hartley (eds) *Readings in Social Psychology*, New York: Holt.

Lang, K. and Lang, G. (1960) 'Decision for Christ: Billy Graham in NYC' in A. Vidich and D. White (eds) *Identity and Anxiety*, New York: Free Press.

Leach, E. (1976) *Culture and Communication*, Cambridge: CUP.

Leacock, E. (1981) 'Myths of Male Dominance', *New York Monthly Review*, April, 3–4.

Lewin, K. (1951) *Field Theory in Social Science*, New York: Harper.

—— (1953) 'Studies in Group Decision', in D. Cartwright and A. Zander (eds) *Group Dynamics: Research and Theory*, Evanston, Ill.: Row.

—— Lippitt, R. and White, R. (1967) 'Patterns of Aggressive Behaviour in Experimentally Created "Social Climates" ', *Journal of Social Psychology*, 10: pp. 271–99.

Lippitt, R., Polansky, N., Redl, F. and Rosen, S. (1952) 'The Dynamics of Power', *Human Relations*, 5: pp. 37–64.

Loftland, D. and Stark, R. (1965) 'Becoming a World Saver: A Theory of Conversion to a Deviant Perspective', *American Sociological Review*, 30: pp. 862–75.

Lott, A. and Lott, B. (1961) 'Group Cohesiveness, Communication Level, and Conformity', *Journal of Abnormal and Social Psychology*, 62: pp. 408–12.

Luckmann, T. (1967) *The Invisible Religion*, New York: Macmillan.

Lyon, D. (1996) 'Religion in the Post-Modern World. Old Problems, New Perspectives', in K. Flanagan and P. Jupp (eds) *Post-Modernity, Sociology and Religion*, London: Macmillan.
—— (2000) *Jesus in Disneyland*, London: Polity Press.
Lyotard, J. (1984) *The Post-Modern Condition*, Manchester: Manchester University Press.
McBain, D. (1978) 'The Spirits Call to the Hard Places', *Renewal*, 74: pp. 28–31.
McLuhan, M. (1996) *The Guttenberg Galaxy*, Toronto: Toronto University Press.
Mann, R. (1959) 'A Review of the Relationship between Personality and Performance in Small Groups', *Psychological Bulletin*, 56: pp. 241–70.
Martin, D. (1990) *Tongues of Fire: The Explosion of Pentecostalism in Latin America*, Oxford: OUP.
Marx, J. and Ellison, D. (1975) 'Sensitivity Training and Communes: Contemporary Quests for Community', *Pacific Sociological Review*, 18 (4): pp. 442–62.
Mauss, A. and Perrin, R. (1992) 'Saints and Seriousness', *Review of Religious Research*, 34: pp. 176–8.
Menzies, I. (1979) 'Staff Support Systems: Task and AntiTask in Adolescent Institutions', in Hinshelwood, R. and Manning, N. (eds) *Therapeutic Communities: Reflections and Progress*, London: Routledge & Kegan Paul.
Millar, S. (n.d.) *Alpha Changing Lives*, Holy Trinity, Brompton.
Myers, R. (1969) *Some Effects of Seating Arrangements in Counselling*, unpublished PhD, University of Florida, Gainsville.
Nugent, R. and Gramick, J. (1989) 'Homosexuality: Protestant, Catholic, and Jewish Issues; A Fishbone Tale' in R. Hasbany (ed.) *Homosexuality and Religion*, New York: Harworth Press.
Ort, R. (1950) 'A Study of Role-Conflicts as Related to Happiness in Marriage', *Journal of Abnormal and Social Psychology*, 45: pp. 691–9.
Palmer, S. (1994) *Moon Sisters, Krishna Mothers*, Rajneesh Lovers, Syracuse, NY: Syracuse University Press.
Percy, M. (1996) *Words, Wonders and Power. Understanding Contemporary Christian Fundamentalism and Revivalism*, London: SPCK.
—— (1998) 'Join the Dots Christianity. Assessing Alpha', *Reviews in Religion and Theology*, May.
—— and Taylor, R. (1997) 'Something for the Weekends, Sir? Leisure, Ecstasy and Identity in Football and Contemporary Religion', *Leisure Studies*, 16: pp. 37–49.
Reitan, H. and Shaw, M. (1964) 'Group Membership, Sex-Composition of the Group, and Conforming Behaviour', *Journal of Social Psychology*, 64: pp. 45–51.
Richter, P. (1995) 'God Is Not a Gentleman!' in S. Porter and P. Richter (eds) (1995) *The Toronto Blessing. Or is It?*, London: Darton, Longman & Todd.
—— and Francis, L. (1998) *Gone But Not Forgotten*, London: Darton, Longman & Todd.
Ritzer, G. (1996) *The McDonaldization of Society*, Newbury Park, CA: Pine Forge Press.
Robertson, R. (1992) *Globalization: Social Theory and Global Culture*, London: Sage.
—— (1993) 'Community, Society, Globality, and the Category of Religion', in E. Barker, J. Beckford and K. Dobbelaere (eds) *Secularization, Rationalism, and Sectarianism*, Oxford: Clarendon.
Roof, W. (1994) *A Generation of Seekers: The Spiritual Journey of the Baby Boom Generation*, San Francisco: Harper & Row.
Sargant, W. (1957) *Battle for the Mind*, London: Heinemann.
Schutz, W. (1955) 'What Makes Groups Productive', *Human Relations*, 8: pp. 429–65.
Sellerberg, M. (1991) 'In Food We Trust: Virtually Necessary Confidence and Unfamiliar Ways of Attaining It', in E. Fursr (ed.) *Palatable Worlds. Sociocultural Food Studies*, Oslo: Solum.

Shaw, M. (1959) 'Acceptance of Authority, Group Structure, and the Effectiveness of Small Groups', *Journal of Personality*, 27: pp. 196–210.

—— (1971) *Group Dynamics*, New York: McGraw-Hill.

Shepherd, S. and Wallis, M. (1989) *Coming on Strong: Gay Politics and Culture*, London: Unwin Hyman.

Smark, P. (1978) 'Mass Marketing God', *Atlas*, 25: pp. 19–209.

Snow, D. and Machelek, R. (1984) 'The Convert as a Social Type', in R. Collins (ed.) *Sociological Theory*, San Francisco: Jossey Bass.

Sommer, R. (1969) *Personal Space: The Behavioural Basis of Design*, Englewood Cliffs, NJ: Prentice-Hall.

Stark, R. and Bainbridge, W. (1980) 'Secularization, Revival and Cult Formation', *Annual Review of the Social Sciences of Religion*, 4: pp. 85–119.

—— and Bainbridge, D. (1985) *The Future of Religion*, Berkeley, CA: University of California Press.

—— Finke, R. and Guest, A. (1996) 'Mobilizing Local Religious Markets: Religious Pluralism in the Empire State, 1855–1865', *Sociological Review*, 61 (2): pp. 203–18.

—— and Iannaccone, I. (1993) 'Rational Choice Proportions About Religious Movements', in D. Bromley and J. Hadden (eds) *Handbook on Cults and Sects*, Greenwich, CT: JAI Press.

—— (1994) 'A Supply-Side Reinterpretation of the "Secularization" of Europe', *Journal for the Scientific Study of Religion*, 33 (1): pp. 230–52.

Steinzor, B. (1950) 'The Spatian Factor in Face-to-Face Discussion Groups', *Journal of Abnormal and Social Psychology*, 45: pp. 552–5.

Stogdill, R. (1948) 'Personal Factors Associated with Leadership: A Survey of the Literature', Journal of Psychology, 25: pp. 35–71.

—— (1959) *Individual Behaviour and Group Achievement*, New York: McGraw-Hill.

Strodbeck, F. and Hook, L. (1961) 'The Social Dimension of a Twelve Man Jury Table', *Sociometry*, 24: pp. 397–415.

Thaibut, J. (1950) 'An Experimental Study of the Cohesiveness of Underprivileged Groups', *Human Relations*, 3: pp. 251–78.

—— and Kelley, H. (1959) *The Social Psychology of Groups*, New York: Wiley.

Torrance, E. (1954) 'Some Consequence of Power Differences on Decision Making in Permanent and Temporary Three-Man Groups', *Research Studies*, Washington State College, 22: pp. 130–40.

Tuddenham, R., MacBride, P. and Zahn, V. (1958) 'The Influence of the Sex Composition of the Group Upon Yielding to a Distorted Norm', *Journal of Psychology*, 46: pp. 243–51.

Wagner, P. (1992) *Warfare Prayer*, Venturer, CA: Regal Books.

Walker, A. (1998) *Restoring the Kingdom*, Surrey: Eagle.

—— (1999) *From Base Metal to Gold: Theological Reflections on the Gold Teeth Filling Phenomena*, www.Ship-of-fools.com

—— (2001) Preface to S. Hunt, *Anyone for Alpha?*

Wallis, R. (1984) *The Elementary Forms of New Religious Life*, London: Routledge.

Walter, T. (1990) 'Why Are Most Church-goers Women?', *Vox Evangelica*, 95: pp. 599–625.

—— (1999) *On Bereavement: The Culture of Grief*, Buckingham: Oxford University Press.

Warner, R. (1993) 'Work in Progress Towards a New Paradigm for the Sociological Study of Religion in the United States', *American Journal of Sociology*, 98 (5): pp. 1044–93.

Weeks, J. (1977) *Coming Out: Homosexual Politics in Britain, From the Nineteenth Century to the Present*, London: Quartet Books.

Westley, F. (1978) 'The Cult of Man: Durkheim's Predictions and Religious Movements', *Sociological Analysis*, 39: pp. 135–45.

Whyte, W. (1943) *The Street Corner Gang*, Chicago: University of Chicago Press.

Wilson, B. (1966) Religion in a Secular Society, London: Weidenfeld & Nicolson.

—— (1968) 'Religion and Churches in Contemporary America', W. McLoughlin (ed.) *Religion in America*, Boston: Beacon Press.

Wright, N. (1996) 'Restorationism and the "House Church" Movement', S. Hunt, M. Hamilton and T. Walter (eds), *Charismatic Christianity: Sociological Perspectives*, Basingstoke: Macmillan.

Wuthnow, R. (1976) *The Consciousness Reformation*, Berkeley: University of California Press.

—— (1993) *Christianity in the Twenty-First Century*, Oxford: Oxford University Press.

Wyer, R. (1966) 'Behavioural Correlates of Academic Achievement: Conformity Under-Achievement and Affiliation-Incentive Conditions', *Journal of Abnormal and Social Psychology*, 6: pp. 255–63.

York, M. (1996) 'Post Modernity, Architecture, Society and Religion: A Heap of Broken Images, or A Change of Heart?' in M. York (ed.) *Post-modernity, Sociology and Religion*, London: Macmillan.

Zajonc, R. and Sales, S. (1966) 'Social Faciliation of Dominant and Subordinate Responses', *Journal of Experimental Social Psychology*, 2: pp. 160–68.

Index